THE
St. Paul
Farmers' Market
PRODUCE COOKBOOK

A collection of
favorite recipes from growers
and their customers

I1052247

St. Paul Growers Association

ST. PAUL, MINNESOTA

2005

Published by the
St. Paul Growers Association
290 East Fifth Street
St. Paul, Minnesota 55101

Cover illustration by Chad Nestor
Illustrations by Joy Kangas
Book design and production by Peregrine Graphics Services

ISBN 0-9669575-0-4

*Dedicated to all of us
who love and appreciate
the bounty of summer*

Contents

Acknowledgments

A SPECIAL THANKS TO: All the growers, their families, producers, and customers of the St. Paul Farmers' Market who shared their recipes; Chad Nestor for the marvelous cover illustration; Joy Kangas for the beautiful interior illustrations; Crystal Bloecher for her wealth of recipes, know-how, and recipe testing; Ulrich Bloecher for the authentic German recipes and testing; Evelyn Kaiser for keeping the entire project on task along with technical writing, recipes, and recipe testing; B. J. Carpenter—cooking instructor, writer, chef, and loyal farmers' market customer—for her technical expertise in proofing the contents of this book; Judy Gilats of Peregrine Graphics Services, our "book coach," for her patience and good advice; Marilyn Herman at the Dakota County Extension Office; The Wisconsin County Extension Office; Der Thao for information about Hmong produce and recipes; and Jack Gerten, Market manager, for unending support.

Preface

COOKBOOK HISTORY

This is a reprint of the 1999 St. Paul Farmers' Market cookbook. We have added a cover that celebrates the 150-year anniversary of the market. But it's still a collection of relatively new recipes, with the exception of a few old favorites from previous cookbooks. The recipes in this cookbook have a colorful and diverse history. Most are favorites collected from the growers and shoppers of the St. Paul Farmers' Market, and their families and friends. This includes gourmet chefs from local restaurants, instructors at the Cooks of Crocus Hill Inc. Cooking School, and members of the Friends of the Market Organization, all of whom are enthusiastic market shoppers and supporters. Some recipes are the unique creation of the contributor. Others have been adapted from various sources. Still others are prized family recipes that have been handed down from generation to generation.

Some growers' families have been coming to the market for generations. If you search the historical records of the market, you would find that many of today's growers carry on their ancestors' tradition of supplying locally-grown products.

A ST. PAUL TRADITION

In 1853 St. Paul was a frontier town with dirt streets, log cabins, and steamboats. As early as 1852 the *Minnesota Pioneer* newspaper called for an organized farmers' market. A two-story brick market house was constructed at Seventh and Wabasha Streets. It was St. Paul's first public market. While fresh produce was only available during the season, dairy products, flour, cakes, and candies could be purchased year-round.

The market has had several homes during its 152-year history, but it was always in the downtown St. Paul area. Its longest tenure was at Tenth and Jackson Streets, opening in 1902. It remained there until freeway construction and downtown development claimed the site, causing a move to Fifth and Wall Streets in 1982. The current market design is reminiscent of the original market—corrugated fiberglass covers the 167 open-air stalls and bricks pave the walkways. The location today is near one of the areas

Built in 1870, the first farmers market in downtown St. Paul was located at 7th and Wabasha Streets. Courtesy Minnesota Historical Society.

selected in 1853 by St. Paul to house the first farmers' market. In 2004 the outdoor market underwent an exciting renovation that is visually inviting, with expanded stalls and better shelter. Plans are in the works for an indoor market hall adjacent to the outdoor market at 5th and Wabasha Streets.

The market is operated by the St. Paul Growers Association, Inc. Day-to-day operations are handled by the market manager and staff, who maintain an office at the downtown St. Paul site. The association allows only fresh, locally-grown produce to be sold directly from the grower to the consumer. Also available are bakery goods, cheese, poultry, a variety of meats, maple syrup, eggs, bagel sandwiches, honey, wild rice, organic plants and produce, flowers, plants, and shrubs, along with the occasional craft or novelty stand.

Introduction

THIS BOOK IS A COLLECTION of favorite recipes from growers, their families, and the customers of the St. Paul Farmers' Market. Its purpose is to help give shoppers ideas for using the produce and products found at the market. All of the recipes in this book reflect the unique seasonal combinations of produce you will find at any given time of the year.

Most of the ingredients can be found right at the market. In addition to fresh fruits and vegetables, look for locally-produced breads, baked goods, wild rice, herbs, eggs, honey, maple syrup, and meats, including beef, chicken, turkey, venison, pork, and buffalo. We also have abundant varieties of local specialty cheeses, goat and sheep cheeses, flavored vinegars for every occasion and whim, and of course, flowers—food for the soul.

We hope that you have as much fun shopping at the St. Paul Farmers' Market as we take pleasure in serving you.

How to Cook Your Vegetables

DEFINITIONS OF COOKING TERMS

Steaming: Steaming is when you cook vegetables over boiling water. Use a steaming basket for this. They are sold at grocery stores. Fill a pot with about one inch of water, place steamer basket in the pot. Bring water to a boil and place vegetables in the basket. The water should not touch the vegetables. Start timing as soon as you put the vegetables in the pot. Test frequently and cook until tender.

Blanching: Blanching is when you immerse vegetables in boiling water until they are tender crisp and then remove them. Use a large pot to insure better water circulation. Bring enough water to boil to generously cover your vegetables. Do no more than one pound at a time. Start timing as soon as you drop the vegetables in the boiling water. After removing vegetables, wait until water returns to a boil before adding the next batch. Black enamel blanching pots are easiest and safest because you simply lift out the insert by the handles to remove vegetables. Tomatoes can also be done this way to loosen skins.

Parboiling: Parboiling is when you immerse vegetables in boiling water to partially cook them. A slotted spoon helps here. You can parboil onions when you want to stuff them and finish cooking them in the oven. Start timing as soon as you drop vegetables in the water.

Stir-frying: Stir-frying is when you heat a little oil in a pan and add vegetables to cook. Make sure you keep stirring to prevent them from becoming to brown on one side. When doing combinations of vegetables, start with the longest-cooking ones first. Often, the sauté period is followed by a steaming period where you add water, cover the pan, and steam vegetables for a time. Woks are ideal for stir-frying because you can push the vegetables that are done up on the sides of the wok, away from the heat, reducing the need for a lot of oil.

Baking: Baking is when you cook vegetables in the oven.

Roasting: Roasting is when you cook vegetables uncovered in the oven, over hot coals, or over a flame, usually charring the outer skin somewhat.

Sautéing: Sautéing is when you cook vegetables in a small amount of oil or fat.

Frying: Frying is when you cook vegetables that are partially immersed in hot oil.

Deep frying: Deep frying is when you cook vegetables that are completely immersed in hot oil.

Grilling: Grilling is when you cook vegetables over hot coals. Foods can be cooked either uncovered or wrapped in a double layer of foil.

COOKING TIMES

Follow your own judgment and personal taste using given cooking times as a guide. Vegetables are done when they are bright in color and tender when put to the bite test. You can also try piercing them with a knife or fork. Overcooked vegetables lose flavor and nutrients. Many factors can vary the cooking time—the size of the pieces, the maturity of the vegetable, and its tenderness, the amounts of both water and vegetables, as well as the size of the pot. Follow your senses. Test frequently.

How to Cut Your Vegetables

DEFINITIONS OF CUTTING TERMS

Slicing: Sliced pieces are round like coins.

Dicing: Diced pieces ⅛–¼-inch wide and are square like cubes.

Cubing: Cubed pieces are ½-inch or more wide and are square like a block.

Chopping: Chopped pieces are small irregular pieces.

Cutting into julienne strips: Julienne cut pieces are about two inches long and ⅛-inch wide, like match sticks.

Shredding: Shredded pieces are long and thin, like threads.

How to Can Your Vegetables

All of the recipes in this book are for boiling-water bath processing. All low acid foods should be processed with a pressure canner. We have included timetables for processing the fruits and vegetables found at the market. Also included are some general steps for canning. This is by no means a complete guide for canning. Please consult your County Extension Office, canning manufactures—such as Kerr or Ball—or local libraries and bookstores for more complete and detailed information.

GENERAL STEPS IN CANNING

1. Read the recipe. Gather together all your canning materials and ingredients.
2. Wash your vegetables under running water.
3. Prepare the food according to the recipe, such as salting and soaking.
4. Wash the jars in soapy water and rinse well. Check the rims for nicks and cracks.
5. Sterilize jars if you are processing food for less than 10 minutes. To sterilize, put the jars mouth up on the rack of a boiling-water bath canner and fill the canner and jars with water to 1-inch above the tops of the jars. Bring the water to a boil and boil for 15 minutes. Leave the jars in the water until you are ready to use them.
6. Prepare the lids according to the manufacturers instructions.
7. Prepare the brine if applicable.
8. Pack the jars leaving the amount of head space called for in the recipe. Pack the vegetables neatly and firmly.
9. Remove air bubbles by running a wooden spoon or a plastic knife down the sides of the jar.
10. Add more boiling liquid if necessary to maintain proper headroom.
11. Wipe the rim of the jar with a clean damp cloth to remove any food particles.
12. Cover the jar with a lid and band, following manufacturer's instructions.
13. Set the hot jar in a preheated canner. The water should be hot but not boiling. Set the jar on the rack of the canner making sure jars do not touch. The water should be 1 to 2 inches above the tops of the jars.
14. Begin timing when the water comes to a boil. Add more boiling water to maintain the water level at 1 to 2 inches above the tops of the jars.
15. Process the jars for the exact time specified in the recipe.
16. Remove jars and set them on a towel to cool. Leave at least 1 inch between jars. Cool thoroughly.
17. Once cooled, check the seals by pressing the center of each lid. It should not pop back.
18. If a jar isn't sealed, repack the contents into a new jar, using a new lid, and process for the full length of time again.
19. Wipe the jars and lids. Label with date and contents.
20. Use food within one year.

JAM AND JELLY MAKING DO'S AND DON'TS

- Use ripe fruit for the best flavor.
- Crush berries 1 cup at a time using a potato masher or similar utensil. If using a food processor, use the pulse button to mash the fruit. Take care not to puree or overprocess. Jam should always have bits of fruit in it.
- For the clearest jelly, allow the cooked fruit to drip naturally into a bowl. Gently squeeze the bag to extract the juice. Overhandling of the bag will result in cloudy jelly.
- Adding ½ teaspoon of unsalted butter or lightly-salted margarine will help prevent or cut down on foaming during the cooking process.
- Melt paraffin in a double boiler over low heat, and use a Pyrex-type measuring cup to pour the hot wax on the jam or jelly. *Never* melt paraffin directly over a flame or an electric burner. If the paraffin is too hot when poured over jam or jelly, it will pull away from the side of the jar, exposing the contents to the air and bacteria.
- *Always* sterilize the jam or jelly jars before filling. Wash the jars, rinse well and place mouth up on the rack (or thick layer of folded terry cloth toweling) in a large pot. Cover with water and boil for 10 minutes. Leave jars in hot water until ready to fill. Carefully remove with a rubber coated canning tongs, or rubber gloves. Lids and rings should be washed, and if sealing in a water bath, sterilized as well.
- *Don't* double recipes, the mixture may not set.
- *Don't* reduce the amount of sugar called for in a recipe, or attempt to use a sugar substitute. The exact amounts of sugar, fruit and pectin are necessary for a good set. The "light" brands of pectin require less sugar.
- *Don't* be alarmed if your jam or jelly doesn't "set" right away. Some may take 2 to 3 weeks, depending on the type of fruit. Apricots, grapes, pears, and cherries may take longer.
- When making jams or jellies from light-colored fruit—apricots, peaches, pears—add a teaspoon of lemon juice to the prepared fruit to prevent browning. There are commercial products available (such as Everfresh) to prevent oxidation.

SOME HELPFUL TELEPHONE NUMBERS

Sure Jell	1-800-431-1001	9 A.M.–4 P.M. (EST) M–F
Ball Kerr	1-800-226-1700	8:30 A.M.–4:30 P.M. (EST) M–F

How to Freeze Your Vegetables

We have included timetables for blanching the vegetables found at the market. You will also find some general steps for freezing. This is not a complete guide for freezing. Please consult your County Extension Office or local libraries and bookstores for complete and detailed information.

GENERAL STEPS FOR FREEZING

1. Gather together your packaging materials, either plastic freezer bags or containers.
2. Make sure you have enough ice. Large blocks are best.
3. Wash vegetables in cold water.
4. Blanch vegetables in at least 4 quarts of boiling water. Do no more than 1 pound at a time. (You can use more than one pot at a time to speed things up.) Start timing as soon as the food is placed in the water. Cover and cook over high heat for the specific time in the chart. An enamel blanching pot is the best for this.
5. Remove the food and quickly plunge it into ice water. Chill the same amount of time it was blanched.
6. Drain well.
7. Put the food into freezer bags or containers and seal. Label the container with the contents and date.
8. Place food in freezer. Spreading the packages or containers out in a single layer will help them freeze more quickly.
9. Use frozen vegetables within 8 to 10 months. Do not thaw before cooking.

How to Freeze Your Fruit

Firm berries may be frozen by using a sugarless dry-pack method. Sort, wash and drain. Pack into freezer containers leaving ½-inch headroom. Seal and freeze. Soft berries can be spread out on a cookie sheet, frozen, and then packed into containers. Cantaloupe chunks can also be frozen by packing chunks, without the rind, into containers and frozen.

Canning and Freezing Timetables

Fruit or Vegetable
Food is listed with amount needed to produce 1 pint. Processing time is given using canning time at 11 psi up to 2,000 feet.

Apples (hot pack only)
1¼ to 1½ lbs., canning
Pints: 20 minutes; quarts: 20 minutes

Asparagus (raw and hot pack)
2¼ to 4½ lbs., canning
1 to 1½ lbs., freezing
Pints: 30 minutes; quarts: 40 minutes
Blanch 2 to 4 minutes

Beans (green or wax, raw and hot pack)
1½ to 2½ lbs., canning
⅔ to 1 lb., freezing
Pints: 40 minutes; quarts: 50 minutes
Blanch 2 to 3 minutes

Beets (hot pack only)
2½ to 3½ lbs., canning
1¼ to 1½ lbs., freezing
Pints: 30 minutes; quarts: 35 minutes
Blanch 3 to 5 minutes

Broccoli
Not recommended for canning
1 lb., freezing
Blanch 3 to 4 minutes

Brussels Sprouts
Not recommended for canning
1 to 1½ lbs., freezing
Blanch 3 to 5 minutes

Cabbage
Not recommended for canning
1 to 1½ lbs., freezing
Blanch leaves 3 to 4 minutes

Carrots (raw and hot pack)
2 to 3 lbs., canning
1¼ to 1½ lbs., freezing
Pints: 25 minutes; quarts: 30 minutes
Blanch 2 minutes for slices,
5 minutes for whole

Cauliflower
Pickle only. Not recommended for canning
1¼ lbs., freezing
Blanch 3 minutes

Celery (hot pack only)
1½ to 2½ lbs., canning
1 lb., freezing
Pints: 30 minutes; quarts: 35 minutes
Blanch 3 minutes

Corn (kernels, cut from cob, raw and hot pack)
3 to 6 lbs., canning
2 to 2½ lbs., freezing
Pints: 55 minutes; quarts: 85 minutes
Blanch 3 minutes

Eggplant
Not recommended for canning
1 to 1½ lbs., freezing
Blanch 2 to 4 minutes

Greens
Not recommended for canning
1 to 1½ lbs., freezing
Blanch 1½ minutes

Kohlrabi
Not recommended for canning
1¼ to 1½ lbs., freezing
Blanch diced pieces 1½ minutes

Parsnips
Not recommended for canning
1½ to 1½ lbs., freezing
Blanch slices 2 minutes

Peas (shelled, raw and hot pack)
3 to 6 lbs., canning
2 to 3 lbs., freezing
Pints: 40 minutes; quarts: 40 minutes
Blanch 1½ minutes

Peppers, bell (roasted and peeled)
2 to 3 lbs., canning
1 to 3 lbs., freezing
Half pints and pints: 35 minutes;
    quarts unsafe
No need to blanch. May be frozen
    whole (seeded) or in slices

Potatoes (1-inch pieces, hot
    pack only)
4 to 6 lbs., canning
2 to 4 lbs., freezing
Pints: 35 minutes; quarts: 40 minutes
Cook until barely tender

Raspberries (raw and hot pack)
¾ to 1½ lbs., canning
¾ to 1½ lbs., freezing
Pints: 15 minutes; quarts: 20 minutes
Freeze with or without sugar

Rhubarb (hot pack only)
⅔ to 1 lb., canning
⅔ to 1 lb., freezing
Pints: 15 minutes; quarts: 15 minutes
Blanch 1 minute. Freeze with or
    without sugar.

Rutabagas
Not recommended for canning
1¼ to 1½ lbs., freezing
Blanch diced pieces 1 minute

Squash, summer (raw and hot pack)
1½ lbs., canning
1 to 1¼ lbs., freezing
Pints: 30 minutes; quarts: 40 minutes
Blanch slices 3 minutes

Squash, winter (hot pack only)
1½ to 3 lbs., canning
1 to 1½ lbs., freezing
Pints: 55 minutes; quarts:
    90 minutes
Cook until soft, then freeze

Strawberries
Not recommended for canning
¾ to 1½ lbs., freezing
Crush or slice. Freeze with or
    without sugar

Tomatoes (raw and hot pack)
1¼ to 2¼ lbs., canning
1¼ to 2¼ lbs., freezing
Pints: 25 minutes; quarts: 25 minutes
Do not need to blanch, but
    probably best to peel.

Vegetables

Asparagus

May–July

PREPARING ASPARAGUS

Wash and snap off the tough ends that are white or pink in color. Leave whole or cut into 1-inch pieces. Eat raw or cook until bright green and tender. Microwave in a covered dish with 2 tbsp. of water. Asparagus cooks quickly so be careful not to overcook. Large diameter stalks may be peeled for a more tender vegetable.

Blanch time: 3–7 minutes

Steam time: 5–8 minutes

Microwave time: 3–5 minutes

Yields: 1 pound of fresh asparagus equals about 20 large spears, 3 cups chopped or diagonally sliced, or 1 cup cooked or puréed.

Nutrition: 1 cup cooked asparagus has about 30 calories and contains potassium and vitamins A and C.

Asparagus Vinaigrette

¾ to 1 lb. asparagus, blanched and chilled
1 tbsp. prepared Dijon mustard
4 tbsp. red wine vinegar
½ tsp. salt
Pinch of cayenne pepper
½ tsp. dried tarragon or 1 small bunch of fresh leaves, minced
½ cup virgin olive oil

Place mustard in a shallow bowl. Whisk in vinegar, salt, pepper, and tarragon.

Put a damp dishcloth under the bowl to hold it in place. Slowly whisk in olive oil until the mixture thickens. Adjust the seasoning to taste. Cover until ready to use. Whisk again before serving.

Arrange asparagus on a serving platter and ladle vinaigrette over the top. Move the spears around a bit so the vinaigrette will cover all the spears.

B. J. Carpenter & Mary Ryan, Cooking Instructors
COOKS OF CROCUS HILL, ST. PAUL

Asparagus Spears with Raspberry Vinegar Dip
So simple, and so good!

2 lbs. asparagus, washed and snapped (to remove woody ends)

Dip:
1 cup light mayonnaise
½ cup raspberry vinegar

Steam asparagus until tender-crisp. Immediately bathe asparagus in ice water to stop cooking and retain its bright green color. Drain and wrap in dry paper towels. May be kept overnight, refrigerated, in ziplock bag.

Mix mayonnaise and raspberry vinegar. Arrange asparagus spears on a platter with bowl of dip. Makes 8 servings.

Doe Hauser-Stowell

ASPARAGUS

Cream of Asparagus Soup

2 lbs. asparagus
3 cups water
1 chicken bouillon cube
3 tbsp. butter or margarine
¼ cup green onions, chopped
1 tbsp. chopped parsley (optional)
3 tbsp. all-purpose flour
⅛ tsp. ground nutmeg
½ tsp. salt
⅛ tsp. black pepper
1 cup 2% or skim milk

Blanch asparagus in boiling water until tender. Reserve liquid. Add bouillon cube to reserved liquid and dissolve. Add extra water if needed, to make 3 cups of broth.

Cut off asparagus tips and reserve. Cut remaining stems into 1-inch pieces. In a blender combine half of the cut stems with 1 cup of broth and process 1 minute until smooth. Repeat with remaining stems. Set aside.

Sauté onions and parsley in butter or margarine until soft. Add flour, nutmeg, salt, and pepper. Cook 1 minute. Add milk and bring to a boil, stirring constantly. Reduce heat and cook until thickened. Stir in asparagus purée, remaining broth and asparagus tips. Heat through, taste, and adjust seasonings. Makes 4 servings.

Pasta with Asparagus

¼ cup olive oil
2 cloves garlic
1 tsp. dried red pepper flakes or 1½ tsp. fresh cayenne pepper when in season
¼ tsp. Tabasco sauce (optional)
1 tbsp. butter or margarine
1 lb. fresh asparagus, tough ends removed and cut into 1½-inch pieces
Salt to taste
¼ tsp. black pepper
½ lb. ziti or penne pasta, cooked and drained
¼ cup Parmesan cheese

ASPARAGUS

Heat olive oil and butter or margarine in a skillet; add garlic, red pepper, and Tabasco sauce if desired. Cook for 2 to 3 minutes.

Add asparagus, salt, and pepper; sauté until asparagus is tender-crisp; about 8 to 10 minutes.

Pour asparagus over hot pasta. Add Parmesan cheese and toss to coat pasta. Serve immediately. Makes 4 servings.

COSTA FARM

Asparagus Filled Crepes

Crepes:
1¼ cups lowfat milk
1 cup all-purpose flour
2 eggs, beaten
2 tbsp. butter or vegetable oil
½ tsp. salt

Filling:
2 bunches asparagus, steamed whole
8 oz. feta cheese
Grated Swiss cheese

To make crepes; in a medium bowl combine milk, flour, eggs, butter or oil, and salt. Beat with a rotary beater until smooth. Let stand 1 hour, if you have the time. Otherwise, heat an 8-inch greased skillet and pour in a scant ¼ cup of batter. Quickly swirl batter to cover pan. Cook over medium-high heat until the top becomes dry and bottom is light brown; about 1 to 2 minutes. Flip with a spatula and brown the other side briefly. Brush the skillet with more olive oil in between each crepe. A paper towel works well. Make remaining crepes, cool on a wire rack and stack.

Preheat oven to 375 degrees. Place 3 to 4 stalks cooked asparagus on each crepe. Crumble portions of feta cheese over asparagus. Wrap up each crepe tightly and place side by side on a lightly-greased cookie sheet. Top with grated Swiss cheese. Bake for about 15 minutes or until cheese is melted and crepes are warmed through. Makes 6 servings.

LENGSFELD'S ORGANIC GARDENS

ASPARAGUS

Asparagus Baked in Foil

½ tbsp. olive oil
1 bunch asparagus
1 clove garlic, cut in slivers
Aluminum foil

Preheat oven to 350 degrees. Wash asparagus and trim off tough ends. Place asparagus on a sheet of aluminum foil, drizzled with olive oil. Sprinkle with garlic slivers. Wrap up to cover all. Bake for 20 to 30 minutes or until tender. Can also be grilled for 15 to 20 minutes.

JoAnn Kaiser

Asparagus Soufflé

1 cup of asparagus, trimmed and cut into 1-inch pieces (approximately
    1 pound)
1 cup milk
5 tbsp. lightly salted butter
1 medium yellow onion, finely chopped
3 tbsp. all-purpose flour
3 egg yolks
¾ cup freshly grated Parmesan cheese
Salt, freshly-ground black pepper and freshly grated nutmeg, to taste
5 egg whites, at room temperature
½ tsp. distilled white vinegar

Preheat oven to 400 degrees and place a rack in the center of the oven.

    Fill a saucepan large enough to hold the asparagus with lightly-salted water and bring to a boil. Add the asparagus pieces and cook until tender to slightly overcooked. Drain and return to the saucepan. Cover with 1 cup of milk, and bring to a boil. Remove from heat, allow to cool slightly, and purée in a food processor or blender.

    Melt butter in a 2-quart saucepan. With a pastry brush, butter a 1-quart soufflé dish or 6 individual dishes, dust with grated Parmesan and set aside. Add the onions and sauté over medium heat until lightly brown. Whisk in the flour and continue to cook for another 2 to 3 minutes.

ASPARAGUS

Add asparagus-milk purée to the onion-roux, stirring constantly over medium heat.

Remove pan from heat, and beat the egg yolks in, one at a time, mixing thoroughly after each yolk is added. Add ⅓ to ½ cup of the remaining Parmesan, reserving some for the top of the soufflé(s). Season with salt, pepper, and nutmeg to taste.

The soufflé can be done to this point ahead of time, and refrigerated for a few hours or overnight. Bring to room temperature before continuing.

Wipe the inside of the mixer bowl with the distilled white vinegar, allowing to air dry a few minutes before adding egg whites. This will help stabilize the whites so they won't collapse during folding and baking. (In lieu of vinegar, a pinch of cream of tartar added to the whites when foamy will do the same thing.) Add the room-temperature egg whites and beat. If you want a firmer soufflé, continue beating until very stiff. For a creamier soufflé, beat egg whites until they just begin to form stiff peaks.

Remove ⅓ of the egg whites and carefully but thoroughly fold them into the asparagus-béchamel. Make sure to fold from the bottom so the egg whites are evenly dispersed. Add remaining egg whites to the top of the mixture, and carefully fold in until just barely incorporated. *Don't over mix.* The color should be somewhat mottled.

Pour into the prepared soufflé dish(es) and sprinkle the top with the remaining Parmesan cheese. Place in the center of the middle rack. If you want a denser soufflé, reduce heat to 375 degrees, for a lighter leave at 400 degrees.

While the soufflé is baking, make the salad and set the table.

For 1 large soufflé: bake for 20 minutes *without opening the door.* Check the soufflé for the doneness by inserting a thin cake tester or a toothpick. It should come out fairly clean. If you desire a more done soufflé, continue baking for another 10 to 15 minutes.

For individual souffles: bake for 10 to 12 minutes *before checking,* and bake for an additional 2 to 3 minutes if desired. Serve immediately. Makes 6 individual servings or 1-quart soufflé.

B. J. Carpenter & Mary Ryan, Cooking Instructors
COOKS OF CROCUS HILL, ST. PAUL

ASPARAGUS

15

Asparagus with Goat Cheese and Morels on Fettuccine

½ cup shallots, minced
2 tbsp. unsalted butter
½ cup dry white wine
½ cup chicken broth
½ lb. fresh morels, or other brown mushrooms, such as porcini, sliced
    cross-wise
½ cup heavy cream
8 oz. mild goat cheese (about 1½ cups)
¾ lb. asparagus, trimmed, cut into ½-inch pieces and cooked in boiling
    salted water for 2 to 3 minutes or until tender
¼ cup fresh chives, minced
¾ lb. fettuccine

In a heavy skillet cook the shallots in butter over moderately low heat, stirring until softened, add wine, and simmer the mixture until the wine is reduced by half. Add the broth and the morels, and simmer the mixture, covered, for 10 minutes or until the morels are tender. Add the cream and the goat cheese and cook the mixture over low heat, stirring until the cheese is melted. Stir in the asparagus, chives, and salt and pepper to taste. Keep the sauce warm. In a kettle of boiling water, cook the fettuccine until it is *al dente*. Drain it well and toss the pasta in a bowl with the sauce. Makes 4–6 servings.

DANCING WINDS FARM

ASPARAGUS

16

Pickled Asparagus

4 lbs. asparagus
7 whole garlic cloves, peeled
1¾ tsp. dried hot red pepper, crushed
3½ tsp. dried dill seed
5 cups white vinegar
5 cups water
½ cup less 1 tbsp. canning salt

Wash asparagus and trim ends. Cut in lengths to allow them to stand upright in pint jars. In each sterilized pint jar, place 1 garlic clove, ¼ tsp. crushed dried hot pepper and ½ tsp. dill seed. Tightly pack asparagus upright leaving 1-inch headroom.

In a large stainless steel kettle, combine vinegar, water, and salt; heat. When mixture boils, pour over asparagus, leaving ½-inch headroom. Adjust clean hot lids. Process in boiling-water bath for 10 minutes. Remove and cool. Makes 7 pints.

ASPARAGUS

Beans

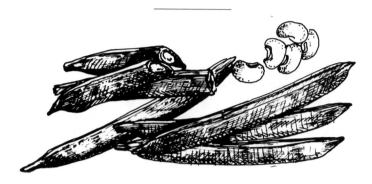

July–October

Green, yellow wax, Italian flat, pole, filet, long asparagus, and fava.

PREPARING BEANS

Wash and snap off tops. Leave whole, slice, or french cut diagonally into 1-inch pieces. Eat raw or cook until bright in color and tender. Microwave in a covered dish with 2 tbsp. water.

Blanch time: 5–7 minutes

Steam time: 7–10 minutes

Microwave time: 3–7 minutes

Yields: 1 lb. fresh beans equals 3 cups sliced beans.

Nutrition: 1 cup cooked beans has 30 calories and contains potassium and vitamin A.

Green and Yellow Bean Salad

1 lb. fresh green beans
1 lb. fresh wax beans
1 large red bell pepper
1 shallot, finely minced
1 bunch fresh tarragon
4 tbsp. tarragon or sherry vinegar
1 tsp. Dijon mustard
½ cup olive oil
Sea salt and freshly-ground black pepper to taste

Wash and clean beans, removing the ends, strings, if there are any, and any bruised spots. Fill a pot large enough to hold the beans ¾ full of water, and bring to a boil. Make an ice water bath large enough to hold the beans and place close to the sink. Place a colander in the sink. Add a pinch of salt to the boiling water. Add the beans and cook until *just barely* tender (about 1 to 1½ minutes depending on the size of the beans), drain in the colander, and immediately place in the ice water bath. This will stop the cooking and fix the color of the beans. Drain after several minutes, and spin in salad spinner to remove excess moisture, or pat dry with paper toweling. Place the beans in a large mixing bowl, and set aside.

Push the core of the red bell pepper in, and split the pepper. Remove the core, and shake all the seeds out of the pepper. Cut the pepper to the same length as the beans, removing any white flesh with the tip of the knife. Julienne into thin strips and add to beans.

Finely mince the shallot. Strip the tarragon leaves from the stem, and finely mince them. Place the shallots and tarragon in a blender, processor, or bowl with the Dijon mustard and the vinegar. Blend, process, or whisk to combine. Slowly add the olive oil while the blender or processor is running, or while whisking constantly. Add salt and pepper to taste. Adjust by adding more vinegar or oil if needed. Thin with water if too thick or vinegary.

Dress the beans and pepper, tossing to combine. Be careful not to overdress. Serve alone, or on a bed of mixed greens, if desired. Makes 6–8 servings.

B. J. Carpenter & Mary Ryan, Cooking Instructors
COOKS OF CROCUS HILL, ST. PAUL

Green Bean and Potato Salad

1 large red onion
1 tbsp. olive oil
¾ lb. green beans, trimmed and blanched
5 medium size potatoes, sliced and blanched
1 to 2 cloves of garlic, chopped
1 red bell pepper, roasted and sliced
2 tbsp. balsamic vinaigrette (see below)

Sauté sliced red onion in olive oil until transparent. Add garlic, sliced potatoes, green beans, and red pepper. Remove from heat and splash with balsamic vinaigrette. Season to taste and serve. Makes 8 servings.

Balsamic Vinaigrette:
¼ cup balsamic vinegar
1 tsp. sugar
¼ cup red wine
1 clove garlic, peeled and chopped
1 shallot, peeled and chopped
2 tbsp. fresh basil, chopped
2 tbsp. fresh parsley, chopped
¾ cup olive oil

Combine all ingredients in blender, pulsing only until garlic and shallots are
finely chopped. Makes 1½ cups.

Kevin Cullin, Executive Chef
GOODFELLOWS RESTAURANT

BEANS

Hungarian Green Bean Soup

3 cups good-quality chicken stock
½ lb. fresh green beans (or one 10½-oz.) pkg. frozen beans, thawed
2 small potatoes, peeled and quartered
½ large onion, quartered
¼ cup (½ stick) butter
2 tbsp. fresh dill, snipped
2 cloves garlic, crushed
Salt and freshly-ground black pepper
¼ cup sour cream, room temperature
Juice of ½ lemon

Combine stock, beans, potatoes, onion, butter, dill, and garlic in large saucepan over high heat and bring to boil. Reduce heat, cover, and simmer until vegetables are tender, about 20 to 24 minutes. Taste and add salt and fresh ground pepper.

Transfer soup to blender in batches and purée until smooth. Return to saucepan. Stir in sour cream and lemon juice. Cook on low until heated through. Makes 4 servings.

Mary Broeker

Basil Green Beans and Cherry Tomatoes

4 cups green and yellow beans, steamed
2 cups red and gold cherry tomatoes, halved
1 tbsp. olive oil
3 cloves garlic, minced
½ tsp. salt
¼ tsp. freshly-ground black pepper
2 tbsp. fresh basil, finely chopped

Cut steamed beans into 1-inch pieces. In a large bowl, combine cherry tomatoes, olive oil, garlic, salt, and pepper. Add hot beans along with basil. Mix well. Makes 8 servings.

Carol Mack & John Stewart

BEANS

Bean Stew and Dumplings

Dumplings:
2 cups all-purpose flour
2 eggs, beaten
½ cup lowfat milk
Pinch of salt

Stew:
4 tbsp. vegetable oil
1 large onion, chopped
4 cups carrots, sliced
8 cups chicken flavored broth
½ tsp. dried thyme
½ tbsp. salt
⅛ tsp. black pepper
4 cups green beans, cut into 1-inch pieces

Make dumplings by mixing flour, eggs, milk, and salt in a medium bowl. Stir until dough becomes very stiff. Cover bowl with a towel and set aside. In a large pot heat oil and sauté the onion until soft. Add remaining ingredients, except beans, and bring to a boil. Then add dumplings. To add dumplings, first stir relaxed dough until it is stiff again. Spoon teaspoon-sized pieces of dough into boiling soup. Cover, reduce heat and cook over medium heat for 45 minutes. Add beans and cook for 20 minutes or until beans are bright in color and tender. Makes 8 servings.

Mary Lengsfeld

Italian Beans with Tomato, Onion, and Garlic

1 lb. fresh flat Italian green beans, washed, ends trimmed, and cut into
    1-inches pieces
Salt to taste
1 tbsp. olive oil
1 onion, halved and sliced thinly
2 cloves garlic, peeled and minced
3 fresh ripe tomatoes, cored, peeled and diced
Salt and black pepper to taste
Pinch of cayenne pepper

BEANS

Wash, trim ends, and cut beans into 1-inch pieces. Cook in a saucepan with 1 to 2 cups of salted water for 12 to 15 minutes or until tender-crisp. Drain and set aside.

Heat oil in large no-stick skillet; add onions and garlic. Sauté for 4 to 5 minutes, until onions are translucent. Add tomatoes, salt, black pepper, and cayenne pepper; heat to simmering. Add beans and simmer 5 minutes longer. Makes 4 servings.

Ulrich Bloecher

Wonderful Green Beans

*The seasonings make the green beans sensational. They are so flavorful
that people who hate green beans love them when prepared this way*

2 lbs. fresh green beans
2 tbsp. olive oil or 1 tbsp. olive oil and 1 tbsp. butter
1 small onion, chopped
2 cloves garlic, minced
½ tsp. ground cumin
¼ tsp. ground coriander
Salt and black pepper to taste
Chopped almonds if desired

Trim ends of green beans and cut into bite-size pieces approximately 1-inch long. Cook the beans in a small amount of water until tender; about 15 to 20 minutes. Drain and set aside.

Place 2 tablespoons oil or butter in saucepan and heat on medium low heat. Add onions and garlic and sauté until onion is tender. Add cumin and coriander and mix well. Add the green beans and stir. Salt and pepper to taste. Chopped almonds can be added if desired but dish is equally as good without. Makes 6–8 servings.

Xelma Q. Pitzl

BEANS

23

Chinese Stir-fried Green Beans

2 tbsp. peanut oil or salad oil
1 lb. fresh young green beans, washed, stem end snipped, and blanched
    2 minutes in boiling water, refreshed in cold water, drained, and dried
1 clove garlic, minced
1 tsp. chili paste (available in Asian markets, may be omitted for a less
    spicy dish)
1 tbsp. soy sauce
1 tbsp. hoisin sauce (available in Asian markets)
2 tbsp. chicken broth or water
1 tsp. cornstarch mixed with 1 tsp. water

Heat wok or cast iron skillet until very hot. Add oil, beans, and garlic. Stir-fry for 1 minute. Add chili paste, soy sauce and stir until mixed. Add chicken broth or water. Cover and cook 1 minute. Add the cornstarch and water mixture. Continue stir-frying until liquid is thickened and coats the beans. Serve immediately with rice. Makes 4 servings.

HILLTOP PRODUCE FARM

Dilled Green Beans

3 lbs. whole green beans
3¼ cups white vinegar
3¼ cups water
6 tbsp. canning salt
1½ tsp. dried hot red pepper, crushed
6 whole garlic cloves, peeled
6 fresh dill heads

Wash beans and trim ends. Cut them in lengths to allow them to stand upright in pint jars. In each sterilized pint jar place ¼ tsp. crushed dried hot red pepper, 1 garlic clove, and 1 dill head. Pack beans upright as tightly as you can, leaving 1-inch headroom.

In a large stainless steel kettle, combine vinegar, water, and salt; heat. When mixture boils, pour over beans leaving ½-inch headroom. Adjust clean hot lids. Process in boiling-water bath for 10 minutes. Remove and cool. Makes 6 pints.

Vi Rothe

BEANS

Beets

July–November

PREPARING BEETS

Wash and trim off greens and tap root leaving 1-inch of both stem and tap root. Cook small beets whole or cut larger ones into slices. Boil whole beets or steam slices until tender. Microwave in a covered dish with 2 tbsp. water. Large beets can be baked whole by pricking several holes with a knife and placing in a covered baking dish with ¼ cup water. Slip skins off after cooking.

Blanch time: 20–25 minutes

Steam time: 20–30 minutes

Microwave time: 9–12 minutes

Bake time: 45 minutes to 1½ hours, depending on size

Yields: 1 lb. fresh equals approximately six 2-inch beets, 4 cups raw or cooked sliced.

Nutrition: 1 cup cooked beets has 55 calories and contains potassium.

Roasted Beet Salad

Dressing:
3 tbsp. raspberry vinegar
2 tbsp. seedless, raspberry jam
1 tbsp. crumbled blue cheese
Salt and freshly cracked ground black pepper
¾ cup (6oz.) flavorless vegetable oil (canola)
2 tbsp. walnut oil

Place vinegar, blue cheese, raspberry jam, salt, and pepper in the bowl of a food processor and blend until smooth. Slowly add the vegetable and walnut oils, and drizzle into mixture through the feed tube. Continue to process until smooth and well blended. Remove and reserve.

Salad:
1 cup walnuts, toasted
4 oz. blue cheese, crumbled
2 bunches beets, about 8 total, cleaned and trimmed
1 pint fresh raspberries
1 red onion, thinly sliced
Mesclun, curly, endive, arugula, or other bitter greens, trimmed washed
    and dried

Preheat oven to 350 degrees. Toast the walnut pieces in the oven for about 3 to 4 minutes, shaking the pan once during this time. Toasted walnuts should remain golden in color with a wonderful nutty aroma. If the skins become too dark, start over. The flavor will be far too bitter for your salad. Once toasted, allow nuts to cool completely.

Increase the oven heat to 375 degrees. Place trimmed beets on a sided-sheet pan and roast for approximately 45 minutes to 1 hour, depending on the size. They should be slightly tender at this point. Next, reduce the oven temperature to 350 degrees, cover the entire contents with aluminum foil, and continue to bake for an additional 20 to 30 minutes. Remove from oven and allow to steam, covered for 10 to 15 minutes. Remove the skins, halve and slice beets into ¼-inch pieces. Reserve.

Trim, wash by scraping with a table knife, and thoroughly dry the greens before use. Reserve greens, wrapped in a kitchen towel, jelly-roll style, in refrigerator until service.

BEETS

To assemble the salad:

Reserve a little crumbled cheese, walnuts, and raspberries to garnish the top of the salad.

Gently toss greens with fresh raspberries, crumbled blue cheese, walnuts, onion slices, and half of the dressing. At this point place the salad on plates individually or place the entire contents in a serving bowl.

Place the reserved beet slices on top of this mixture and garnish with the remaining walnuts and raspberries. Drizzle a little more dressing on the top of the beets and garnish with the remaining blue cheese. Finish with a little freshly cracked pepper. Makes 4 servings.

B. J. Carpenter & Mary Ryan, Cooking Instructors
COOKS OF CROCUS HILL, ST. PAUL

Beet and Apple Salad

4 medium beets
1 cup apples, peeled and diced
2 tbsp. vegetable oil
2 tbsp. red wine vinegar
2 tbsp. lemon juice
¼ cup honey
½ tsp. salt

In a covered saucepan, cook beets in boiling water until tender, about 20 minutes. Peel and dice. In a medium bowl, whisk together oil, vinegar, lemon juice, honey and salt. Add beets and apples and toss to coat. Makes 4 servings.

BEETS

Beet Borscht

5 cups water
1½ cups beets, peeled and diced
1 cup potatoes, peeled and diced
1 cup carrots, peeled and diced
1 tsp. salt
2 tbsp. butter or vegetable oil
1 onion, chopped
2 cloves garlic, minced
1 cup green or red cabbage, shredded
½ cup tomato, chopped
½ cup beet, peeled and grated
1 tsp. dried dill
1 tsp. honey
½ tsp. Worcestershire
Salt and black pepper

Bring 5 cups water to boil and add diced beets, potato, carrot, and salt. Reduce heat and cook covered over medium heat for 30 minutes or until vegetables are soft.

In a saucepan, heat butter or oil and sauté onion and garlic until soft. Add the cabbage and sauté for 3 minutes. Stir in tomatoes, grated beet and remaining ingredients. Mix well. Add sauté mixture to boiled vegetables. Simmer for 10 to 20 minutes or until vegetables are tender. Salt and pepper to taste. Makes 6–8 servings.

Evelyn Kaiser

BEETS

German Beets

6 medium beets
2 tbsp. red wine vinegar
¼ cup red wine
3 tbsp. butter
1 tbsp. all-purpose flour
1 cup meat flavored stock
½ tsp. salt
1 tsp. sugar
1 tsp. whole caraway seed

In a medium saucepan, cook beets in boiling water until tender, about 20 to 30 minutes. Peel and slice beets into sticks, place in a bowl. Add vinegar and wine. Marinate 30 minutes.

Melt butter, add flour, and cook over low heat for 1 minute, stirring. Pour in stock and simmer for 10 minutes, stirring. Add remaining ingredients and stir. Drain beets, add to hot sauce, and stir gently. Makes 4–6 servings.

Honey Baked Beets

6 medium beets
Juice of 1 lemon
2 tbsp. ghee (clarified butter) or butter
¼ cup honey

Preheat oven to 350 degrees. Trim off tops of beets and put on a lightly greased cookie sheet. Bake until very soft, about 45 to 60 minutes. Cool, remove loose skin and slice thinly.

In a skillet melt ghee or butter. Add honey and lemon juice and mix well. Add beets and mix. Cook over low heat until heated through. Makes 4–6 servings.

Geoffrey Saign

Granny's Quick Pickled Beets

1 bunch fresh beets, tops removed
Water for cooking
1 cup sugar
1 cup water
¾ cup white vinegar
1 tsp. salt
2 bay leaves
8 whole cloves
2 allspice berries

Place beets in a large saucepan, cover with water and bring to a boil. Lower heat and simmer until done, about 20 to 30 minutes.

While beets are cooking, combine remaining ingredients in a saucepan and bring to a boil; simmer 5 minutes. Drain, peel, and cut beets in slices or chunks. Put into a jar or bowl and pour hot pickling liquid over beets. Cover and refrigerate overnight. Makes about 1 quart.

Kim Pinkham

Pickled Beets

13 cups whole beets
1½ cups white vinegar
1½ cups water
1 cup sugar
¼ tsp. ground cinnamon
¼ tsp. ground cloves
3 tsp. canning salt (optional)

Scrub beets well, place them in a pot, cover with water and bring to a boil. Reduce heat and simmer, covered, for 20 to 30 minutes or until beets are tender. Dunk in cold water, strip off skins, and slice.

In a large stainless steel kettle, combine vinegar, water, sugar, cinnamon, and cloves. Bring to a boil.

Fill hot sterilized pint jars with hot beet slices, leaving ½-inch headroom. Add ½ tsp. salt (optional) to each jar. Add boiling syrup leaving ½-inch headroom. Adjust clean hot lids. Process in boiling-water bath for 30 minutes. Remove and cool. Makes 6 pints.

Broccoli

PREPARING BROCCOLI

Wash and remove outer leaves. Leaves may be cooked and eaten as well for a tasty treat. Cut florets and stems into ½-inch pieces. Stems may be peeled or not. Eat raw or cook until bright in color and tender. Microwave in a covered dish with 2 tbsp. water.

Blanch time: 4–6 minutes

Steam time: 8–12 minutes

Microwave time: 4–7 minutes

Yields: 1 lb. fresh equals 2 three-inch heads of broccoli which equals 5 cups florets and chopped stems.

Nutrition: 1 cup cooked broccoli has 40 calories and contains substantial amounts of calcium, potassium and vitamins A and C.

Creamy Broccoli Salad with Raisins and Bacon

1 bunch broccoli, 3 stalks
½ cup red onion, chopped
1 cup roasted sunflower seeds
½ cup raisins
8 strips bacon, fried crisp, drained and crumbled

Dressing:
1 cup mayonnaise, light or regular
½ cup sugar
2 tbsp. vinegar or raspberry vinegar

Wash and cut up broccoli into bite-size florets. Peel and cut the stems into bite-size pieces as well. Add onion, sunflower seeds, raisins, and crumbled bacon. In a small bowl combine mayonnaise, sugar, and vinegar. Mix well until sugar is dissolved. Add to vegetables and mix well. Serve immediately. Makes 8–10 servings.

Janet Kogler

Broccoli Vegetable Pasta Salad

Amounts given are approximate, but fresh tomatoes are a must.

2 quarts water for cooking
4 oz. spaghetti or vermicelli
2 cups broccoli florets
1 burpless cucumber, sliced
1 small onion, diced
2–3 fresh tomatoes, diced
½ bottle Italian dressing
Mixed Italian herbs

Break spaghetti into 4 to 5 pieces before cooking. Cook in 2 quarts boiling water. Drain and rinse.

In a large bowl combine spaghetti with remaining ingredients. Mix well. You will need at least half of the dressing bottle. Add Italian herbs. Makes 4–6 servings.

Ann DesLauriers

BROCCOLI

Szechwan Broccoli Beef Salad

This spicy salad is a delicious luncheon meal and may be prepared a day ahead

2 lbs. fresh broccoli
¼ cup peanut oil—add 1 tbsp. sesame oil
1 large sweet red bell pepper, seeded and cut into strips
1 cup fresh mushrooms, sliced
½ cup rice wine vinegar
2 tbsp. soy sauce
1 tsp. dried red peppers, crushed (or to taste)
1 tsp. fresh ginger grated
2 cloves garlic, crushed
1 lb. rare lean roast beef, julienned
1 (8oz.) can water chestnuts, drained and sliced
1 (8oz.) can bamboo shoots, drained

Wash broccoli and cut into florets in a large bowl. Peel and slice stems. In a large skillet or wok heat 2 tbsp. oil. Stir-fry broccoli stems first, then add florets for 1 to 2 minutes. Cover pan and cook 2 minutes more. Transfer to the bowl. Stir-fry the sweet red pepper strips in fresh oil 1 to 2 minutes; add to broccoli. Stir-fry mushrooms in fresh oil 1 to 2 minutes; add to broccoli and peppers.

 Combine vinegar, soy sauce, red pepper, ginger and garlic. Pour over the stir-fried vegetables. Add beef, water chestnuts and bamboo shoots. Marinate, refrigerated, overnight. Makes 6 servings.

Kim Pinkham

Broccoli Cheese Soup

2 tbsp. chopped onion
3 tbsp. butter
3 tbsp. all-purpose flour
¼ tsp. black pepper
2 cups milk, lowfat
1 cup cheddar cheese, grated
2 chicken bouillon cubes dissolved in 1½ cups boiling water
1 head partially cooked broccoli, chopped

BROCCOLI

In a large pot, sauté onion in butter until transparent. Blend in flour and pepper. Blend in milk and bouillon and bring to a boil. Stir in cheese. Add broccoli. Simmer, covered, until vegetables are tender, about 20 to 30 minutes. Makes 6 servings.

JORDAN RANCH

Easy Broccoli Stir-fry with Tempeh

4 cups cut broccoli florets and sliced stems
1 (8oz.) pkg. of tempeh, diced ½-inch cubes
3 tbsp. vegetable oil
1 small onion, chopped
1 clove garlic, minced

Binder:
2 tsp. cornstarch
¼ cup cold chicken flavored broth
2 tbsp. soy sauce

Cut broccoli into bite-size pieces. Peel stems if desired and slice into very thin slices. Set aside.

In a large saucepan heat 1 tbsp. oil. Add tempeh cubes and fry over medium heat until golden brown on all sides, turning when needed. Pour tempeh cubes on a plate and set aside.

In the same large sauce pan, heat the remaining 2 tbsp. oil. Sauté onion and garlic over medium heat until soft, about 3 minutes. Stir in broccoli and stir-fry over medium heat until bright green, about 5 to 7 minutes.

Make binder. In a small bowl mix cornstarch with cold chicken flavored broth and soy sauce. Pour into broccoli mixture, along with tempeh cubes. Stir and cook until tender. Serve with rice. Makes 6–8 servings.

LENGSFELD'S ORGANIC GARDENS

BROCCOLI

Broccoli Frittata

Any leftover cooked vegetable may be used in a frittata. Double or triple the recipe for more servings.

3 tbsp. onion or 2 tbsp. chopped shallots, finely chopped
1 tbsp. butter or vegetable oil
1 small clove garlic, minced
1 cup potatoes, cooked and sliced
1½ cups broccoli, cooked and chopped
3 tbsp. grated Parmesan cheese
2 eggs, beaten lightly
¼ cup 2% milk
Salt and black pepper to taste
⅓ cup mozzarella cheese, grated

Sauté onion or shallots in butter or oil until tender but not brown, using an 8 or 10-inch nonstick skillet. Stir in garlic and potatoes; sauté lightly. Add broccoli and stir to mix. Combine Parmesan cheese, eggs, milk, salt, and pepper. Pour over the broccoli-potato mixture, lower heat, and cover. Cook slowly until eggs are partially set. Sprinkle mozzarella cheese over the top, cover, and cook slowly until cheese is melted and eggs are completely set. Using a spatula, ease the frittata out of the pan and onto a serving plate. Cut in wedges and serve. Makes 2 servings.

Crystal Bloecher

Broccoli Rice Casserole

1 large head fresh broccoli
1 lb. lean hamburger
2 tbsp. butter
1 small onion, sliced
½ cup celery, sliced
1 (10½ oz.) can cream of mushroom soup
½ cup whole or 2% milk
1 cup raw quick-cooking rice
½ cup cheddar cheese, grated

Preheat oven to 350 degrees. Wash, cut up, and cook broccoli until tender-crisp; drain. Brown hamburger in a nonstick skillet; drain. Melt butter in the same skillet and sauté onion and celery until semisoft. Add remaining ingredients and broccoli; pour into a greased baking dish and bake, covered, for 45 minutes. Makes 6 servings.

HILLTOP PRODUCE FARM

BROCCOLI

Brussels Sprouts

PREPARING BRUSSELS SPROUTS

Wash and trim outer leaves and tough stem ends. Cut an X in the stem. Leave whole or cut in half and cook until tender. Microwave in a covered dish with 2 tbsp. water.

Blanch time: 5 minutes

Steam time: 10–15 minutes

Microwave time: 4–6 minutes

Yields: 1 lb. fresh equals 40 Brussels sprouts or 3½ cups whole.

Nutrition: 1 cup cooked sprouts has 30 calories and contains potassium and vitamins A and C.

Marinated Brussels Sprouts

1½ lb. Brussels sprouts, cooked or steamed tender-crisp
½ cup tarragon vinegar (or may use plain vinegar with 1 tsp. chopped
    fresh tarragon)
½ cup salad oil
1 small clove garlic, crushed
1 tbsp. sugar
1 tsp. salt
Dash of Tabasco sauce
I green onion, thinly sliced

In a medium bowl whisk together vinegar, oil, garlic, sugar, salt, and Tabasco sauce. Add Brussels sprouts and green onion. Toss well. Cover and refrigerate 8 hours or overnight, stirring occasionally. Makes 6 servings.

HILLTOP PRODUCE FARM

Roasted Brussels Sprouts

5 tbsp. extra virgin olive oil
1½ lbs. Brussels sprouts
5 or 6 fresh herb sprigs such as rosemary or thyme
1 tbsp. garlic, minced
Freshly ground salt & black pepper to taste

Preheat oven to 425 degrees. Heat olive oil in small sauté pan. Add Brussels sprouts, herbs, and garlic. Toss to coat. Place in a shallow roasting pan. Cook for 35 minutes shaking pan 2 or 3 times during roasting process. If no browning occurs, increase heat by 30 degrees. Sprinkle with salt and pepper. Makes 6–8 servings.

GOLDEN FIG EPICUREAN DELIGHTS

BRUSSELS SPROUTS

Lemon Garlic Brussels Sprouts

1 lb. Brussels sprouts
3 tbsp. butter
2 shallots, finely chopped
2 cloves garlic, minced
3 tbsp. lemon juice
Salt and black pepper to taste

Wash and clean Brussels sprouts, making a crosscut in the base of each for more even cooking. Steam the sprouts for 10 minutes or until desired doneness is reached. Meanwhile, melt butter in a skillet; add shallots. Sauté until shallots are transparent; add garlic and sauté a bit longer. Add lemon juice and Brussels sprouts. Add salt and pepper to taste. Lower heat and steam sprouts until they are reheated. Makes 4 servings.

HILLTOP PRODUCE FARM

Creamed Brussels Sprouts

3 cups Brussels sprouts, washed and trimmed
3 tbsp. butter or margarine
3 tbsp. all-purpose flour
1½ cups warm lowfat milk, use less for a thinner sauce and more for a
    thicker one.
1 tsp. salt
½ cup cheddar or Swiss cheese (optional)

Steam Brussels sprouts until tender, about 15 minutes. In a medium saucepan, melt butter or margarine, stir in flour and cook over low heat, stirring constantly for 2 minutes. Add warm milk all at once, and bring to a boil, stirring. Reduce heat and stir until sauce thickens. Stir in salt. Pour over Brussels sprouts.
    Variation: For a cheese sauce, stir in ½ cup grated cheddar or Swiss cheese along with the salt. Stir until melted. Makes 4–6 servings.

Duane Lengsfeld

BRUSSELS SPROUTS

for _new_ recipes

- green onions
- asparagus - 2 lbs
- Chic. bouillon
- fresh parsley
- canola oil
- brocoli
- bell pepper
- bread crumbs
- ½ lb. Kielbasa sausage
- 1 lb. lentils
- 15 oz. canned tom. (diced)
- small cabbage
- caraway seed

<u>

Savory Brussels Sprouts

1½ lb. fresh Brussels sprouts
4 tbsp. butter
1 tbsp. whole mustard seed

Clean Brussels sprouts and make a small crosscut in the base of each (for more uniform cooking). Cook or steam sprouts in a small amount of water for 7 to 10 minutes, depending on the desired doneness. Drain and keep warm. Meanwhile, melt butter in a small skillet and add mustard seeds. Sauté seeds over low heat for 3 to 5 minutes or until lightly browned; some seeds will pop open from heat—this is good. Pour seeds and butter over the drained sprouts, stir to coat, and serve immediately. Makes 6 servings.

HILLTOP PRODUCE FARM

Honey Braised Brussels Sprouts

2 lbs. Brussels sprouts
1 tbsp. garlic, chopped
1 tbsp. olive oil
1 tbsp. honey
Juice of 1 lemon
Salt and cayenne pepper

Preheat oven to 375 degrees. Steam Brussels sprouts until tender. In a bowl combine olive oil, honey, garlic, and lemon juice. Add Brussels sprouts and coat well. Spread the coated Brussels sprouts on a baking sheet and sprinkle with salt and cayenne pepper. Roast in oven for 20 minutes. Makes 8–10 servings.

Geoffrey Saign

BRUSSELS SPROUTS

Brussels Sprouts Meatballs

24–30 Brussels sprouts
1 lb. ground beef, ground turkey, or soy hamburger
¼ cup onion, chopped
1 egg, beaten
2 slices bread, torn up in 1-inch pieces
1 tsp. salt
⅛ tsp. black pepper
⅛ tsp. garlic powder
Vegetable oil for frying
Spaghetti sauce

Steam Brussels sprouts until tender, about 15 minutes.

In a large bowl, mix all ingredients, except Brussels sprouts. Press mixture around each sprout until covered. Fry in an oiled skillet until golden brown. Simmer in spaghetti sauce and serve over pasta. Makes 6 servings.

Evelyn Kaiser

BRUSSELS SPROUTS

Pickled Brussels Sprouts

4 lbs. Brussels sprouts
4 cups water
1 tbsp. salt
7 whole garlic cloves, peeled
3½ tsp. dried dill seed
1¾ tsp. dried hot red pepper, crushed
5 cups white vinegar
5 cups water
½ cup less 1 tbsp. canning salt

Wash Brussels sprouts and soak for 10 minutes in a bath of 4 cups water and 1 tbsp. salt to drive out bugs. Rinse. Cut an X deeply into the core of each Brussels sprout.

In each sterilized pint jar, place 1 clove garlic, ½ tsp. dill seed, and ¼ tsp. crushed dried hot red pepper. Tightly pack Brussels sprouts leaving ¾-inch headroom.

In a large stainless steel kettle, combine vinegar, water, and salt; heat. When mixture boils, pour over Brussels sprouts, leaving ½-inch headroom. Adjust clean hot lids. Process in boiling-water bath for 10 minutes. Remove and cool. Makes 7 pints.

BRUSSELS SPROUTS

Cabbage

WHEN AVAILABLE

July–Frost

SOME VARIETIES

Green, red, savoy, and Chinese

PREPARING CABBAGE

Wash, peel outer leaves, and cut in half. Cut each half into 4 wedges or chop into 1-inch pieces or shred. Eat raw or cook until tender. Microwave in a covered dish with 2 tbsp. water.

Blanch time: 6–8 minutes

Steam time: 6–10 minutes

Microwave time: 4–6 minutes

Yields: 1 lb. fresh equals ½ medium head cabbage or 4 cups chopped.

Nutrition: 1 cup cooked has 30 calories and contains potassium and Vitamins A and C.

Vinegar Coleslaw

3 cups cabbage, shredded
½ cup green pepper, chopped
¼ cup white vinegar
¼ cup sugar
2 tbsp. water or vegetable oil
½ tsp. salt
½ tsp. whole celery seed
½ tsp. dried mustard

In a small bowl combine vinegar, sugar, water or oil, salt, celery seed, and mustard. Combine cabbage and chopped pepper in a large bowl. Pour dressing over cabbage mixture and mix well. Chill. Makes 6 servings.

Mrs. Bernice Beulke

Oriental Cabbage Raman Noodle Salad

1 (3oz.) pkg. chicken-flavored raman noodles
½ medium sized head cabbage, shredded
3 tbsp. toasted sunflower seeds or slivered almonds
2 green onions, thinly sliced

Dressing:
Raman noodle seasoning packet
2 tbsp. sugar
3 tbsp. white vinegar
⅓ cup vegetable oil
½ tsp. salt
¼ tsp. black pepper
1 tsp. MSG (optional)
1 small clove garlic, pushed through a garlic press or crushed

Break up raman noodles into a medium bowl. Add the remaining ingredients. In a small bowl, combine dressing ingredients and pour over salad. Chill 1 to 2 hours before serving. Makes 8 servings.

Crystal Bloecher

CABBAGE

4th of July Pineapple Coleslaw
Our yearly holiday tradition for the summer's first cabbage!

4 cups green cabbage, shredded
1 cup Miracle Whip
1 tbsp. white vinegar
1 (8oz.) can crushed pineapple, drained

In a large bowl, stir together Miracle Whip, vinegar, and pineapple until smooth. Stir in cabbage until well coated. Makes 8 servings

Duane Lengsfeld

Cabbage Soup

1 small head green cabbage (3–4 cups shredded)
2 slices bacon, diced
1 large onion, chopped
2 small leeks, white part only, sliced
2 carrots, sliced
1 potato, peeled and diced
1 tbsp. all-purpose flour
6 cups brown stock (beef or ham)
2 tbsp. parsley, chopped
1 bay leaf
Salt and black pepper to taste
Pinch of ground nutmeg
2 tsp. fresh dill, chopped
3 or 4 frankfurters, sliced and fried
Vegetable oil for frying

Put shredded cabbage into a saucepan of boiling, salted water. Cook 5 minutes; drain and rinse under cold water. Set aside.

Meanwhile, in a large soup pot, heat bacon over gentle heat and fry for a few minutes, until some fat is rendered. Add onion, leeks, carrots, and potato; stir a few minutes to heat vegetables. Sprinkle in flour; blend well. Add stock, parsley, bay leaf, salt, and pepper; bring to a boil. Reduce heat and simmer 10 minutes. Add cabbage. Cook 30 minutes or until vegetables are tender but not mushy. Adjust seasoning by taste; add nutmeg and dill. Remove bay leaf.

CABBAGE

While soup is cooking, heat oil in a skillet and sauté frankfurter slices until brown. Serve soup in bowls, adding a few slices of frankfurter to each one. Makes 6 servings.

HILLTOP PRODUCE FARM

Grilled Cabbage

1 small head green cabbage
2–4 tbsp. butter
Seasoned salt
Aluminum foil, heavy duty

Preheat grill. Cut cabbage into 8 wedges. Place a cabbage wedge on a 12-inch square piece of heavy duty aluminum foil. Dot with butter and sprinkle with seasoned salt. Fold in edges of foil to seal. Repeat with remaining cabbage wedges.

Place over hot coals on the rack of the grill. Cook for 20 to 30 minutes, turning several times, until tender. Makes 8 servings.

Ann DesLauriers

Cabbage Succotash

3 ears fresh sweet corn, peeled
3 cups green cabbage, chopped
2 cups lima beans, cooked
2 tbsp. butter or margarine
1 medium onion, chopped
1½ tsp. balsamic vinegar
1 tsp. salt
¼ tsp. black pepper

In a large pot, cook corn in boiling water until tender, about 7 to 10 minutes. Cut kernels off the cobs with a sharp knife.

Steam chopped cabbage until tender, about 7 to 10 minutes. In a large skillet, heat butter or margarine and sauté onion until soft. Add the cooked corn kernels, cabbage, balsamic vinegar, and mix well. Salt and pepper to taste. Makes 8 servings.

CABBAGE

Sweet-Sour Savoy Cabbage Rolls

1 sweet red pepper, seeded, cut in strips and blanched 30 seconds in
   boiling water
1 small onion, peeled, cut in thin strips and blanched 30 seconds in
   boiling water
1 large head savoy cabbage
2 tbsp. corn starch
½ cup sugar
¼ cup white vinegar

Pork filling:
1 lb. lean ground pork
¼ cup raisins
½ cup onion, finely diced
¼ cup uncooked rice
½ tsp. salt
¼ tsp. black pepper
1 tbsp. ginger root, minced or grated
1 clove garlic, minced
1 tbsp. soy sauce

Bring a large saucepan of water to a rolling boil. Blanch red pepper and onion strips and remove to drain in a colander. Carefully, and without tearing, remove twelve leaves from the savoy cabbage head (may have to blanch the whole head to loosen leaves). Blanch each leaf about 1½ minutes, until limp. Rinse in cold water and drain thoroughly. Cut the large midrib out of each leaf and discard. Fill each leaf with 3 tbsp. of pork filling and roll up, tucking the sides in to enclose the filling completely. Place the rolls on a steamer rack with 1-inch of water in the pan below. Steam 25 minutes. Remove rolls and keep warm. Add water to steaming liquid to make 1½ cups. Return to pan and heat. Mix corn starch, sugar, and vinegar; stir to dissolve sugar. Add to cooking steaming liquid and stir until thickened. Add red pepper and onion. Return cabbage rolls to pan and reheat. Serve with cooked rice. Makes 6 servings.

HILLTOP PRODUCE FARM

CABBAGE

Savoy Cabbage and Beef Hotdish

6 strips of bacon, cut into 1-inch pieces
1½ lbs. lean round steak, cut into ½-inch cubes
1 onion, finely chopped
6 cups savoy cabbage, finely chopped
2 cups beef broth or bouillon
6 cups potatoes, peeled and cubed
1 large clove garlic, crushed
⅛ tsp. freshly grated nutmeg
½ tsp. salt or to taste
¼ tsp. black pepper

Preheat oven to 350 degrees. In a large, heavy 3 or 4 quart casserole, fry bacon until almost crisp. Add beef and onion; brown lightly. Add cabbage and broth. Cook for 10 minutes. Add potatoes, crushed garlic, nutmeg, salt and pepper, and mix well. Bake, covered, in a preheated oven at 350 degrees for 1½ hours. Check after 1 hour to make sure that there is enough moisture. Add ½ cup water if necessary. Makes 6 servings.

Ulrich Bloecher

Sweet and Sour Red Cabbage with Bacon

8 slices of bacon
1 large onion, chopped
⅓ cup cider vinegar
4 tbsp. brown sugar
1 tsp. salt
1 tsp. dried mustard
1 medium head red cabbage
2 tbsp. cornstarch
⅔ cup water

Fry bacon, drain, reserving 2 tbsp. fat, and crumble. Brown onions in bacon grease, remove from pan. Mix vinegar, sugar, salt, and mustard in ⅔ cup water. Pour mixture into pan. Add cabbage and cook for 15 minutes. Mix cornstarch with ⅔ cup water. Add crumbled bacon and onions to vinegar mixture. Simmer until liquid is clear. Makes 8 servings.

Jan Heaberlin

CABBAGE

German Sweet-Sour Red Cabbage with Apples
A prized family recipe

1 medium head red cabbage
1 tbsp. butter
1 large onion, diced
1 cup apple cider or water
1 bay leaf
1 tsp. salt
4 medium apples, Macintosh or any other tart-sweet Minnesota apple
½ cup white vinegar
¼ cup sugar
⅛ tsp. ground cloves
⅛ tsp. black pepper
¼ cup red wine (optional)

Shred and chop cabbage. Melt butter in a large saucepan. Sauté onion until transparent, but do not brown. Add cabbage and mix well, sautéing lightly. Add cider or water, bay leaf and salt. Bring to a boil, lower heat, and allow to simmer. Meanwhile, peel and chop apples. Add to cabbage and simmer 45 minutes to one hour, until apples are soft and cabbage is well cooked. Add vinegar, sugar, cloves, pepper, and red wine, if desired. Simmer 15 minutes longer to blend flavors. Adjust sweetness and sourness with more sugar and/or vinegar to taste.

Note: For best flavor, may be made one or two days ahead and reheated. Recipe may be doubled. This cooked red cabbage keeps up to two weeks in the refrigerator, or it may also be frozen for future use. Makes 8–10 servings.

Helene Bloecher

Purple Cabbage Potato Salad

3½ cups new potatoes
2 tbsp. extra light virgin olive oil
2 tbsp. red wine vinegar
½ tsp. salt
½ cup black olives, sliced
2 cups purple cabbage, shredded
¼ cup baby dill pickles, chopped
⅔ cup mayonnaise
1 tbsp. Dijon mustard
2 tbsp. onions, minced
Black pepper

Boil potatoes with jackets on. Break up while still hot. Stir together olive oil and vinegar. Add to potatoes. Refrigerate until potatoes have cooled. Combine salt, olives, cabbage, dill pickles, carrots, and green peppers. Combine mayonnaise and mustard. Add onions and black pepper. Mix all of above. Refrigerate, preferably overnight, to develop flavor. Makes 6 servings.

Deb McNeely-Goodell

CABBAGE

51

Carrots

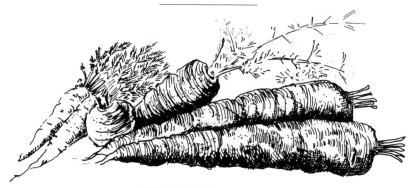

PREPARING CARROTS

Wash, trim ends, scrub or peel. Cut in ¼-inch slices, strips, chunks or cubes. Eat raw or cook until tender. Microwave in a covered dish with 2 tbsp. water.

Blanch time: 6–8 minutes

Steam time: 8–10 minutes

Microwave time: 9–11 minutes

Yields: 1 lb. fresh equals eight 6-inch carrots, 3½ cups sliced or 4 cups grated.

Nutrition: 1 cup cooked has 50 calories and contains potassium, a substantial amount of vitamin A and is a good source of fiber.

Carrot and Ginger Soup

6 tbsp. unsalted butter
1 large yellow onion, chopped
¼ cup ginger root, finely chopped
3 cloves garlic, minced
6 cups vegetable bouillon broth
1 cup dry white wine
2 lbs. carrots, peeled and cut into ½-inch pieces
2 tbsp. fresh lemon juice
Pinch of curry powder
Salt and black pepper to taste
Parsley, fresh and chopped

Melt butter in large stock pot over medium heat. Add onion, ginger, and garlic and sauté 15 to 20 minutes. Add stock, wine, and carrots. Heat to boiling. Reduce heat, cover, and cook over medium heat until carrots are tender, about 45 minutes. Purée soup in a blender or food processor. Season with lemon and parsley and a dollop of yogurt. Makes 6 servings.

Carol Neumann

Carrot Slaw

3 cups carrots, shredded
¾–1 cup mayonnaise
1 tbsp. white vinegar
1 (8 oz.) can crushed pineapple, undrained
½ cup raisins (optional)

In a large bowl, stir together mayonnaise and vinegar. Add undrained pineapple and raisins, if desired, and mix well. Add to shredded carrots and mix well. Cover and chill.

Variations: Cabbage–carrot slaw. Substitute shredded green cabbage for ½ of the carrots. Add ¼ cup chopped red pepper. Makes 6 servings.

Evelyn Kaiser

CARROTS

Pickled Carrot & Celeriac Salad

5 large carrots, matchstick julienne
1 large celeriac (2lbs.), peeled and matchstick julienne
2 onions, sliced into thin rings
2½ tbsp. salt
2 tbsp. dill seed
Zest and juice of 1 orange
2 cups cider vinegar
⅔ cup water
1 tbsp. sugar

Mix the carrots, celeriac, and onions in a bowl with 2 tbsp. of the salt. Mix well and let stand for about 2 hours.

Rinse the vegetables under cold running water, then drain well. Stir in the dill seed and orange zest, then pack loosely into container(s).

Place the orange juice, vinegar, water, sugar, and remaining salt into a saucepan. Bring to a boil and boil for 2 to 3 minutes, then skim well. Pour the liquid into the container(s) to cover the vegetables, close the containers and refrigerate for 1 week.

Jim Trenter

Ginger Glazed Carrots

¼ cup margarine
¼ cup brown sugar, packed
2 tsp. fresh ginger root, grated
2 cups sliced carrots, cooked until just tender
2 cups small onions, cooked until just tender

In a medium saucepan, melt margarine and add brown sugar and ginger. Simmer over low heat 2 minutes then add carrots and onions. Stir to coat all pieces with margarine and sugar. Cook over low heat, stirring often, 15 minutes, or until carrots and onions are well glazed. Makes 6 servings.

Ann Fox

Carrots Lyonnaise

1 lb. carrots (6–8), peeled and julienned
½ cup chicken broth
3 tbsp. butter
3 medium onions, thinly sliced
1 scant tbsp. all-purpose flour
Salt and black pepper to taste
¾ cup water or chicken broth
Pinch of salt
Pinch of sugar

Cook carrots in chicken broth, covered, for 10 minutes. Melt butter in saucepan; add onions and cook, covered, over low heat, stirring occasionally, for 15 minutes. Stir in flour, salt and pepper, and the water or broth. Bring to boil. Add carrots and broth. Simmer uncovered for 5 to 10 minutes, until desired doneness. Add pinch of sugar. Makes 6 servings.

HILLTOP PRODUCE FARM

Carrot Delight

A good company carrot dish!

6 large carrots, cut in julienned strips
½ cup mayonnaise
2 tbsp. horseradish
4 tbsp. water
Freshly ground black pepper
Sliced almonds for topping

Preheat oven to 350 degrees. Boil carrots in saucepan with a little water for 8 minutes; drain. Mix mayonnaise, horseradish, water and black pepper; add to drained carrots. Pour into a baking dish, top with sliced almonds and bake for 10 minutes, until heated through. Makes 4 servings.

Doe Hauser-Stowell

CARROTS

Basil Carrots

6 carrots, peeled and sliced
¼ cup onion, chopped
1 tbsp. butter or vegetable oil
¼ cup fresh basil, chopped

Steam carrot slices until tender, about 10 minutes. In a medium saucepan, sauté onion in butter or oil, add carrots and basil. Mix well. Makes 6 servings.

Carrot Hash Browns

1½ cups carrots, shredded
1½ cups potatoes, peeled and shredded
¼ cup onion or green onion, finely chopped
1 tbsp. all-purpose flour
2 tbsp. Parmesan cheese
½ tsp. salt
Vegetable oil for frying

In a medium bowl, combine ingredients. Spoon into a heated and oiled skillet and pat flat. Cook over medium-low heat until brown and crisp. Turn and cook until golden. Makes 3 servings.

LENGSFELD'S ORGANIC GARDENS

Sweet and Tangy Carrots

5 cups carrots, sliced
½ cup green pepper, chopped
⅓ cup onion, chopped
⅔ cup sugar
1 (10¾ oz.) can tomato soup
½ cup cider vinegar
⅓ cup vegetable oil
1 tsp. prepared mustard
1 tsp. Worcestershire sauce
1 tsp. dried dill weed

CARROTS

In a large serving bowl, combine carrots, green pepper, and onion. In medium saucepan, combine the remaining ingredients. Bring to a boil over medium heat, stirring occasionally; pour over vegetables. Mix will. Chill thoroughly. Serve cold. Makes 12, ½-cup servings.

GENE SCHWARTZ FARM

Whole Baked Baby Carrots

12 whole baby carrots
Vegetable oil
Aluminum foil

Preheat oven to 400 degrees. Place carrots side by side on oiled foil and fold in edges to seal. Bake for 20 to 30 minutes, until tender. Can also be grilled for 20 to 30 minutes, until tender. Makes 6 servings.

JoAn Kaiser

Fresh Carrot Cake

3 cups carrots, shredded
2 cups all-purpose flour
1 tsp. baking powder
1 tsp. baking soda
2 tsp. ground cinnamon
4 eggs
1 cup canola oil
2 cups sugar
1 cup chopped pecans (optional)

Preheat oven to 350 degrees. Chop the shredded carrots with a knife to make them extra fine.

In a medium bowl, whisk together flour, baking powder, baking soda, and cinnamon. In a separate large bowl, beat eggs until light and fluffy. Add oil and sugar and mix well. Add flour mixture and beat until well incorporated. Add carrots and nuts, if desired, and mix well; about 250 strokes.

Pour into a greased and floured 9x13-inch baking pan. Bake for 30 to 35 minutes or until a toothpick inserted near the center comes out clean.

CARROTS

Carrot Pineapple Cake

1 cup vegetable oil
2 cups sugar
3 eggs
2 cups all-purpose flour
2 tsp. ground cinnamon
2 tsp. baking soda
1 tsp. salt
1 pkg. (7 oz.) shredded coconut
1 cup walnuts, chopped
1 can (13½ oz.) crushed pineapple, drained
2 cups carrots, shredded
2 tsp. vanilla
1 cup raisins (optional)

Frosting:
4 oz. cream cheese, softened
1 stick margarine, softened
1 tsp. vanilla
½ lb. powdered sugar, sifted
¼ cup coconut (optional)
¼ cup chopped nuts (optional)

Preheat oven to 350 degrees. Combine ingredients in order given until well blended. Grease and flour a 9x13 pan and pour batter into pan. Bake 50 to 60 minutes. Cool and frost, if desired.

Frosting:
In a medium bowl, beat together cream cheese, margarine, and vanilla until light and fluffy. Gradually beat in 1 cup of powdered sugar. Beat well. Beat in enough remaining sugar to make frosting spreading consistency. Add optional coconuts and nuts, if desired.

Esther Mundt
Pat Jordan
May Collova

CARROTS

Carrot Marmalade

Based on an old Shaker recipe

3 (1 oz.) pkg. fruit pectin
3 tbsp. cold water
3 cups carrots, shredded
Juice and grated rind of 2 lemons
Juice and grated rind of 2 large oranges
6 cups sugar
½ tsp. ground cinnamon (optional)

In a small bowl, dissolve pectin in water and allow to stand 3 minutes. Juice lemons and oranges. Grate outer portion of the lemon and orange rinds making sure not to grate the inner white portion.

In a heavy saucepan combine juices, carrots, sugar, and lemon and orange zest. Bring to a boil and boil 3 minutes, stirring. Add fruit pectin mixture and continue to boil for 2 more minutes while stirring. Ladle hot liquid into sterilized jars leaving ½-inch headroom. Adjust clean hot lids and cool. Store in refrigerator.

CARROTS

Cauliflower

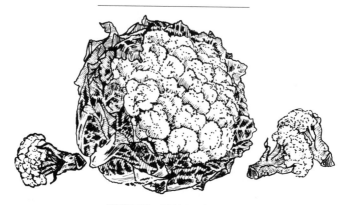

July–October

White, green broccoflower, purple, orange, and romanesco.

Wash, trim outer leaves, and core. Leave whole or break into florets. Eat raw or cook until tender. Microwave in a covered dish with 2 tbsp. water.

Blanch time: 3–5 minutes

Steam time: 7–12 minutes

Microwave time: 4–6 minutes

Yields: 1 lb. fresh equals one 4-inch head cauliflower, trimmed, 4 cups florets or chopped cauliflower, or 2 cups cooked and puréed. 1 large head equals 6 cups florets, 1 medium head equals 4 cups florets, 1 small head equals 2½–3 cups florets.

Nutrition: 1 cup cooked cauliflower has 30 calories and contains potassium and vitamin C.

Cauliflower-Radish Salad

1 medium head of cauliflower, thinly sliced
8–10 radishes, shredded
1 cup parsley, finely chopped
7–8 scallions, thinly sliced
1 cup Parmesan cheese, grated
1 lb. bacon, fried and crumbled

Dressing:
1 cup mayonnaise or Miracle Whip
1 tsp. sugar
¼ cup half & half

Fold all ingredients together with dressing. Makes 4–6 servings.

Donna Cavanaugh
A GOURMET THYME, DISTINCTIVE CATERING

Colorful Cauliflower Salad

1 head iceberg lettuce, chilled
1 small head cauliflower, chilled
½ cup vegetable oil
¼ cup white vinegar
½ tsp. salt
1 tbsp. sugar
¼ tsp. white pepper
Pinch of cayenne pepper
2 tbsp. fresh parsley, snipped
⅓ cup onion, chopped
⅓ cup pimento stuffed olives, chopped
1½ cups mozzarella cheese, coarsely grated

Break lettuce into bite-size pieces. Separate cauliflower into florets and cut into thin vertical slices. *For dressing:* In a screw top jar, combine oil, vinegar, and seasonings. Cover, shake well, and toss with vegetables, olives, and cheese just before serving. Makes 10–12 servings.

Sue Zelickson

CAULIFLOWER

Marinated Cauliflower with Roasted Red Pepper

4 cups cauliflower florets
1 red bell pepper, roasted, peeled and seeded
1 medium red onion, sliced and separated into rings

Marinade:
¼ cup white vinegar
¼ cup olive oil
2 tsp. sugar
1 tsp. dried oregano
¼ tsp. salt
⅛ tsp. black pepper

Steam cauliflower until just tender. Slice roasted pepper into thin strips. Cook onion in a small amount of boiling water for 5 minutes until tender-crisp. In a large bowl, combine onion, cauliflower, and pepper.

In a screw top jar combine marinade ingredients. Cover and shake well. Pour over vegetables. Cover and chill overnight. Stir before serving. Makes 8 servings.

Cauliflower with Cheese Sauce

3 cups cauliflower, broken into florets
3 tbsp. butter or margarine
3 tbsp. all-purpose flour
1–1½ cups warm lowfat milk, more for a thinner sauce and less for a
    thicker sauce
1 tsp. salt
½ cup cheddar or Swiss cheese, grated

Steam cauliflower florets until tender, about 10 minutes. Melt butter or margarine, stir in flour, and cook over low heat, stirring constantly, for 2 minutes. Add warm milk all at once, and bring to a boil, stirring. Reduce heat and stir until sauce thickens. Stir in salt and grated cheese. Stir until cheese is melted. Pour over the cooked cauliflower. Makes 6 servings

LENGSFELD'S ORGANIC GARDENS

CAULIFLOWER

Indian Cauliflower and Mixed Vegetables

1 medium head cauliflower
2–3 medium potatoes
2 tbsp. vegetable oil
1 medium onion, finely chopped
3 cloves garlic, minced
½ tbsp. fresh ginger, finely chopped
1 tsp. ground cumin
1 tbsp. ground coriander
1 tsp. turmeric
¼ tsp. ground cayenne
2 cups tomatoes, chopped
1 tsp. salt
2 cups hot vegetable broth or water
1 cup peas, beans or greens, chopped (whatever is in season)

Cut cauliflower into 1–1½ -inch pieces. Cut potatoes into bite-size pieces. Sauté onions, garlic, and ginger in oil until soft. Stir in cumin, coriander, turmeric, and cayenne. Add potatoes and cauliflower and cook, stirring, about 5 minutes. Add tomatoes and salt. Add 2 cups hot broth and bring to a boil. Reduce heat, cover, and cook for 15 minutes. Add peas and cook until vegetables are soft. Makes 6 servings.

Evelyn Kaiser

Cream of Cauliflower Soup

1 large head cauliflower, broken into florets
3 cups chicken broth
2 tbsp. butter or margarine
2 tbsp. all-purpose flour
½ tsp. salt
Dash black pepper
1 cup warm lowfat milk

Steam cauliflower until tender, about 8 minutes. Combine cooked cauliflower pieces with a little broth in a blender. Cover and process until smooth. Set aside.

In a large pot melt butter or margarine. Stir in flour and cook on low heat for 2 minutes. Add warm milk all at once. Bring to a boil, stirring constantly. Turn down heat and continue stirring until slightly thickened. Add the rest of the broth, purée and seasonings. Heat through. Adjust seasonings and consistency. Makes 8 servings.

JoAn Kaiser

Cauliflower Casserole

1 large head cauliflower
1 can sliced mushrooms
¼ cup green pepper, chopped
¼ cup melted butter
½ cup all-purpose flour
2 cups lowfat milk
1 tsp. salt
1 cup cheddar cheese, grated
2 tbsp. pimentos, chopped

Preheat oven to 325 degrees. Separate head of cauliflower into florets and cook in boiling salt water until tender, about 7 to 10 minutes. Drain and set aside. In a saucepan, sauté drained mushrooms and green peppers in butter. Cook and stir over medium heat for 5 minutes. Do not let vegetables get brown. Blend in flour and gradually stir in milk. Cook and stir until mixture thickens. Stir in salt, cheese, and pimentos. Put half of cooked cauliflower into 2-quart lightly greased casserole. Spoon half of the cream sauce over the cauliflower. Repeat. Bake the casserole for 15 minutes. Makes 8 servings.

Betty Adelmann

CAULIFLOWER

Turmeric Cauliflower Pickles

3 heads cauliflower (about 5 lbs.)
6 cups white vinegar
3 cups water
1½ cups sugar
3 tbsp. whole mustard seeds
3 tbsp. whole pickling spices
1 tbsp. canning salt
1 tsp. turmeric

Wash cauliflower and break into florets. Steam for 1 minute. Do not over-cook. In a large stainless steel kettle, combine vinegar, water, sugar, mustard seeds, pickling spices, salt, and turmeric. Bring to a boil. Reduce heat and simmer for 3 minutes.

   Pack cauliflower pieces into sterilized hot pint jars up to shoulder of jar. Pour hot brine over cauliflower, leaving ½-inch headroom. Adjust clean hot lids. Process 15 minutes in boiling-water bath. Remove and cool. Makes about 6–7 pints.

Corn

July–Frost

SOME VARIETIES

Yellow, bicolor, white, sugar enhanced or supersweet. "Sugar Enhanced" will keep its sweetness for about 2 days and tends to have more tender kernels. "Super Sweet" will keep its sweetness for about 7 days and tends to have crisper kernels.

PREPARING SWEET CORN

Peel outer husk and remove silk. Cook until just tender. Corn can be roasted on the grill with husks off or on. Microwave with husks on or peel and wrap ear in a damp paper towel. To use cooked corn kernels for a recipe, stand a cooked ear of corn on its stem end and shave the kernel off with a knife, cutting from top to bottom.

Blanch time: 3–7 minutes

Steam time: 5–10 minutes

Microwave time: 3–4 minutes (one ear)

Grilling time: 25 minutes (in husk); 15 minutes (in foil)

Yields: 1 lb. fresh equals 5 to 6 ears of corn or 3 cups of kernels.

Nutrition: 1 ear has about 70 calories and contains potassium and vitamin A. It is a good source of fiber.

Preparing Homegrown Popcorn

In the fall you can find this for sale at the Farmers' Market.

Mini popcorn can be popped on the cob. Place the whole cob in a paper bag and microwave on high until the popping stops.

Larger-sized cobs should be shucked. Use your fingers and thumbs to pry the kernels off the cob. Pop the kernels in an air popper or as you would normally pop popcorn.

Indian corn can be partially popped by cooking the whole cob in the microwave. It makes an interesting ornament!

Cajun Corn Roast

Fresh shucked corn
Cajun seasoning
Unsalted butter, slightly softened
Aluminum foil in sheets large enough to wrap corn in

Place one ear corn diagonally on a large square of foil. Smear with butter, about 1½ tsp. per ear. Sprinkle Cajun seasoning on lightly. Loosely wrap corn, keeping foil seam up. Roast over hot, prepared grill about 20 to 25 minutes. Makes 1 serving.

Carlen Arnett & Keith A. Parker

Savory Corn

2 cups cooked corn kernels
1 small onion, diced
1 small pepper, chopped
2 tbsp. ghee (clarified butter) or butter
¼ cup maple syrup

Steam onion and pepper pieces until tender. In a bowl, mix warm corn, onion, pepper, and melt in ghee or butter. Add maple syrup to taste. Makes 4 servings.

Geoffry Saign

CORN

Marinated Corn Salad

8 ears fresh corn
½ red onion, diced
½ red pepper, diced
½ green pepper, diced
4 scallions, chopped
3 cloves garlic, minced
1 jalapeño pepper, diced small
½ cup olive oil
½ cup white vinegar
¼ cup cilantro, chopped
1 tsp. ground cumin
1 tsp. salt
1 tsp. freshly-ground black pepper

Shuck corn and remove silk. Blanch cobs in boiling water 3 to 5 minutes. Rinse in cold water and drain. Cut corn from cob and put in a large bowl. Add diced onion, peppers, scallions, garlic, and remaining ingredients. Mix well, cover, and chill overnight to blend flavors. Makes 6–8 servings.

HILLTOP PRODUCE FARM

Southwestern Corn and Black Bean Salad

Serve on lettuce, on grilled chicken or as a salsa for tortilla chips

1 (15oz.) can black beans
2–3 cups cooked corn (cut from 3 large or 6 small ears of yellow corn)
½ cup fresh cilantro, chopped
6 tbsp. fresh lime juice (about 2 large whole limes)
6 tbsp. vegetable oil, combination of olive oil and vegetable oil
⅓ cup red onion, finely chopped
1½ tsp. ground cumin
½ cup ripe tomatoes, chopped
Few drops hot sauce to taste (optional)

In a large bowl combine all ingredients except tomatoes. Taste and season with salt and pepper if desired. Cover and refrigerate until cold. May be prepared 1 day ahead. Add tomatoes prior to serving. Makes 3½ to 4 cups.

Carlen Arnett & Keith A. Parker

CORN

Fresh Corn Chowder

1 onion, chopped
3 tbsp. butter or oil
4 cups cooked corn kernels
2 cups potatoes, diced (smaller cooks faster)
4 cups lowfat milk
2 bay leaves
¼ tsp. dried sage
Salt and black pepper

In a large pot, sauté onions in butter until soft. Add remaining ingredients, bring to a boil, cover, and simmer until potatoes are tender, about 30 minutes. Season with salt and pepper. Remove bay leaves. If desired, process half of the cooled soup in a blender and return to the pot. Makes 8 servings.

Variations: Chicken corn chowder: Add 1½ cups cooked diced chicken after blending soup. Curry corn chowder: Add 1 tbsp. ground curry powder to sautéed onions. Cheesy corn chowder: Add 2 cups grated cheese after blending. Tomato corn chowder: Add 1½ cups chopped tomatoes to sautéed onions.

Carol Neumann

Corn and Chicken Chowder with Hazelnut Butter

2 cloves garlic
1½ cups corn kernels
1½ cups chicken stock
½ cup sweet potatoes, ¼-inch diced
½ cup russet potatoes, ¼-inch diced
¼ cup cooked bacon, diced
¼ cup red and green peppers, diced
¼ cup onion and celery, diced
12 oz. chicken meat (cooked) cut into ½-inch pieces (white or dark)
Salt
Tabasco
Worcestershire sauce

Hazelnut butter:
½ cup butter
⅓ cup roasted hazelnuts, chopped
Tabasco
Salt

In a large saucepan, boil the garlic, corn kernels, and chicken stock for approximately 5 minutes. Remove from heat and purée ¾ of the mixture in blender until fairly smooth. Then return purée to the pan with remaining ¼ of corn (make sure garlic is puréed). Return pan to heat and bring to a boil. When mixture is boiling, add potatoes, and cook until potatoes are just barely soft, then add remaining vegetables and boil for 3 minutes. Add chicken, lower heat to simmer, and cook for 1 minute. Season with salt, Tabasco and Worcestershire and ladle into bowls. Garnish with hazelnut butter and serve. If soup is too thick, add more chicken stock.

Instructions for hazelnut butter: Put soft butter and chopped hazelnuts into food processor and process until smooth. Season with salt and Tabasco and chill lightly. Makes 4 servings.

Kevin Cullen
EXECUTIVE CHEF, GOODFELLOWS RESTAURANT

Corn Pudding with Chives

2½ cups fresh corn
¼ cup sugar
1 tsp. salt
3 large eggs
1½ cups whole or 2% milk
2 tbsp. butter, melted and cooled
3 tbsp. all-purpose flour
¼ cup fresh chives, chopped
⅛ tsp. nutmeg, freshly grated, if possible
Dash of white pepper

Preheat oven to 325 degrees and butter a 1½ quart shallow oven-proof casserole dish. Coarsely chop half of the corn in a food processor. Combine chopped corn and remaining corn in a bowl; add sugar and salt. In a separate mixing bowl, whisk eggs; add milk, butter, flour, chives, nutmeg, and pepper, mixing well. Add corn mixture and pour into buttered casserole. Bake for one hour or longer, until the center of the pudding is set and top is lightly browned. Makes 6–8 servings.

HILLTOP PRODUCE FARM

Frozen Corn

Quick and easy with a very fresh buttery taste

8 cups corn (cut off uncooked cob)
½ stick butter
1½ tsp. sugar (optional)
1½ cups water

Put all ingredients in large kettle. Bring to a boil and cook for 5 minutes. Spread onto cookie sheets to cool. Put into containers and freeze. Be sure to use only fresh picked corn for the freshest possible flavor. Makes about 5 pints.

Nan Gianoli

Corn Fritters with Corn Cob Syrup

Fritters:
2 cups cooked corn kernels (about 6 ears)
3 eggs, beaten
2 tbsp. lowfat milk
1 tbsp. butter, melted
1 tsp. baking powder
½ tsp. salt
⅛ tsp. black pepper
1¼ cups all-purpose flour
½ cup vegetable oil for deep frying

In a large skillet heat oil to 375 degrees. Mix ingredients for fritters. Drop by tablespoons in hot oil and deep fry in 1-inch of oil for 3 to 5 minutes.

Syrup:
6 corn cobs, broken into chunks
4 cups water
1¼ cups brown sugar

To make the syrup, cook corn cobs uncovered for 30 to 45 minutes, until liquid is reduced to 2 cups. Remove cobs and stir in sugar. Cook another 20 to 30 minutes or until liquid is reduced to 1 cup. Strain and serve with fritters. Makes 6 servings.

Corn Relish

4 cups corn kernels (about 9 ears)
1 cup green pepper, diced
1 cup red pepper, diced
1 cup celery chopped finely
1 medium onion, chopped
1 cup white vinegar
¾ cup sugar
½ tsp. turmeric
1 tbsp. whole mustard seed

Boil husked ears of corn for 5 minutes. Cool and cut kernels from the cob, using a sharp knife. Do not scrape.

In a large stainless steel kettle, combine all ingredients, except corn. Bring to a boil and boil for 5 minutes. Add corn and simmer for 10 minutes. Fill clean hot jars with hot mixture, leaving ½-inch headroom. Adjust clean hot lids. Process in boiling-water bath for 15 minutes. Remove and cool. Makes 4 pints.

Corny Corn Bread

1 cup yellow cornmeal
1 cup all-purpose flour
¼ cup honey
½ tbsp. baking powder
½ tbsp. baking soda
½ tsp. salt
1 cup buttermilk or lowfat milk
4 tbsp. butter or margarine, melted
1½ cups cooked corn kernels
1–2 tbsp. jalapeños, sliced (optional)

Preheat oven to 375. In a large bowl, combine dry ingredients. Stir in liquid ingredients. Stir in corn and optional jalapeños. Do not overmix! Pour batter into a greased 8x8-inch pan. You may top with jalapeño slices if desired. Bake for 25 minutes or until a toothpick inserted comes out clean.

Evelyn Kaiser

Cucumbers and Pickles

WHEN AVAILABLE

June–Frost

SOME VARIETIES

Slicing, Pickling, European, Middle Eastern, and Asian

PREPARING CUCUMBERS

Wash, peel if desired and slice or dice. Cucumbers are mostly eaten raw. European types have smoother skins and a more delicate texture. Pickles have more crunch. Cucumbers can be included in stir-fry or soup if desired.

Yields: 1 lb. fresh equals 2 6-inch cucumbers or 3 cups sliced cucumbers.

Nutrition: 6 large slices has 5 calories and contains potassium and some vitamin A.

Austrian Cucumber Salad

An old family recipe

2 12-inch long burpless cucumbers
1 green pepper, seeded, cut into strips or rings
1 sweet Walla Walla onion, cut into rings
1 tsp. salt

Dressing:
1 cup sugar
½ cup white vinegar
1 clove garlic, crushed
1 tbsp. fresh dill, chopped

Strip-peel cucumbers, then serrate with a fork on unpeeled strip areas. Slice diagonally in ¼-inch thick slices. Layer slices in a colander, lightly salting each layer. Add green pepper and onion. Allow to drain for at least ½ hour. Meanwhile combine sugar, vinegar, and garlic in a saucepan. Heat to dissolve sugar. Remove from heat and add chopped dill. Cool to room temperature. Put drained cucumber, pepper, and onion slices in a bowl; pour syrup over and stir to coat. Cover and refrigerate 2 hours or overnight. Makes 6 servings.

Stephen Michael Farkas

Refrigerator Pickles

7 cups cucumbers, sliced thin
1 cup green peppers, chopped
1 cup onion, sliced
1 tsp. whole celery seed
2 tbsp. salt
2 cups sugar
1 cup white vinegar

In a large bowl, combine vegetables, celery seed, and salt. In a small bowl mix together sugar and vinegar and pour over vegetables. Cover and refrigerate. Keeps well. May also be frozen.

Alice Mossong

Egyptian Cucumber Cheese Salad

1 large cucumber, peeled and halved lengthwise, seeds removed
Salt
12 oz. feta cheese, drained if necessary
½ cup mild onion, finely chopped
¼ cup lemon juice
¼ cup olive oil
Freshly ground black pepper
Mint sprigs for garnish

Score cucumber with a fork. Sprinkle with salt and let stand for 20 minutes. Crush cheese with fingertips or fork and mix thoroughly with onion, lemon juice, and oil. Season with pepper. Drain, rinse, and slice cucumber about ⅓-inch thick. Combine with cheese mixture. Place in shallow serving dish and decorate with mint sprigs. Chill about 30 minutes before serving. Makes 6 servings.

Mary Broeker

Grandma's Creamy Cucumber Salad

We serve German style over mashed potatoes

5 medium cucumbers
1 tsp. garlic powder
1½ tsp. salt

Dressing:
1 cup mayonnaise
1 tbsp. white vinegar
1 tbsp. sugar
2 tsp. paprika

Peel cucumbers. Slice very thinly with a cabbage cutter into a large bowl. Sprinkle with garlic powder and salt, mix well. Cover and refrigerate for 3 to 24 hours. Drain by squeezing out as much excess liquid as possible.

In a bowl, stir together, mayonnaise, vinegar, and sugar. Add cucumbers and stir to coat. Sprinkle with paprika. Makes 6 servings.

Duane Lengsfeld

Sunomono

Japanese shrimp and cucumber salad

1 (6oz.) can small salad shrimp, rinsed, drained, and chilled
2 large cucumbers (8–10 inches), peeled and seeded, sliced very thinly
2 tsp. salt
2 tbsp. sesame seeds, toasted (may be done in a dry skillet over low heat, stirring frequently)

Rice vinegar dressing:
¾ cup rice wine vinegar
3 tbsp. sugar
1 tbsp. light soy sauce

Dressing: In a small bowl, combine ingredients and stir until sugar dissolves.
   Salad: Sprinkle cucumber with salt. Allow to drain ½ hour in colander. Squeeze out all remaining moisture. Toss lightly with chilled shrimp. Just before serving, combine with rice vinegar dressing. Sprinkle with toasted sesame seeds. Makes 6–8 servings.

HILLTOP PRODUCE FARM

French Cucumber Soup

2 lbs. cucumbers (about 6 8-inch long)
½ cup shallots, minced
3 tbsp. butter
6 cups chicken broth
2 tsp. white wine vinegar
1 tsp. fresh dill or tarragon, finely chopped
4 tbsp. quick Cream of Wheat
Salt and white pepper to taste
1 cup sour cream (may use lowfat or fat free, if desired)

Peel cucumbers, discard large seeds and cut into ¼-inch chunks. In a large saucepan, cook shallots in butter until soft (do not brown). Add cucumbers, broth, vinegar, and dill or tarragon. Bring to a boil, add cream of wheat slowly, stirring, and simmer 25 minutes. Purée and season with salt and pepper. May be served hot or cold. Before serving add sour cream. Makes 6–8 servings.

Kim Pinkham

CUCUMBERS AND PICKLES

Cucumber Relish

A good use for those oversized, end-of-the-season cukes

10–12 large cucumbers
2 lbs. onions (3 cups ground)
2 small hot red peppers (4 tsp. ground)
1 large bunch celery (3 cups ground)
2 sweet red and green peppers (1 cup ground)
¼ cup canning salt
6 cups water
4 cups white vinegar
3 cups sugar
2 tbsp. whole mustard seed
1 tbsp. whole celery seed
1 tsp. turmeric

Wash vegetables and seed peppers, peel onions, remove celery leaves. In a meat grinder, grind the vegetables using a medium blade. Combine in a large stainless steel kettle. Add salt and water; mix well. Cover and let stand overnight in the refrigerator. Remove from refrigerator and drain well; approximately 1 hour. In a large stainless steel kettle, combine vinegar, sugar, and mustard and celery seeds. Bring to a boil. Add drained vegetables and bring to a simmer. Add turmeric and cook 10 minutes, stirring frequently. Fill sterilized pint jars with relish, leaving ½-inch headroom. Adjust clean hot lids. Process for 10 minutes in a boiling-water bath. Remove from bath and cool at room temperature. Makes 6–7 pints.

Hazel Dial

Turmeric Bread and Butter Pickles

Our family makes these with the last cucumbers of summer for a winter treat

25 pickling cucumbers, washed
12 onions
½ cup canning salt
4 cups white vinegar
4 cups sugar
4 tsp. whole mustard seed
4 tsp. whole celery seed
4 tsp. turmeric powder

Soak cucumbers in cold water for 6 hours. Drain and slice thinly along with the onions. (A cabbage cutter comes in handy here). In a five gallon plastic container, mix vegetables with salt. Let stand 1 hour. Drain well, but don't rinse.

In a large stainless steel kettle, combine vinegar, sugar, and spices. Bring to a boil. Add cucumber and onion slices and bring to a boil. Ladle boiling mixture into clean hot pint jars, leaving ½-inch headroom. Adjust clean hot lids. Process in boiling-water bath for 10 minutes. Remove and cool. Makes 10 pints.

Evelyn Kaiser

Sweet Dill Pickle Halves

30 5-inch cucumbers
1 quart vinegar
1 quart water
¾ cup sugar
¾ cup canning salt
1 tsp. turmeric
3 tbsp. whole pickling spices
6 cloves garlic, peeled
6 fresh dill heads

Wash the cucumbers and set aside. In a large stainless steel kettle, combine vinegar, water, sugar, salt, and turmeric, and bring to a boil. Tie pickling spices up in a clean white cloth and drop in pot. Boil 10 minutes, remove and discard spice bag.

CUCUMBERS AND PICKLES

Slice each pickle in half lengthwise. Put a garlic clove in each sterilized pint jar. Pack jars as tightly as you can with the cut cucumbers, coming up to the shoulder of the jar. Place a dill head on the top of each jar. Pour boiling vinegar mixture over cucumbers leaving ½-inch headroom. Adjust clean hot lids. Process in boiling-water bath for 10 minutes. Remove and cool. Makes 6 pints.

Dried and Seasoned Cucumber Chips
Just like potato chips!

8 6-inch cucumbers
Seasoned salt
Dehydrator

Peel cucumbers and slice thinly. Thinner slices dry faster. Arrange slices on dehydrator racks and sprinkle with seasoned salt. Use whatever flavors you wish. Dehydrate according to instructions until brittle. Zucchinis work well for this too.

Carol Lovingfoss

Mom's Celery Pickles
Use this when you can't find dill!

5 stalks celery, cut into 6-inch lengths and split in two, lengthwise
25 6-inch cucumbers
1 quart white vinegar
1 quart water
3 cups sugar
½ cup canning salt
2 onions, peeled and cut into wedges

Wash cucumbers thoroughly and cut off stem end. Combine vinegar, water, sugar, and salt in a stainless steel kettle; bring to a boil. Sterilize quart jars and lids in boiling water. Pack cucumbers into sterilized jars along with two pieces of celery and two wedges of onion for each jar. Fill with boiling brine. Adjust clean hot lids. Process 10 minutes in a boiling-water bath. Remove carefully from bath and allow to cool at room temperature. Makes about 5 quarts.

Hazel Dial

Kosher Dill Pickles

20–25 4- to 6-inch cucumbers

For each quart:
⅛ tsp. powdered alum
1 clove garlic
2 heads dill
1 small dried hot red pepper
Grape leaf

Brine:
1 quart vinegar
1 cup canning salt
3 quarts water

Wash cucumbers; soak in cold water overnight. Pack into sterilized quart jars. To each quart add alum, garlic, dill, and red pepper. Combine vinegar, salt and water in a large stainless steel kettle; heat to boiling. Fill each jar with brine, leaving ½-inch headroom. Place grape leaf on top of each jar. Adjust clean hot lids. Process 10 minutes in a boiling-water bath. Remove and cool. Makes about 6 quarts.

Hazel Dial

Eggplant

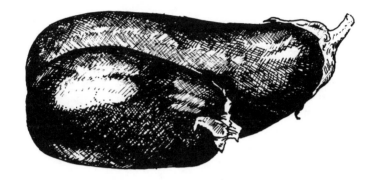

WHEN AVAILABLE

August–Frost

SOME VARIETIES

Large cylindrical, Japanese and miniature round

PREPARING EGGPLANT

Wash and trim stem. Peel if desired. Slice or cut into cubes. Salting draws out bitterness and somewhat reduces the oil-absorbing capacity of the eggplant. To salt, sprinkle slices or cubes with salt, drain in a colander for 30 minutes, rinse with water and pat dry. Pieces or whole eggplant can be fried, broiled or baked. Microwave pieces in a covered dish with 2 tbsp. of water. Eggplants can be grilled whole until equally charred on all sides and limp.

Pan fry time: 10–14 minutes (slices)

Broil time: 10–14 minutes (slices)

Bake time: 30–40 minutes (whole)

Microwave time: 5–8 minutes (slices)

Grilling time: 10–14 minutes (slices)

Yields: 1 lb. fresh equals 1 large eggplant, 5 cups sliced or diced or 2 cups cooked and puréed.

Nutrition: 1 cup cooked has 96 calories and is an excellent source of potassium and iron.

Marinated Eggplant Salad

6 cups eggplant, unpeeled and diced
2 tbsp. olive oil
½ cup water
2 tbsp. red wine vinegar
2 large green bell peppers, roasted, peeled, and seeded
2 large red bell peppers, roasted, peeled, and seeded
½ cup red or white onion, minced
1 clove garlic, minced
½ cup olive oil
¼ cup white vinegar
2 tbsp. sugar
2 tbsp. fresh lemon juice
2 tbsp. fresh parsley, chopped
1 tbsp. fresh basil, chopped
2 cups cooked garbanzo beans
1 cup tomatoes, chunked
Salt and black pepper

In a large nonstick pan, heat olive oil, add eggplant, and toss to coat. Add water and wine vinegar. Simmer about 7 minutes, covered, until eggplant is tender. Pour mixture into a large bowl. Slice peppers into strips and add to eggplant mixture along with onions and garlic.

In a small bowl combine vinegar, sugar, lemon juice, parsley, and basil. Mix well and pour over eggplant. Add garbanzo beans and tomatoes. Salt and pepper to taste and mix well. Chill and marinate at least 30 minutes. Makes 12 servings.

Baba Ghanooj

Egyptian eggplant spread

1 lb. eggplant (about 4 Japanese type or 1 medium globe type)
4 tbsp. sesame tahini
¼ cup fresh lemon juice
1 tsp. honey
2 cloves garlic, minced
2 tbsp. olive oil
Salt and black pepper to taste
Chopped fresh parsley for garnish, if desired

EGGPLANT

To roast the eggplant, place directly on wire rack of barbeque over hot coals. Roast until skin appears black and charred and begins to crack and blister. Turn so that all sides are equally charred and insides become limp. Place on a platter to cool. Peel skins off with your fingers, dipping eggplant in cold water to rinse off bits of charred skin.

Place pulp in a bowl. Set aside. Combine tahini, lemon juice, and honey; mix well. Add to eggplant pulp along with olive oil, salt, and pepper. Mix well and adjust seasonings. Garnish with parsley and serve with pita bread, or as a sandwich or cracker spread. Makes 6 servings.

Roasted Eggplant with Garlic

Make this when eggplant is abundant, fresh, and inexpensive at the Farmers' Market.
Keep it frozen in zip-lock bags for use all winter

6 large globe eggplants, washed and dried
6–12 cloves garlic, peeled, and sliced lengthwise into slivers
Sunflower or olive oil to coat baking sheets and outsides of eggplant

Preheat oven to 400 degrees. Rub 2 large baking sheets with oil. Make slits all around eggplant with tip of paring knife. Push slivers of garlic into eggplant slits. Rub oil all over eggplant. Place on baking sheets. Roast in oven until eggplant is very tender throughout. Time will vary with size of eggplant, but check after 30 minutes and add time as needed.

When eggplants are very soft, remove from oven and let cool until you can remove the stem and most of the skin You can leave a little on if you like the full flavor—you decide. Mash the pulp with a potato masher if you like it course, or blend with on-off pulses in a blender until texture is the way you like it. When eggplant is cooled to room temperature, pack into zip-lock bags, label with date and contents, and freeze. Lay bags horizontally, like magazines.

Uses: blend into rice pilaf during the last 5 to 10 minutes of cooking. Season as a side dish or grilled seafood or poultry. Stuff tomatoes or mushrooms with eggplant, bread crumbs, and seasonings. You can probably think of your own favorite way of using this delicious prepared vegetable.

Jeanne Quan

EGGPLANT

85

Caponata

1 large eggplant
6 tbsp. vegetable oil
1 clove garlic, minced
1 onion, chopped
½ cup tomato sauce
½ cup celery, chopped
½ green pepper, diced
2 tbsp. capers
¼ cup red wine vinegar
2 tbsp. sugar
Salt and black pepper

Peel eggplant and cut into slices ½-inch thick. Cut slices into cubes ½-inch thick. In a large skillet, heat 5 tbsp. of the oil and sauté the eggplant until brown. Remove the eggplant and set aside. Add the remaining 1 tbsp. of oil to the pan and sauté the garlic and onion. Add tomato sauce, celery, and green pepper. Simmer, covered, for 15 to 20 minutes, adding water if needed. Return eggplant to skillet with capers. Stir in vinegar and sugar. Add salt and pepper to taste. Simmer 15 minutes longer, stirring occasionally to prevent sticking. Chill well and serve on lettuce leaves for a salad, or on crackers or Italian bread for an hors d'oeuvre. Makes 6 servings.

Nan Gianoli

Gratin of Eggplant and Tomato

3 medium eggplants
Salt and black pepper
4 tbsp. olive oil, or more
2 medium onions
⅔ cup water
4 large tomatoes
1 large clove garlic
½ cup white wine
2 tsp. fresh thyme leaves, chopped
½ cup Parmesan cheese

EGGPLANT

Cut eggplants in slices ⅓-inch thick. Sprinkle with salt and drain for 30 minutes. Pat dry, then sauté in oil until golden. Drain on paper towels.

Dice onions (not too finely) and sauté in 1 tbsp. oil until soft. When oil is absorbed, add water and continue to cook slowly until almost a purée or paste.

Preheat oven to 375 degrees. Slice tomatoes. Arrange slices of eggplant and tomato alternately in oiled gratin dish. Chop or crush garlic over dish and add white wine. Season with salt, pepper, and thyme leaves. Arrange onion purée over dish and sprinkle with Parmesan cheese. Bake for 30 minutes. Serve warm or cold. Makes 4–6 servings.

Mary Broeker

Eggplant Parmesan
This is our special occasion dinner with homemade tomato sauce!

1 small eggplant
1 egg, beaten
¼ cup all-purpose flour
1 cup soda crackers, finely crushed
4 tbsp. vegetable oil
¼ cup Parmesan or grated Romano cheese
Spaghetti sauce
Mozzarella cheese, grated

Cut the eggplant in ¼-inch thick rounds or lengthwise into ¼-inch thick steaks. Dip slices first in egg, then in flour then in cracker crumbs. Press the cracker crumbs on with your fingers to coat evenly. In a large skillet, heat oil and fry eggplant until golden brown on both sides. Drain on a paper towel.

Preheat oven to 400 degrees. In a 9x13 lightly greased pan, make a single layer of eggplant, and sprinkle with Parmesan or Romano cheese. Top with spaghetti sauce and grated mozzarella. Bake for 10 to 12 minutes or until cheese is melted. Makes 4 servings.

Evelyn Kaiser

EGGPLANT

Ratatouille

1 medium eggplant, cut into ½-inch chunks
1 tbsp. salt
3 medium zucchini, sliced
1 large green pepper, chopped
1 large onion, halved, then sliced
4 tomatoes, peeled and cut in eighths
3 tbsp. olive oil
2 cloves garlic, crushed
1 tsp. salt
¼ tsp. black pepper
2 tsp. fresh basil, chopped
1 tsp. fresh oregano, chopped
2 tbsp. fresh Italian parsley, chopped

Sprinkle eggplant with salt; let stand 30 minutes. Dry on paper towels. Heat 1 tbsp. oil in large, deep skillet; sauté onions and garlic 2 minutes. Add peppers and sauté 2 more minutes; remove from pan. Heat the remaining 2 tbsp. oil in pan and add eggplant; brown on all sides. Add zucchini, tomatoes, and seasonings, except parsley. Add the pepper-onion mixture and Italian parsley; cover and cook on low heat, stirring occasionally, until vegetables are just tender, about 10 minutes. Serve as a vegetable side dish or as a main dish. Put cheese on a roll or toast, spoon ratatouille on top, top with more cheese, and broil to heat and melt the cheese. Serve cold as an appetizer or salad. Makes 6 servings.

Variation: Sausage Ratatouille: brown 1 lb. bulk Italian sausage, drain on paper towels, and add to vegetables before cooking.

Joan Schellinger

Zakouska

This eggplant spread comes from a Romanian friend. It's the best!

4 lbs. eggplant
2 lbs. red peppers
2 lbs. onions
2 cups vegetable oil
2 lbs. tomatoes (Roma are best)
3 tbsp. salt
2 tbsp. black pepper
10 bay leaves

Preheat grill. Roast eggplant directly on wire rack of barbeque grill. Turn until all sides are equally charred black and inside becomes limp. Cool. Peel off skins with fingers, chop eggplant, and place pieces in a strainer to drain.

Roast peppers on barbeque grill or place on a cookie sheet and broil in oven. When skins are blackened, put peppers in a paper bag to loosen skins. Peel off charred skins and chop into 1-inch chunks.

Preheat oven to 250 degrees. Dice the onion and sauté in oil until soft. Add chopped eggplant and peppers and mash. Bring to a boil. Place pot in oven or transfer mixture to a shallow baking dish and bake for about 1 hour or until oil rises to the top. You can also cook the mixture on top of the stove but plan on a lot of stirring.

Dip tomatoes in boiling water, then cold water, peel, and crush. Place tomatoes in a saucepan and bring to a boil; lower heat and simmer until thickened. Add eggplant mixture, salt, pepper, and bay leaves. Simmer for 30 minutes or until good and thick. This can be frozen. Makes about 6 pints.

Connie Korolchuk

Breaded Eggplant Steaks

1 large eggplant
1 cup crushed soda crackers
1 tsp. salt
½ tsp. dried thyme
¼ tsp. black pepper
3 eggs
2 cups lowfat milk
1 cup all-purpose flour, in a bowl
½ cup vegetable oil for frying
Spaghetti sauce (optional)

Slice the eggplant into ¼-inch slices; set aside. In a medium bowl, mix cracker crumbs, salt, thyme, and pepper. In a separate small bowl, beat eggs until fluffy. Beat in milk.

In a large skillet heat oil. Dip eggplant slices first in the egg mixture, then in flour and then in the cracker crumbs. Press cracker crumbs on with your fingers to coat evenly. Fry over medium heat until golden brown on both sides and tender. Top with spaghetti sauce, if desired. Makes 6 servings.

Pat Jordan

EGGPLANT

Garlic

PREPARING GARLIC

Peel outer paper and chop with a knife. A garlic press is a fast way to crush garlic. Garlic cloves can be sautéed whole until soft and then mashed with a fork. This prevents the burning or sticking that can occur when sautéing minced garlic.

Roasting garlic: Whole garlic bulbs can be roasted for an easy way to have garlic on hand. Cut out the root core and place the whole unpeeled bulb in an oiled baking dish. Bake at 375 degrees for 45 minutes. The garlic will be cooked and soft. Whenever you need garlic, just squeeze the bulb and the garlic comes out the root end like a tube of toothpaste. Store the bulb in the refrigerator. To roast individual garlic cloves, place unpeeled cloves on a nonstick cookie sheet and bake for 30 to 35 minutes or until very tender. Longer baking will caramelize the garlic. The flesh can be squeezed out of the skin.

Garlic oil: Garlic oil can be made by placing peeled garlic cloves in olive oil. The oil will take on a wonderful garlic flavor. Both the oil and the cloves can be used for cooking and salads. Store the garlic oil in a jar in the refrigerator.

Yields: 1 lb. fresh equals 4 cups chopped garlic.

Garlic Butter Sauce

Serve over vegetables or pasta

4 tbsp. butter or olive oil
6 cloves garlic, peeled, crushed or minced
Salt
Black pepper

In a saucepan, melt butter or olive oil. Add garlic and simmer over low heat, stirring constantly. Cook until garlic turns golden and becomes very aromatic. Do not overcook. Remove from heat and season to taste. Makes ½ cup.

Fresh Garlic Soup Brisighella
Zuppa di Aglio Fresco

Don't be put off by the amount of garlic. The soup is mellow and mild, yet full-flavored. it is one of my favorite dishes–easy to do and substantial enough to make a light supper main dish on its own.

Soup:
2 heads large-clove garlic
4 cups water
2 small to medium onions, finely chopped
½ cup extra virgin olive oil
6 medium fresh sage leaves, or 6 small dried sage leaves
3½ cups poultry or meat stock
Salt and freshly-ground black pepper to taste

Croutons:
4 ½-inch thick slices good quality Italian baguette style bread
⅔ cup (about 3 oz.) Italian parmigiano-reggiano cheese, grated

Working ahead: The soup comes together quickly once the garlic has been peeled and boiled 10 minutes. This could be done 1 day ahead and the garlic refrigerated in a sealed container. The croutons can be prepared at the same time, then wrapped and stored at room temperature. Rewarm them in a 300 degree oven for 5 minutes. Make the soup itself, without puréeing, within 2 hours of serving. Reheat to a boil, purée, and serve.

Preparing the garlic: Separate the cloves from each head of garlic, but do not peel them. Bring the water to a rolling boil in a 2-quart saucepan. Drop in the garlic cloves and boil 10 minutes. Drain them in a sieve and peel. If you are using fresh green garlic, do not peel the cloves.

Making the soup: Return the garlic cloves to the saucepan, add the onion, olive oil, sage, and stock. Bring to a lively bubble over medium-high heat. Partially cover and cook 5 minutes. Uncover, adjust the heat so the liquid bubbles slowly, and cook another 5 minutes.

Making the croutons: Preheat the broiler. While the soup is simmering, arrange the bread slices on a baking sheet. Toast them under the broiler 1 to 2 minutes per side, or until the slices are crisp and golden. Set aside a few spoonfuls of the cheese to top the soup. Sprinkle the rest over the bread slices. Slip the baking sheet back under the broiler only a second or two, to melt the cheese but not brown it. Keep warm.

Finishing and serving: Have four soup dishes warming in a low oven. The garlic cloves will be meltingly soft when the soup finishes cooking. Remove all but 1 sage leaf, and purée the soup in a blender or food processor. Season to taste. Arrange the croutons in the soup dishes, and pour the purée over them. Sprinkle each serving with a few shreds of cheese, and serve immediately. Makes 4 servings

This unique and delicious recipe is reprinted with the kind permission of Lynne Rossetto Kasper, excerpted from her book, *The Splendid Table, Recipes from Emilia-Romagna, the Heartland of Northern Italian Food.* Copyright 1992 by Lynne Rossetto Kasper, published by William Morrow and Company, Inc.

GARLIC

Braised Chicken with Garlic and Fennel

5 tbsp. virgin olive oil
1 whole frying chicken, cut up, skin removed (reserve back for broth
  or stock)
1 large head garlic, cloves separated, and peeled
3 carrots, peeled and cut into strips
3 fennel bulbs, tops cut off and reserved for garnish
8 small yellow new potatoes (1½-inches in diameter)
1½ tsp. salt (or to taste)
½ tsp. freshly-ground black pepper
1 tbsp. fennel fronds, chopped

Preheat oven to 350 degrees. Halve fennel bulbs lengthwise and cut halves
lengthwise into ¼-inch slices. Pour olive oil into a 5-quart heavy ovenproof
kettle with a tight-fitting lid; add chicken and vegetables, salt and pepper;
toss to coat. Cover kettle and bake until chicken is cooked through and vegetables are tender, about 1½ hours. Stir in chopped fennel fronds and serve
with fresh French bread. Makes 4 servings.

Modified from *The Best of Gourmet, 1999*
HILLTOP PRODUCE FARM

Roasted Garlic Mashed Potatoes

6 cups potatoes, peeled, and cut into 1-inch cubes
1 cup whole milk
2 tbsp. butter
1–2 tbsp. roasted garlic paste
¼ tsp. salt
¼ tsp. fresh ground pepper (optional)

Cook potatoes in water until soft, about 20 minutes. Heat the milk and butter together. Drain potatoes and press through ricer or mash, add all other
ingredients and beat with hand mixer until well blended and smooth. Do
not over beat or potatoes will get pasty. Makes 6 servings.

Ulrich Bloecher

GARLIC

Roasted Garlic Custard

4 large* firm head of garlic
1 cup unsalted chicken stock
1 tsp. unsalted butter
½ teaspoon salt
¼ tsp. freshly-ground white pepper
2 large eggs, at room temperature
1 large egg yolk, at room temperature
⅔ cup half & half, warmed
1 cup whole milk, warmed
Unsalted butter for the ramekins, and boiling water

Preheat oven to 350 degrees. Remove the excess peel from the heads of garlic, and slice the top ¼ of the bulb off. Wrap the heads of garlic in aluminum foil, and place in the preheated oven to roast. It should take about 30 to 45 minutes for the garlic to roast, depending on how large and how fresh the heads are. The foil packet should be very soft and pliable. Remove the garlic from the foil, and squeeze the roasted flesh out onto a plate while it is still warm, taking care to remove any skin that may adhere. This step can be done a day ahead, and the roasted garlic refrigerated.

Reduce the oven heat to 300 degrees. Heat the chicken stock. Add the roasted garlic, butter, salt and pepper, and simmer for 30 minutes, or until the liquid is reduced to a glaze consistency.

Beat the eggs and yolk together until light. Beat in the warmed cream and milk. Mix in the garlic-chicken stock mixture. Press this mixture through a fine sieve.

Ladle mixture evenly into 6 buttered ramekins. Place the ramekins in a baking pan, spacing them evenly apart. Place on the middle rack of the preheated oven, and add boiling water to ¼-inch below the rims of the ramekins. Bake for 30 minutes, or until the custards are firm. They should be lightly puffed. Remove from oven, and allow to stand in the water for 10 minutes before turning out. Makes 6 servings.

*May be prepared several hours ahead, and reheated in the oven before unmolding.

B. J. Carpenter & Mary Ryan
COOKING INSTRUCTORS AT COOKS OF CROCUS HILLS

Garlic Cream Sauce For Pasta

¼ cup garlic, finely chopped
½ cup butter
2 tbsp. fresh basil, finely chopped
¼ tsp. dried thyme
¼ tsp. dried rosemary
¼ tsp. black pepper
2 cups light cream
¼ cup fresh parsley, finely chopped
Salt

In a medium saucepan, melt butter. Add garlic and sauté for 2 minutes. Add remaining ingredients and simmer over low heat for about 5 minutes or until sauce is thickened. Salt to taste. Serve over pasta. Makes about 3 cups. Makes 8 servings.

Greens

WHEN AVAILABLE

May–Frost

SOME VARIETIES

Beet greens, collards, kale, mustard greens, sorrel, Swiss chard, and turnip greens

PREPARING GREENS

Wash and trim stems. Serve whole or chop. Eat raw or cook until tender. Microwave in a covered dish with 2 tbsp. water. The cooking times vary greatly depending on type of green and the maturity of the leaf. Different types of greens can be used interchangeably in recipes.

Blanch time: 2–8 minutes

Steam time: 5–10 minutes

Microwave time: 2–4 minutes

Yields: 1 lb. fresh greens equals 8 cups sliced or diced or 1½–2 cups cooked. These vary depending on the variety.

Nutrition: Kale, 1 cup cooked, has about 45 calories. Greens are excellent sources of calcium, potassium, and vitamins A and C.

Fig and Endive Salad

⅔ cup pecans, chopped
⅓ cup pecan oil
1 bunch endive or escarole, leaves separated
2 cups sprouts, such as alfalfa or radish
4 fresh figs, thinly sliced crosswise
2 scallions, thinly sliced
3 tbsp. raspberry or blueberry vinegar
½ cup fresh raspberries or blueberries
Salt and black pepper to taste

In a small skillet toss pecans with 1 tbsp. pecan oil and toast for about 5 minutes. Remove with a slotted spoon and place on paper towel to drain. Reserve any leftover oil in pan.

Arrange endive leaves on plates. Top with sprouts. Place fig slices over sprouts. Sprinkle pecans, berries, and scallions on top of figs.

In same skillet from toasting pecans, add vinegar, salt, pepper, and remaining oil. Whisk vinaigrette for 3 minutes over low heat. Drizzle vinaigrette over salads. Serve immediately. Makes 4 servings.

Laurie McCann

Swiss Chard Sauté

2 tsp. vegetable oil
2 tsp. garlic, minced
½ cup leeks, sliced
1 cup chard stems, sliced
1 tbsp. broth
4 cups Swiss chard, coarsely chopped
Salt and freshly-ground black pepper to taste

Heat oil in a large nonstick skillet; add garlic, leeks, and chard stems. Sauté, stirring for about 2 to 3 minutes. Add broth and chard. Season with salt and pepper to taste, stirring to combine ingredients. Cover and simmer, stirring occasionally, for about 5 minutes or until the chard is tender. Makes 4 servings.

HILLTOP PRODUCE FARM

Maple Syruped Greens

1 lb. kale or chard, coarsely chopped
2 tbsp. olive oil
4–5 cloves garlic, minced
2 tbsp. lemon or orange juice
¼ cup maple syrup
1 tbsp. sesame oil
1 tbsp. fresh ginger, grated or minced (or 1 tsp. dried)
Soy sauce or tamari, to taste
1 tbsp. sesame seeds (optional)

In a large frying pan, heat oil to medium hot. Sauté garlic a minute or two; cool slightly and add the juice, syrup, half of the sesame oil, and ginger. Mix together. Add greens and cover. Turn up the heat and cook, stirring occasionally, until greens are wilted but not mushy.

Add tamari to taste and drip on remaining sesame oil. Transfer to warm serving dish and garnish with sesame seeds.

Mary Broeker

Dancing Winds Sautéed Chard Threads with Goat Cheese

Quick to prepare, this vegetarian dish can be served atop pasta or polenta. During the winter, leafy greens are available in abundance; experiment with substituting red or green mustard, kale, red chard or even spinach for the green chard.

1 large bunch green Swiss chard with stalks intact
3 tbsp. olive oil
2 cloves garlic, minced
¼ cup chicken or vegetable stock
½ tsp. salt
½ tsp. freshly-ground black pepper
3–4 oz. low-salt feta (½ to ⅔ cup)

To prepare the chard, cut out the white stalk, or spine, in each leaf by cutting along either side of it, creating a V shape. Coarsely chop the stalks and set them aside. Stack the leaves, one on top of the other, and roll them up, creating a log. Cut the log crosswise into ½-inch wide sections. When the sections are unfurled, they will form long, narrow strips.

Heat olive oil in a large skillet over high heat. Add the garlic and chopped chard stalks and sauté until tender, about 5 minutes. Add the stock and allow to cook down for 1 to 2 minutes. Reduce the heat to medium and mix in the chard leaves, salt, and pepper. When the leaves just begin to wilt, after 1 to 2 minutes, fold in the feta cheese. When the cheese begins to soften, after about 1 minute, remove from the heat. Transfer to a serving dish and serve immediately. Makes 4 servings.

Mary Doerr

Collard Greens with Onion and Bacon

½ lb. bacon, cut into 1-inch pieces
3 medium onions, coarsely chopped
1¼ cups chicken broth
¼ cup white vinegar
2 tbsp. packed dark brown sugar or to taste
½ tsp. dried hot red pepper flakes or to taste
4 lbs. collard greens, coarse stems, and ribs removed, washed, drained, and coarsely chopped

In a deep heavy kettle cook bacon in 2 batches over medium heat until crisp. Drain on paper towels. Pour off all but about 3 tbsp. drippings. Add onions to drippings and cook, stirring occasionally, until browned slightly and softened. Transfer with a slotted spoon to a bowl.

Add broth, vinegar, brown sugar, red pepper flakes, and about half of bacon to the kettle, stirring until sugar is dissolved. Add half of the collards, stirring until wilted; add remaining collards and do the same. Simmer, covered, 30 minutes. Stir in onions and simmer, covered, 30 to 45 minutes more, or until collards are very tender. Serve collards topped with remaining bacon. Makes 8 servings.

HILLTOP PRODUCE FARM

Collards and Black-eyed Peas

6 cups collard greens, coarsely chopped
1 medium onion, chopped
1 tbsp. olive oil
2 cloves garlic, minced
2 cups tomatoes, chopped
2 tsp. ground cumin
2 tbsp. fresh lemon juice
1 tsp. salt
1 tsp. black pepper
1 tbsp. tomato paste or ketchup (optional)
1 cup cooked black-eyed peas

Steam collard greens until tender, about 7 to 10 minutes. In a large skillet, sauté onion and garlic in oil until soft. Add tomatoes, cumin, lemon juice, salt, pepper, tomato paste or ketchup if desired, and black-eyed peas. Mix well. Stir in cooked collards until mixed. Serve over rice. Makes 3 servings.

Evelyn Kaiser

Curried Kale and Squash Soup

4 cups kale, with stems removed, washed, and chopped
3 cups winter squash, peeled and diced
4 tbsp. olive oil
1 large onion, chopped
1 clove garlic, minced
1 cup uncooked wild rice
1 cup dried lima beans
6 cups vegetable or chicken broth
1 tbsp. curry powder
Salt and black pepper

In a large pot, sauté onion in oil until soft. Add garlic and cook for 1 more minute. Add remaining ingredients, cover, and bring to a boil; reduce heat. Simmer for 2 to 3 hours, stirring occasionally, until rice and beans are tender and soup is good and thick. Season with salt and pepper. Makes 8 servings.

LENGSFELD'S ORGANIC GARDENS

GREENS

Kale Colcannon

5 medium potatoes, peeled and quartered
4–6 cups kale, with stems removed, washed, and chopped
2 tbsp. butter or margarine
1 small onion, chopped
⅓ cup lowfat milk
1 tsp. salt (or to taste)
⅛ tsp. black pepper

Boil potatoes until tender. Steam kale separately until tender, about 10 minutes. While potatoes and kale are cooking, heat butter or margarine in a large pot. Sauté onion until soft. Mash potatoes, add kale, onion, milk, salt, and pepper. Mix well. Reheat and adjust seasonings. Makes 4–6 servings.

French Cream of Sorrel Soup

4 cups sorrel, chopped (stems removed)
3 tbsp. butter
3 cups chicken stock
2 egg yolks
¼ cup cream
½ cup sour cream
Salt and white pepper to taste

Melt butter in heavy saucepan. Sauté sorrel until wilted. Add chicken stock and simmer 10 minutes. Mix egg yolks with cream; while whisking, add ¼ cup of the sorrel-stock mixture; then slowly add this to the remaining sorrel-stock mixture, whisking constantly. Heat until thickened. Do not boil. Remove from heat and add sour cream. Add salt and white pepper to taste. Makes 4 servings.

HILLTOP PRODUCE FARM

GREENS

Hortopita

A traditional greens pie of Greece

1 lb. fresh spinach
1 lb. mixed greens (arugula, mustard, sorrel or dandelion)
½ cup extra virgin olive oil
2 medium-sized leeks, whites, and 1-inch of green, finely chopped
1 cup scallions, finely chopped
1 tsp. minced fresh chili pepper, or ½ tsp. dried
1½ cups feta cheese, crumbled
1½ cups fresh Parmesan or pecorino Romano, grated
2 large eggs, lightly beaten
¼–½ cup (depending on personal preference) fresh dill weed, minced
1 cup fennel bulb, thinly sliced and chopped
1 cup golden raisins
Sea salt and freshly-ground white pepper
Extra virgin olive oil
16–18 sheets phyllo dough

Preheat oven to 375 degrees. Wash all greens, and roughly chop. Heat 1 cup of water in a heavy bottomed sauté pan, and add about half of the chopped greens. Cover and cook for several minutes, until the greens are wilted. Add remaining greens, stir together, and place in a colander to drain. Press with the back of a spoon to extract the liquid.

Dry the sauté pan, add ½ cup of the olive oil, and place over medium heat. Sauté the chopped leeks and scallions until soft, about 5 minutes. Add the remaining oil, wilted greens, and the chili pepper. Sauté for an additional 2 to 3 minutes. Remove from heat and allow to cool for several minutes.

Mix the cheeses together and taste for saltiness. Beat the eggs until light. Mix the cheese, minced dill weed, and fennel bulb into the eggs. Plump the raisins in some warm water, drain, and add to the egg mixture. Add the egg mixture to the greens, mix well and salt to taste, adjusting the amount to the saltiness of the cheese.

Bring the phyllo sheets to room temperature, according to the directions on the package. Brush a 10-inch springform pan with olive oil. Layer 8 to 9 sheets of the phyllo in the bottom of the pan, brushing each individually with oil and overlapping one another. Tuck into the bottom edge of the pan.

Spread the filling evenly into the phyllo, pressing and smoothing the top with the back of the spoon. Fold the overhanging layers of phyllo onto the top of the filling. Layer the remaining leaves of phyllo onto the top, oiling each. Trim some of the excess, but leave enough to tuck into the side of the pan, using a thin spatula or butter knife.

Place in a cookie sheet so the oil won't drip in the oven. Bake for 40 to 50 minutes or until golden and slightly puffed. Remove from oven, place on a cooling rack, and allow to cool for 10 minutes before releasing the spring.

This dish can be served warm or cold, and is also good at room or picnic temperature. Makes 6–8 servings as full course or 10–12 servings as a side dish.

B. J. Carpenter & Mary Ryan, Cooking Instructors
COOKS OF CROCUS HILL, ST. PAUL

GREENS

Seared Scallops with Baby Greens and Orange Vinaigrette

2 tsp. orange zest
2 tbsp. orange juice
1 tsp. red wine vinegar
⅛ tsp. salt
¼ cup and 1 tsp. olive oil
4 cups of baby greens, washed and dried
1 small shallot, minced
¾ tbsp. butter
¾ lb. sea scallops
Ground black pepper

For the vinaigrette, whisk zest, juice, vinegar, salt, and a pinch of pepper in a small bowl. Slowly whisk in ¼ cup of the oil. Set vinaigrette aside.

Put the greens into a bowl. Salt and pepper the scallops on both sides.

Heat a large sauté pan over medium-high heat until hot. Add butter to coat the bottom of the pan. Continue heating the pan until the butter turns golden brown. Add the scallops to the sauté pan. Cook until the scallops are well browned, then turn scallops and cook until opaque. Remove the scallops and wipe the fat from the pan. Add the remaining tsp. of the oil, shallot and thyme. Cook until the shallot softens lightly. Remove the pan from the heat and let cool for 1 minute.

Pour vinaigrette into the pan scraping the bottom to remove caramelized bits. Spoon ⅔ of the vinaigrette over the baby greens, toss the greens and then divide onto plates. Place a portion of the scallops on each bed of greens. Spoon the remaining vinaigrette over the scallops. Serve immediately. Makes 2 servings.

Jim Trenter

Herbs

WHEN AVAILABLE

May–Frost

PREPARING HERBS

Wash, pat dry with a towel, trim stems, and chop. When substituting fresh herbs for dried in a recipe, the general rule is to use 3 times as much fresh herbs as dried, or 1 tbsp. fresh equals 1 tsp. dried for the same flavor. Cutting basil with a knife makes it turn black. This is fine for cooking dishes but for fresh salads, simply tear up.

DRYING HERBS

Herbs with long stems such as marjoram, sage, savory, mint, and rosemary can be dried in bunches. Tie the stem ends together into small bunches and hang them upside down in a dry shaded area. An herb with large leaves, such as basil, can be tray dried. Spread the leaves on a screen or tray one layer deep. Cover with cheese cloth to protect from insects. Stir or turn leaves daily. The herbs should be dry in 1 to 2 weeks, depending on temperature and humidity.

Herb List

ARUGULA ❧ Italian spicy salad herb with a flavor reminiscent of radish, walnuts, and bacon. Use in tossed salads, in chicken, beef or ham sandwiches. Also called rucola and rocket.

BASIL (SWEET BASIL) ❧ For all tomato and pasta cookery. Add a touch to hamburger and sprinkle over beef during cooking to enhance the flavor. Add a pinch to cheese dishes and sausage.

CHERVIL ❧ A deliciously-flavored herb. Use on meat and fish. Add to soups and salads. Makes a tasty herb vinegar. Fresh lacy leaves are a nice garnish.

CORIANDER ❧ Use the leaves in soup and stew. Enjoy a fresh spicy flavor in chili dishes and curries. Add to cream cheese and cottage cheese. Used extensively in Asian and Mexican cooking.

DILL WEED ❧ Excellent with vinegar as a basis for salad dressing. Sprinkle over meat and fish. A snappy treat with salads and zucchini dishes.

FENNEL ❧ Especially appreciated when cooked with fish and fish chowders. Good with eggs, salads, and stews.

LEMON BALM ❧ Desirable in hot drinks, when flavored with honey. Gives mild lemon flavor to foods. Excellent in salads, and salad dressing.

LOVAGE ❧ This celery herb has a rich savory celery flavor. Use with chicken, cabbage, potatoes, salad, meats, seafood, and soups. Essential for cooking broths.

MARJORAM ❧ Sprinkle this herb over meats, especially lamb and mutton, before cooking. Add a bit to sausage, soup, sauces, and cheese dishes.

MINT ❧ Will aid in the digestion of lamb and mutton. Add to green peas and carrots for a lively taste treat. Make a fresh mint jelly. Use in tea and lemonade.

HERBS

108

OREGANO ✆ A great favorite in pizza pie. Try it over cheese sandwiches and hamburgers before broiling. Very popular in Italian, Mexican and French foods.

PARSLEY ✆ Use for garnishing and flavor. This nutrient rich herb may be mixed with melted butter for potatoes and creamed vegetables. Curly parsley dresses up salads and vegetable trays. Italian, or flat-leaved parsley is a more intensely, flavored herb for soups and sauces.

ROSEMARY ✆ Good in creamed soups. Place a leaf in a potato before baking. Excellent in stuffing. Use with lamb, pork, and stew.

SAGE ✆ How many memories are linked to the fragrant, homey aroma of sage used in stuffing of Thanksgiving turkey or Christmas goose? Is also good with veal and pork, perhaps because of their bland nature. Try a pinch or two in soft cheese or sausage.

SAVORY ✆ Called the "bean herb." Has an affinity for dishes with peas or beans. Add a bit to stew, egg dishes, and poultry stuffing.

SORREL ✆ A spring and summer herb that has a sour lemony flavor. The leaves are used in soups, salads, and sauces. Sorrel is good paired with fish.

TARRAGON ✆ Make a tarragon vinegar to use as a basis for salad dressing. It will enhance the flavor of seafood and egg dishes.

THYME ✆ Use the leaves. Excellent for flavoring stew and soup. Add a pinch or two to creamed or scalloped onions and fresh peas.

HERBS

Some Tips for Using Herbs in Cooking

Myrl and Dan Moran offer some good tips on using herbs in their book, *The Herbal Solution,* from Melon Patch Herbs.

For the cook who wants to learn more about using herbs, they ask three questions: 1. What herbs do you like? Try all of the herbs that interest you and decide which ones you like best. Start with a very small amount of an herb in a dish you are making and increase the amount according to your taste. 2. Fresh or dried? Fresh is best, but dried will do. Generally use about 3–4 times as much fresh herb as dried in the recipe. 3. What are you cooking? Some dishes team up well with particular herbs, for example, chicken and tarragon, eggs and chives, or fish and dill. Parsley compliments almost everything.

Two classic herb combinations often seen on recipe ingredient lists are bouquet garni and fines herbs. Bouquet garni is usually made up of bay leaf, parsley, thyme, peppercorns, and garlic, which are tied in a cheesecloth bundle. The bundle is put into the stew pot during cooking and removed when cooking is finished. Fines herbs consist of equal parts parsley, chives, French tarragon, and chervil, chopped finely and is added toward the end of cooking.

Another tip: Do not cook herbs too long—they will lose their flavor. Add them in the last few minutes of cooking.

FLOWERS IN YOUR FOOD

Some flowers are eminently edible, and they really dress up your plate! Nasturtium, Johnny jump-ups, geranium, marigold, calendula, dianthus, rose, and pansy, to name a few, are beautiful edible garnishes. Herb flowers are wonderful in salads because they taste like the herbs themselves, for example arugula, borage, chive, burnet, dill, thyme, basil, hyssop, and sage. Always be sure the flower you wish to use is edible (some are poisonous), use only unsprayed flowers, and check for insects before using.

HERBS

Basil and Garlic Herb Butter

½ cup butter, softened
2 tbsp. fresh basil, chopped
1 clove garlic, minced
2 tbsp. fresh oregano, chopped
2 tbsp. fresh parsley, chopped
Salt and black pepper to taste

Cream butter together with herbs. Form into a long cylinder. Wrap in wax paper and aluminum foil and freeze. Slice off pats as needed. Makes about ¾ cup.

Myrl & Dan Moran
Reprinted from *The Herbal Solution* published by Melon Patch Herbs, 1989

Nasturtium Salad

4 cups mixed lettuce leaves
12 nasturtium leaves
2 hard boiled eggs, chopped
10 nasturtium flowers
Oil and vinegar dressing (your choice)

Mix lettuce, nasturtium leaves, and eggs in a salad bowl. Toss with dressing and garnish with nasturtium flowers and serve. Makes 2 servings.

Myrl & Dan Moran
Reprinted from *The Herbal Solution* published by Melon Patch Herbs, 1989

HERBS

Edible Flower Lemonade

3 cups cold water
¾ cup freshly squeezed lemons
⅔ cup rosepetal sugar
¼ cup roseflower water
Lemon slices for garnish

Flowered ice cubes:
For flowered ice cubes you will need one ice cube tray, various edible flowers, and water. Place one or two flowers in each ice cube square. Fill each square ½ full of water. Freeze. Top frozen half cubes off with water. Freeze. You can make the flower cubes in one freezing but the flowers will not freeze in the middle. They will float to the top before the cube freezes solidly.

Lemonade:
Combine lemon juice with sugar and roseflower water. Stir to dissolve sugar. Add 3 cups water and mix well. Garnish with lemon slices and serve with flowered ice cubes. Makes 1 quart.

GOLDEN FIG EPICUREAN DELIGHTS

Basil and Arugula Oil

Flavored oils are quite expensive, so here's a real value. The fragrance, flavor, and beauty of this oil is worth the effort! It makes simple ingredients like sliced tomatoes, steamed potatoes or green beans taste and smell like heaven (and earth). This recipe is inspired by Charlie Trotter's (great Chicago chef) public television series—basil adds that beautiful verdant green color!

1 bunch fresh basil, genovese or other varietal, washed and dried, leaves
    removed from stems
1 oz. arugula leaves, washed and dried
1 cup cold pressed canola or sunflower oil
2–3 tbsp. extra virgin olive oil
Blender
Coffee filter for straining

HERBS

Blanch basil and arugula leaves in boiling water for 10 to 15 seconds only. Chill in bowl of ice (stops cooking and enhances color). Dry on towel or in salad spinner. Chop coarsely in food processor or blender. Add oil and blend for a full 3 to 4 minutes. Pour into a glass jar and let settle for 48 hours. If the ambient temperature is very warm you may wish to refrigerate the jar, though the original method utilizes room temperature only.

Strain oil mixture through a coffee filter to remove solids. Pour into a glass jar and let settle another 24 hours, to clarify before using. Store at room temperature, or refrigerate if you wish.

Drizzle on tomatoes and mozzarella cheese, green beans, on grilled crusty bread or even steamed corn on the cob.

Jeanne Quan

Melon Patch Basil Pesto

⅓ cup olive oil
3 cloves garlic, peeled and chopped
2 tbsp. pine nuts
½ tsp. salt
2 cups fresh basil leaves
½ cup fresh parsley, stems removed
½ cup grated Parmesan cheese

In a blender combine olive oil, garlic, pine nuts, and salt. Blend until smooth. Add basil and parsley. Blend well. Place mixture in a bowl. Gently fold in Parmesan cheese. Toss with hot spaghetti and serve at once. Makes about 2 cups.

MELON PATCH HERBS

HERBS

Mint Chutney
Serve with spicy dishes and meat

1 cup packed fresh mint leaves (no stems)
½ cup green onion, chopped
1½ tsp. ginger root, peeled, and chopped
1 small hot chili pepper, seeded, and minced
1 tsp. salt
½ cup plain yogurt

Blend all ingredients in blender until smooth. Pour into a bowl and serve.
Makes 2 cups.

Tabouli

1 cup bulgur
4 cups cold water
1½ cups fresh parsley, finely chopped
1 cup fresh mint, finely chopped
½ cup green onion, finely chopped
1 cucumber, chopped
2 tomatoes, chopped and drained

Dressing:
1–2 cloves garlic, minced
¼ cup extra virgin olive oil
¼ cup fresh lemon juice
1 tsp. salt
Dash black pepper

Soak bulgur in water for 45 minutes. Drain and place in an unbleached cotton towel. Squeeze out excess water by wringing the towel with your hands.
This is the secret to good tabouli. Now the grain will better absorb the other
flavors.

    In a large bowl, mix dressing ingredients. Add the bulgur and the rest of
the ingredients and mix well. Chill. Makes 4 servings.

Evelyn Kaiser

HERBS

114

Scarborough Fair Potatoes
Parsley, sage, rosemary, and thyme

1 lb. boiling potatoes (a yellow potato like Yukon Gold is especially good)
2 tbsp. olive oil
½ medium or 1 small onion
2 tsp. parsley, chopped
1½ tsp. fresh sage (or ½ tsp. dried)
1½ tsp. fresh rosemary (or ½ tsp. dried)
½ tsp. fresh thyme (or ¼ tsp. dried)
Freshly ground black pepper

Boil or steam the potatoes until tender. Drain and cut into about 1-inch chunks. Chop the onion. Mince the sage, rosemary, and thyme.

Heat the oil in a skillet and sauté the onion for 2 to 3 minutes. Add the potatoes, minced herbs (except the parsley), and pepper. Mix together and cook 3 to 5 minutes or until the potatoes are starting to brown and are heated through. Add the parsley, stir, and serve. Makes 4 servings.

Don Feeney

Herb Goat Cheese Quesadillas

1 lb. chevre (fresh goat cheese)
½ cup lowfat milk
1 tbsp. fresh basil, chopped
1 tbsp. fresh cilantro, chopped
1 tbsp. fresh parsley, chopped
1 tbsp. fresh sage
8 flour tortillas
½ cup olive oil

Preheat oven to 375 degrees. Combine goat cheese and milk in a bowl. Mix together and add the fresh herbs. Spread ¼ cup cheese mixture onto each flour tortilla and fold in half. Brush tortillas with olive oil and place on a baking sheet. Bake for 8 to 10 minutes or until golden brown. Cut each in half and serve warm. Makes 8 servings.

Jay Liberman, Chef
FOODSTUFFS, EVANSTON, ILLINOIS

HERBS

Baked Chicken Breast with Herb Pesto

The pesto also works very well with pork tenderloin

8 boneless and skinless chicken breasts

Pesto:
2 cups fresh basil
1 cup fresh mint
½–1 cup fresh cilantro
4 cloves garlic
1 2-inch piece ginger
2 jalapeño peppers, seeded
¼ cup soy sauce
1 tsp. white pepper
2 tbsp. molasses
1 cup olive oil

Combine all ingredients in a blender and purée.

Arrange chicken breasts in a glass baking dish and top with pesto, covering chicken breast on sides. Cover the dish with plastic wrap and marinate several hours or overnight.

Preheat oven to 350 degrees and bake chicken 30 to 45 minutes until chicken is done. Makes 6–8 servings.

Donna Cavanaugh
A GOURMET THYME, DISTINCTIVE CATERING

Eggs Benedict with Rosemary Hollandaise

2 fresh eggs, poached
2 slices Canadian bacon, cooked and drained
½ cup rosemary hollandaise, recipe below
2 toasted crumpets (English muffins work nicely also)
Capers
Fresh rosemary sprigs

Place cooked Canadian bacon on tops of toasted crumpets. Rest poached eggs on top of each bacon piece. Pour rosemary hollandaise sauce over the eggs. Garnish with capers and fresh rosemary.

HERBS

Rosemary hollandaise:
2 tbsp. rosemary, lemon and garlic vinegar
¼ tsp. freshly-ground black pepper
¼ cup hot water
3 egg yolks
¾ cup clarified butter
1½ tsp. freshly-squeezed lemon juice
1 tsp. ground rosemary
Salt and black pepper

In a saucepan reduce vinegar and pepper by half. Cool. Add hot water. Whisk egg yolks with vinegar reduction until tripled in volume. Gradually add clarified butter. Add lemon juice and ground rosemary. Salt and pepper to taste. Makes 2 servings.

GOLDEN FIG EPICUREAN DELIGHTS

Moran's Fresh Basil in Oil

For freezing. This is the best way to preserve fresh basil.

2 cups firmly packed fresh basil, stems removed
½ cup vegetable oil

Blend basil and oil in a food processor or blender until smooth. Pour into freezer containers, cover and freeze. Use the same amount of thawed frozen basil mixture as you would fresh basil. It will keep in a freezer for up to 6 months. Makes 1½ cups.

MELON PATCH HERBS

HERBS

Rosemary Sorbet

This is so refreshing as a dessert or palate cleanser!

Other herbs, such as mint, lemon thyme, or lemon balm could be used instead of rosemary.

Note before starting: Liquids should stand overnight.

First Mixture:
5 cups water (filtered is best)
2 cups granulated sugar
1–2 oz. fresh rosemary, more or less, to taste

Second Mixture:
2 cups dry white wine
6 tbsp. lemon juice
3 tbsp. aquavit

Combine water, sugar, and rosemary in a saucepan and boil gently for 5 minutes. Remove from heat and steep 1 hour or overnight.

Combine white wine, lemon juice, and aquavit; chill overnight.

Next day strain out the herb from the first mixture, squeezing as much liquid out as possible—this is where the flavor is. Combine liquids and process in an ice cream machine, according to manufacturer's instructions.

Serve garnished with small sprigs of rosemary, sugared or not, or rosemary flower petals. Makes 8 servings.

Susan Dietrich, Pastry Chef
PRAIRIE SWEETS

Kohlrabi

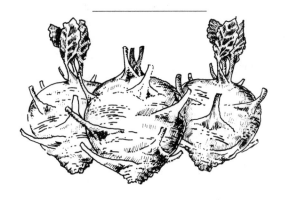

June–Frost

SOME VARIETIES

Green and purple

PREPARING KOHLRABI

Remove leaves and stems, peel outer skin, using a knife. Eat raw like an apple or cut into pieces and cook until tender. Microwave in a covered dish with 2 tbsp. water.

Blanch time: 5–7 minutes

Steam time: 7–10 minutes

Microwave time: 5–8 minutes

Yields: 1 lb. fresh equals 2–4 medium kohlrabi or 3 cups diced or 4 cups grated.

Nutrition: 1 cup cooked has 50 calories and has moderate sources of potassium and Vitamin C.

Kohlrabi Slaw

3 cups kohlrabi, peeled and shredded

Creamy Dressing #1:
¾–1 cup mayonnaise
1 tbsp. white vinegar
1 (8oz.) can crushed pineapple, undrained

In a large bowl, mix mayonnaise, vinegar, and undrained pineapple. Add shredded kohlrabi and mix well.

Vinegar Dressing #2:
¼ cup white vinegar
¼ cup sugar
2 tbsp. water
¼ tsp. salt
½ tsp. whole celery seed
½ tsp. dry mustard
1 shallot, minced

In a medium saucepan, combine vinegar, sugar, water, salt, celery seed, mustard, and shallot. Cover and boil for 3 minutes. Remove from heat and cool. Put shredded kohlrabi in a large bowl. Pour cooled dressing over kohlrabi and toss to coat. Makes 6 servings.

Evelyn Kaiser

Autumn Kohlrabi Salad with Apples

½ cup sour cream
¼ cup creamy French dressing
2½ cups kohlrabi, grated
2 small apples, chopped
1 small onion, minced

In a large bowl mix sour cream and French dressing. Add kohlrabi, apples, and onion. Coat well. Makes 4 servings,

Ann DesLauriers

Kohlrabi Chowder

6 strips bacon, diced
1 medium onion, chopped
1 clove garlic, minced
4 cups chicken broth
4 cups kohlrabi, peeled and cubed
4 cups potatoes, peeled and cubed
1 cup heavy cream
Salt and white pepper to taste
2 tbsp. parsley, chopped

Fry bacon in heavy soup pot over medium heat until done; remove and drain on paper towels. Drain off all but about 1 tbsp. bacon fat. Add chopped onion and sauté until glassy—do not brown. Add garlic and sauté one minute longer. Add chicken broth, kohlrabi, and potatoes. Bring to a boil and simmer, partially covered, over medium heat until potatoes and kohlrabi are soft and soup becomes thick. Stir frequently so soup does not scorch. Remove from heat. Mash or purée if a less chunky soup is desired. Add cream, salt, white pepper, and parsley. Add bacon. Reheat (do not boil) and serve. Makes 8 servings.

HILLTOP PRODUCE FARM

Honey Mustard Kohlrabi

2 cups kohlrabi, peeled and sliced
2 tbsp. olive oil
2 tbsp. honey
1–2 tbsp. Dijon mustard

Steam kohlrabi until tender, about 10 minutes. In a bowl mix together oil, honey, and mustard. Taste and adjust for flavor. Toss with cooked kohlrabi pieces. Makes 4 servings.

Geoffrey Saign

KOHLRABI

Easy Creamed Kohlrabi
Cooked Kohlrabi are sweeter than cauliflower!

3 cups kohlrabi, peeled and sliced
3 tbsp. butter or margarine
3 tbsp. all-purpose flour
1–1½ cups warm lowfat milk, less for a thicker sauce or more for a
    thinner sauce.
1 tsp. salt

Steam kohlrabi slices until tender, about 10 minutes. In a medium saucepan, melt butter or margarine, stir in flour, and cook over low heat, constantly stirring, for 3 minutes. Add warm milk, all at once, and bring to a boil, stirring. Reduce heat and stir until sauce thickens. Stir in salt. Pour over the cooked kohlrabi. Makes 6 servings.

LENGSFELD'S ORGANIC GARDENS

Cajun Kohlrabi

6 kohlrabi
1 tbsp. vegetable oil
1 tsp. butter
1 small onion, diced
1 small green pepper, seeded and diced
1 clove garlic, minced
2 small to medium tomatoes, peeled and diced
1 tsp. Cajun spice

Peel and dice kohlrabi. Cook in a covered saucepan in 4 cups boiling water until tender, about 8 to 10 minutes. Drain. In a large saucepan, sauté onions and green pepper in oil and butter until tender. Add minced garlic and sauté 1 minute longer. Add tomatoes and bring to a simmer. Add cajan spice. Add cooked kohlrabi and reheat. Makes 6 servings.

Stuffed Kohlrabi

8 kohlrabi, 3 to 4-inches in diameter
1 lb. ground meat, half pork and half beef
1 medium onion, peeled and diced
2 eggs
½ cup bread crumbs
¼ tsp. salt
¼ tsp. black pepper
1 pinch ground nutmeg
4 tbsp. butter
2½ cups beef broth or bouillon
3 tbsp. sour cream
2 tsp. cornstarch

Peel kohlrabi, cut flat end on bottom, and cut a lid off the top. Reserve the lids. Hollow out kohlrabi with a melon baller or sharp spoon leaving ¼-inch wall. In food processor or with a fork combine meat, half of the onion, eggs, bread crumbs, salt, pepper, and nutmeg. Fill kohlrabi with meat mixture, put lid on top and tie with a string or secure with toothpicks to hold lid in place.

In heavy casserole melt butter, add kohlrabi flat end down and remaining onion, brown lightly, add 1 cup of beef broth, cover, and bake in oven at 325 degrees. Bake for one hour, as needed add remainder of the broth. Remove kohlrabi to serving platter and remove strings or toothpicks. Over medium heat combine sour cream and cornstarch with remaining liquid in casserole to make gravy. Serve with cooked potatoes.

Reserve the kohlrabi pulp from the cavities for other uses. Makes 8 servings.

Ulrich Bloecher

KOHLRABI

Easy Kohlrabi and Carrots with Tempeh

2 cups kohlrabi, peeled and cut into ¼-inch slices
1 cup carrots, peeled and cut diagonally into ¼-inch slices
1 (8oz.) package tempeh, diced ½-inch cubes
3 tbsp. canola oil
1 small onion, finely chopped
2 tbsp. soy sauce

Steam kohlrabi and carrot slices until tender, about 10 minutes. In a large skillet, heat 1 tbsp. oil and add tempeh cubes. Fry over medium heat until brown on all sides, turning when needed. Pour cubes into a bowl and set aside. In the same skillet heat remaining 2 tbsp. oil. Add onion and garlic and sauté over medium heat until soft, about 3 minutes. Add soy sauce and mix. Add cooked kohlrabi, carrots, tempeh, and stir to coat. Add more soy sauce if needed. Serve with rice or potatoes. Makes 6 servings.

Evelyn Kaiser

Lettuce

May–Frost

SOME VARIETIES

Boston bibb, Belgian endive, curly endive, escarole, iceberg, green and red leaf lettuce, oak leaf, romaine, lambs lettuce, and mesclun, which is a mix of baby lettuces and, if desired, other greens.

PREPARING LETTUCE

Wash off dirty leaves under running water or by dunking in water. Shake off excess water and use a salad spinner to dry the leaves. They work great! Tear lettuce in bite-size pieces.

Yields: 1 lb. fresh equals 6 cups chopped lettuce leaves or greens.

Nutrition: 1 head has 25 calories and contains some potassium and Vitamin A. Endive and escarole has 10 calories in 1 cup and contains potassium and Vitamin A.

Honey Herb Salad Dressing for Greens

¼ cup vegetable oil
½ cup honey
⅓ cup white vinegar
1 tsp. dry mustard
½ tsp. salt
2 tsp. onion, minced
½ tsp. lemon balm, dried
½ tsp. tarragon, dried

Place all ingredients in a shaker bottle. Shake at intervals until thoroughly blended. Refrigerate to cure for 24 hours. Shake before each use. Makes about 1 cup.

Lil Lindig

Maple Dressing for Tossed Salads

½ cup corn oil
¼ cup white vinegar
¼ cup maple syrup
1–2 tbsp. tomato paste
½ tsp. salt
Dash black pepper
½ tsp. dried basil, crushed
¼ tsp. dried oregano, crushed

In a medium bowl, whisk together all ingredients, cover, and refrigerate at least 2 hours. Stir well before serving on tossed salad. Makes 1 cup.

Joan Schellinger

Grandma's Lettuce Salad

Grandma used cream from their cow before Miracle Whip was invented

4 cups torn lettuce
1 cup light mayonnaise
1 tbsp. white vinegar
1 tbsp. sugar

In a medium bowl, stir together mayonnaise, vinegar, and sugar. Add torn lettuce and stir until well coated. Makes 8 servings.

Duane Lengsfeld

Caesar Salad

A delicious alternative to the raw egg dressing in classic Caesar salads

1 large head romaine lettuce
2 cups seasoned croutons (you can make your own by drying two slices
    of French bread, cubed, in a warm skillet or oven, sprinkled with
    seasoned salt)
¼ cup grated Parmesan cheese
Dressing (follow recipe)

Dressing:
¼ cup lemon juice
2 tbsp. salad oil
2 tbsp. salad dressing or mayonnaise (regular or lowfat)
½ tsp. Worcestershire sauce
1 small clove garlic, mashed with salt or put through a garlic press
1½ tsp. anchovy paste
⅛ tsp. freshly-ground black pepper
2 tsp. Italian parsley, finely ground

Wash and drain Romaine lettuce. Combine dressing ingredients in a covered jar and shake well. Tear or cut lettuce into bite-size pieces; sprinkle with croutons and Parmesan cheese. Toss with dressing and serve immediately. Makes 6–8 servings.

HILLTOP PRODUCE FARM

LETTUCE

Citrus Endive Salad

1 bunch curly endive or escarole
1 large red grapefruit
2 oranges
½ cup citrus juice
⅓ cup honey
2 tbsp. salad oil
3 tbsp. raspberry vinegar
Toasted slivered almonds for garnish (optional)

Wash endive or escarole and put into colander to drain well.

Catch the dripping juices in a large salad bowl while peeling the grapefruit and oranges—this will be used for making the dressing later. Carefully peel grapefruit and oranges so that the inner membranes are cut off with the peels, exposing the sections. Manually squeeze the peels to extract whatever juice they may contain, then discard. Carefully cut out each citrus section, separating it from the membranes, again catching the juice; set sections aside. Add more orange or grapefruit juice to the saved juices to make about ½ cup. Whisk in honey, salad oil, and raspberry vinegar.

Tear endive or escarole into bite-size pieces, add to dressing in bowl and toss well to coat. Add reserved grapefruit and orange sections; toss lightly. Garnish with toasted slivered almonds. Makes 6 servings.

HILLTOP PRODUCE FARM

Seven Layer Salad

1 head iceberg lettuce, broken into bite-size pieces
1 cup celery, diced
1 green pepper, diced
1 large onion, cut in rings
1 cup green snap peas, chopped
2 cups mayonnaise
2 tbsp. sugar
6 oz. grated cheddar cheese
¾ lb. bacon, fried crisp, drained, and crumbled

LETTUCE

In a large bowl, layer lettuce, celery, green pepper, onion, and green peas to make 5 layers.

In a small bowl, combine mayonnaise and sugar. Spread over the five layers of vegetables. Top with cheese and crumbled bacon. Cover and refrigerate at least 8 hours. Makes 8 servings.

Elaine Lundberg

Dancing Winds Greek Salad

Olive oil, feta cheese, Calamata olives and garlic–all scrumptious staples of Mediterranean countries–are showcased in a traditional Greek salad

8 cups torn romaine lettuce
1 small red onion, thinly sliced
1 medium tomato, diced
¼ cup olive oil
1 tbsp. red wine vinegar
2 tsp. lemon juice
4–8oz. crumbled feta cheese (choose either plain or tomato basil)
1 tbsp. fresh oregano, finely snipped
½ tsp. garlic, minced
½ tsp. salt
⅛ tsp. coarsely ground black pepper
½ cup drained calamata olives

In a large salad bowl, combine romaine, onion, and tomato; refrigerate.

In a small bowl, combine olive oil, vinegar, lemon juice, oregano, garlic, salt and pepper; whisk to blend.

To serve: Drizzle dressing over greens; add olives and toss lightly. Sprinkle with feta cheese. Makes 8 servings

Mary Doerr

LETTUCE

Taco Salad

1 lb. ground beef
1 medium onion, finely chopped
2 cloves garlic, minced
1 (16oz.) can kidney beans, undrained
½ cup taco sauce
½ tbsp. ground chili powder
1 medium head of lettuce, torn
3 large tomatoes, diced
1 green pepper, chopped
8 oz. cheddar cheese, grated
1 cup taco chips, crushed
Taco sauce or salsa (optional)
French dressing (optional)

In a large skillet, brown ground beef and drain off fat. Add onion and garlic and cook for 3 minutes. Add undrained kidney beans, taco sauce, and chili powder. Bring to a boil; reduce heat. Cover and simmer for 10 minutes or until onions are tender.

In a large bowl, combine torn lettuce, tomatoes, green pepper, and cheddar cheese. Add hot hamburger mixture. Toss to mix. To serve, top with crushed chips, taco sauce, salsa or French dressing, if desired. Makes 8 servings.

Donna Schueller

Lettuce Soup

6–10 cups lettuce, chopped (any kind)
½ cup onion or green onion, chopped
2 tbsp. butter or olive oil
3 cups chicken flavored broth
2 tsp. salt
½ tsp. black pepper
½ cup light cream or 6 oz. cream cheese, diced
Croutons or chopped parsley for garnish

LETTUCE

In a large pot, sauté onion and lettuce in butter or olive oil until limp. Add broth, salt, and pepper. Simmer 5 minutes and taste for salt. Purée 2 cups at a time in a blender and process until smooth. Return purée to pot to reheat. Add cream or cream cheese cubes and heat until melted. Top with croutons or parsley. Makes about 6 servings.

Rice Stuffed Lettuce Rolls

Rice stuffing:
1 cup uncooked Basmati rice
2 cups water

Dressing:
1 clove garlic, crushed
1 tbsp. honey
1 tbsp. vinegar or lemon juice
1 tbsp. olive oil
¼ cup fresh parsley, chopped
¼ cup fresh green onions, including tops, chopped
2 tbsp. fresh mint, chopped
Salt and black pepper
12–18 large romaine lettuce leaves
1 cup tomato, chopped

Preheat oven to 375 degrees. In a covered saucepan, bring rice and 2 cups water to a boil. Reduce heat to low and cook for 20 minutes.

In a large bowl, combine garlic, honey, vinegar or lemon juice, olive oil, parsley, green onions, and mint; mix well. Add cooked rice, salt, and pepper. Taste and adjust seasonings.

Steam lettuce leaves briefly until tender, about 2 minutes. Using a sharp knife, remove large ribs of romaine leaves. Place a couple spoonfuls of stuffing in each leaf. Fold in sides and roll up. May be served cold topped with chopped tomato. To bake, place rolls, seam side down in a greased baking dish. Top with chopped tomato and bake for 20 minutes.

Mixed Vegetables

Vinegar and Oil Dressing for Cooked Vegetables

½ cup white vinegar
1 cup water
¼ cup salad oil
½ cup sugar

In a small bowl, whisk together the vinegar, water, salad oil, and sugar. Cover and chill. Pour over cooked vegetables of your choice.

Variation:
5 tbsp. olive oil
5 tbsp. vegetable oil
2 tbsp. red wine vinegar
1 tbsp. freshly cut oregano
1 tbsp. freshly cut chives
1 tbsp. freshly cut parsley
Salt
Freshly ground black pepper

In a bowl, whisk together the olive oil and vegetable oil with the vinegar. Add oregano, chives, parsley, and salt and pepper to taste. Pour dressing over vegetables. Enough dressing for ½ lb. each broccoli, cauliflower, carrots plus onions and green peppers. Makes 4 servings.

Marilyn Heschke
Nancy Jordan
Mrs. Melvin Poppitz
Diane McLagan

Mock Hollandaise Sauce

The classic use for this sauce is steamed asparagus,
but it is also good on just about any green or yellow vegetable

1 cup beef broth or bouillon
½ stick unsalted butter
1 cup whole milk
1 tbsp. corn starch
2 egg yolks
1 tbsp. lemon juice
1 tsp. sugar
Salt and white pepper to taste
1 tiny pinch of cayenne pepper

In saucepan bring broth to a boil, add butter, and remove from heat. Beat milk, cornstarch, and egg yolks together. When butter is melted add milk mixture, bring to a boil over medium heat, stirring constantly, boil for one minute and remove from heat. Stir in lemon juice, sugar, salt, and pepper to taste, add cayenne pepper. Makes 2½ cups.

Ulrich Bloecher

Eichten's Vermicelli Salad

1 lb. vermicelli pasta
1 small jar green pimento stuffed olives, sliced
1 large cucumber, peeled, and sliced
4 stalks celery, diced
1 medium green pepper, diced
1 bunch green onions, sliced
1 box cherry tomatoes, halved
⅓ cup grated parmesan or romano cheese
1 package salad seasonings
1 (8-oz.) jar Italian dressing

Break vermicelli into quarters, then add to boiling water, and bring back to boil. Remove from heat. Let stand 2 minutes, drain. Place in large bowl and add other ingredients. Cover and marinate at least 4 hours in refrigerator. Overnight is better. Makes 6 servings.

EICHTEN'S CHEESE

Crudités Salade

9 spears fresh asparagus, cut in small pieces
¾ cup raw cauliflower, chopped
¾ cup raw broccoli, chopped
¾ cup celery, slivered
1 small zucchini, thinly sliced
½ cup raw mushrooms, thinly sliced
1 small cucumber, thinly sliced
4 green onions, thinly sliced
¼ cup radishes, thinly sliced
1 cup cherry tomatoes

Vinaigrette Dressing:
1½ cups vegetable oil
½ cup white wine vinegar
1 tsp. salt
¼ tsp. black pepper
½ tsp. sugar
¼ tsp. dried rosemary

Place all vegetables in bowl and toss. In a small bowl, blend ingredients for dressing and pour over raw vegetables. Cover and refrigerate for one hour or longer. Makes 2 cups.

Sue Zelickson, Editor
Minnesota Heritage Cookbook Volume I: Hand Me Down Recipes
AMERICAN CANCER SOCIETY

Perfection Molded Vegetable Salad

1 envelope unflavored gelatin (1 tbsp.)
¼ cup cold water
1¼ cup boiling water
1 tsp. salt
½ cup sugar
¼ cup lemon juice
¼ cup vinegar or sweet pickle juice
1 small onion, minced
1 cup cabbage, shredded
1 cup celery, chopped
½ cup carrots, grated
2 tbsp. green pepper, chopped
¼ cup sliced stuffed olives (optional)

Soften gelatin in cold water (2 to 3 minutes). Add boiling water and stir until gelatin is completely dissolved. Add salt, sugar, lemon juice, and vinegar or sweet pickle juice. Stir to dissolve sugar. Chill until partially set—about 1 to 2 hours. Add remaining ingredients, pour into oiled mold or serving bowl, and chill until set. Serve with mock Russian dressing. Makes 6 servings.

Mock Russian Dressing:
½ cup mayonnaise or salad dressing
3 tbsp. cream
3 tbsp. chili sauce

To mayonnaise or salad dressing add cream and chili sauce. Mix well. Chill. Makes ¾ cup.

HILLTOP PRODUCE FARM

Fresh Vegetable Broth

2 celery stalks with leaves
2 carrots
2 leeks
1 onion, unpeeled, studded with 4 whole cloves
2 cloves garlic, slightly crushed
8 white mushrooms, halved
4 tomatoes, quartered
4 potatoes, halved
8 sprigs fresh parsley
2 sprigs fresh dill
1 bay leaf
8 whole peppercorns
1 tsp. salt
9 cups water

Wash and drain vegetables. Cut celery and carrots into chunks. Put all ingredients into a large, heavy soup pot. Bring to a boil; simmer over low heat, uncovered, for 1½ hours. Strain broth, reserving vegetables for another use, if desired. Cool to room temperature; refrigerate or freeze. Makes 6 cups.

HILLTOP PRODUCE FARM

Minestrone Soup

6 cups beef broth
1 (15-oz.) can great northern, cannelini or lima beans
1 large potato, peeled and diced
2 carrots, sliced
2 ribs celery, sliced
1 white or yellow onion, chopped
2 cloves garlic, minced
1 small green pepper, chopped
1 tbsp. olive oil
1½ cups green cabbage, shredded
1 cup zucchini, cubed
1 cup green beans, cut in 1-inch lengths
½ lb. spinach or Swiss chard, chopped
3 cups Italian plum tomatoes, chopped
½ cup small shell macaroni or other pasta, uncooked
½ tsp. each dried oregano and rosemary (or 1 tsp. each, fresh, chopped)
1 tsp. dried basil (or 2 tsp. fresh, chopped)
1 tsp. salt
½ tsp. black pepper
Grated Parmesan cheese

In a large stockpot, bring beef broth to a boil. Add canned beans, potato, carrots, and celery. Simmer 15 minutes. Meanwhile, heat olive oil in a skillet and sauté onion, garlic, and green pepper for 5 minutes. Add to broth mixture and simmer another 15 minutes. Add cabbage, zucchini, green beans, and spinach or Swiss chard. Simmer 10 minutes. Add chopped tomatoes, pasta, oregano, rosemary, basil, salt, and pepper. Simmer another 15 minutes or until pasta is cooked. Serve sprinkled with Parmesan cheese. Makes 15 servings.

Modification of a recipe submitted by Joan Schellinger

Vegetable Appetizer Bars

2 8-oz. pkgs. crescent rolls
8 oz. cream cheese, regular or reduced fat
¾ cup mayonnaise or salad dressing
1 package dry ranch salad dressing mix
¾ cup green pepper, finely chopped
¾ cup green onion, finely chopped
¾ cup tomatoes, peeled, seeded, and finely chopped
¾ cup carrots, finely chopped
¾ cup mushrooms (canned or fresh), finely chopped
¾ cup cauliflower, finely chopped
¾ cup broccoli, finely chopped
¾ cup cheddar cheese, grated

Preheat oven to 375 degrees. Cover the bottom of an 11x17-inch ungreased cookie sheet with the crescent rolls, pushing the dough with your fingers to seal the seams. Bake 7 to 8 minutes at 375 degrees. Cool. In a small bowl, mix cream cheese, mayonnaise or salad dressing, and dry dressing mix. Spread on baked, cooled crust. Sprinkle chopped vegetables on top; then sprinkle cheese on top of vegetables. Chill at least an hour or two. Serve cold. Cut into squares. Makes 4 dozen bars.

Crystal Bloecher

MIXED VEGETABLES

End of the Season

This vegetable medley is beautiful and healthful

12 Italian turkey sausages, cut in 1-inch pieces
¼ cup olive oil
1 onion, sliced
1 green pepper, seeded and sliced
1 yellow pepper, seeded and sliced
1 red pepper, seeded and sliced
1 carrot, thinly sliced
4 purple potatoes, cooked, peeled, and sliced
1 medium zucchini, sliced
¼ cup fresh basil leaves
1 tbsp. each fresh mint and oregano leaves

In a large skillet, cook sausage pieces; remove and drain. Add olive oil to skillet and sauté onions, peppers, carrots, potato, and zucchini, stirring frequently, until vegetables are tender-crisp. Add basil, mint, and oregano. Add the sausage pieces and reheat. Makes 8 servings.

Doe Hauser-Stowell

Oven-Roasted Vegetables with Garlic

These easy-to-make vegetables are served at Chamberlain's Prime Chop House in Dallas, Texas

6 parsnips, peeled, halved crosswise, then lengthwise
6 carrots, halved crosswise, then lengthwise
6 shallots, peeled, cut in half
2 medium-size red onions, peeled, each cut into 8 wedges
1 large head garlic, separated into cloves, peeled
3 tbsp. fresh rosemary, chopped or 1 tbsp. dried
3 tbsp. fresh thyme, chopped or 1 tbsp. dried
2 tbsp. olive oil
2 tbsp. (¼ stick) butter, melted

Preheat oven to 400 degrees. Mix first 7 ingredients in large roasting pan. Drizzle with oil and butter and toss to coat. Roast vegetables until golden and tender, stirring occasionally, about 1 hour 20 minutes. Season with salt and pepper. Transfer vegetables to platter and serve. Makes 6 servings.

Bon Appetit, *September 1995*

MIXED VEGETABLES

Panzanella (Italian Bread Salad)

4 cups slightly dried-out bread (it is important that this be a hearty, substantial, dense country-style bread), cubed or torn apart, with or without the crust
4–5 tomatoes, medium-sized, firm, meaty and ripe, cored, and chopped into 1-inch chunks
1 red onion, thinly sliced
½ to 1 cucumber, cut into ½-inch chunks
½ cup basil leaves, loosely packed
Salt and freshly-ground black pepper to taste

Optional additions:
Thinly sliced celery hearts
Diced sweet pepper
Pitted Mediterranean olives

Vinaigrette:
½ cup olive oil
2 tbsp. red wine vinegar
1 tsp. garlic, finely minced
½ tsp. salt
4–6 mashed anchovy fillets (optional)
2 tbsp. drained capers

Whisk together vinaigrette ingredients. Mix salad ingredients in a bowl. Add vinaigrette and toss gently to blend. Add more salt and black pepper to taste. Once again, toss gently, cover, and refrigerate for 30 minutes or so, to allow flavors to come together.

Lynne Alpert

Saturday Market Focaccia

Preheat oven to 375 degrees. On a round of focaccia, spread seasoned tomato sauce, sprinkle with mozzarella and Parmesan cheese, and choose from topping suggestions. Bake for 15 to 20 minutes or until cheese is melted and toppings are a bit roasted.

Spring Toppings
Cooked, chopped, and drained spinach, sliced green onions, sliced and fried or raw radishes, chopped fresh herbs, cooked flat peas, and marinated asparagus.

Early Summer Toppings
Halved red and yellow cherry tomatoes, steamed zucchini strips, chopped onion, minced garlic, cooked corn kernels, cooked new potato slices, cooked chopped green beans, and chopped fresh herbs.

Late Summer Toppings
Tomato slices, still more steamed zucchini strips, chopped sweet or hot peppers, chopped Spanish onions, chopped fresh herbs, cooked chopped chard, and grilled eggplant slices.

Autumn Toppings
Spread focaccia with cream sauce or cooked mashed squash, chopped onions, cooked chopped kale or spinach, cooked Brussels sprout halves, cooked parsnip slices, cooked apple slices, and apple butter.

Evelyn Kaiser

Vegetable Quiche Muffins

4 cups all-purpose flour
2 tbsp. baking powder
1 tsp. garlic salt
1 tsp. ground white pepper
1 tsp. dried dill weed
4 eggs, beaten
½ cup canola oil
1 cup grated cheddar cheese
1½ cups skim or lowfat milk
½ cup bread crumbs
2 cups grated or finely chopped raw vegetables (1 small zucchini, ½ bell pepper, ½ cup broccoli florets, 1 small onion or green onions, ½ cup grated carrots, for example)

Preheat oven to 350 degrees. Grease two muffin pans. In a bowl, combine flour, baking powder, garlic salt, white pepper, and dill weed. Set aside. In a large bowl, combine eggs, oil, cheese, milk, breadcrumbs, and vegetables; blend well. Add the flour mixture and mix just to combine. Fill muffin pans ⅔ full and bake 25 to 30 minutes or until muffin springs back when pushed gently with your finger. Makes 18 muffins.

HILLTOP PRODUCE FARM

MIXED VEGETABLES

Late Summer Linguine

This is a quick and light pasta sauce that can only be made with really fresh vegetables

1 lb. linguine
¼ cup fresh basil
¼ cup parsley
2 tsp. fresh oregano
1 tsp. fresh thyme
1 tsp. fresh rosemary
1 medium onion
2 cloves garlic (more to taste)
1 small eggplant
1 bell pepper, preferably red or yellow
1 small zucchini
3 to 4 cups chopped ripe tomatoes
¼ cup olive oil
Salt
Black pepper
Parmesan cheese

Cook linguine according to package directions. Mince the herbs and set aside. Chop onion. Mince garlic. Peel and dice eggplant, pepper, zucchini, and tomatoes. Heat oil in large frying pan. Add onion, garlic, pepper, eggplant, and zucchini, and sauté for 5 minutes. Add tomatoes, stir and heat for 10 minutes, stirring occasionally. Add herbs, salt and pepper, stir to heat through briefly. Serve over hot linguine and top with grated Parmesan. Makes 4 servings.

Don Feeney

Teriyaki Veggie Kabobs
I made this recipe up. It's delicious and easy!

4 12-inch wooden skewers, soaked in water
1 lb. firm tofu, drained
½ cup teriyaki sauce
1 medium zucchini, sliced
1 green pepper, seeded and chunked
1 small red onion, chunked
½ cup mushrooms, sliced

Preheat grill to medium heat. Cut tofu into 1-inch cubes and combine with teriyaki sauce in a container. Cover and marinate for at least 30 minutes. Cut up vegetables. Put the tofu cubes and vegetables on the skewers, alternating between the different vegetables and tofu as you go. Brush with teriyaki sauce. Place skewers directly on rack of grill. Roast over medium heat, turning as needed, until vegetables and tofu are cooked and slightly charred. Makes 4 servings.

Rene LaBore

Kohlrabi, Apple and Spinach Salad
with Hazelnuts and Blue Cheese

2 cups (2 medium handfuls) fresh baby spinach
1 large kohlrabi bulb
2 apples, any good sweet-tart variety, such as McIntosh or Haralson
¼ cup hazelnuts, chopped and toasted (10 minutes in a 350 degree oven)

Vinaigrette:
3 tbsp. extra virgin olive oil
2 tbsp. sherry or champagne vinegar
Salt and freshly-ground black pepper to taste

Wash and dry spinach. Toast hazelnuts. Peel and julienne the kohlrabi and apple. Whisk together olive oil and sherry or vinegar. Salt and pepper to taste. Toss with kohlrabi, apple, and spinach. Place on two serving plates and sprinkle with cheese and toasted hazelnuts. Makes 2 servings.

Philip Dorwart, Executive Chef
TABLE OF CONTENTS, MINNEAPOLIS

MIXED VEGETABLES

Okra

August–Frost

PREPARING OKRA

Wash and trim ends. If using okra whole, don't trim so much off that you cut into the seed cavity. Otherwise, slice into quarter inch wheels and cook until tender. Microwave in a covered dish with 2 tbsp. water. Cut okra releases a gooey juice that thickens soups and stews.

Pan fry time: 5–8 minutes

Blanch time: 5–6 minutes

Steam time: 8–10 minutes

Microwave time: 3–5 minutes

Yields: 1lb. fresh equals 8 cups whole okra or 4 cups sliced.

Nutrition: 1 cup boiled has 60 calories and contains potassium, calcium, vitamin A and folacin.

Chicken, Shrimp or Vegetable Gumbo Soup

Omit the chicken and shrimp for a vegetarian soup

1½ tbsp. vegetable oil
1 large yellow onion, peeled and diced
1 cup carrots, diced
1 cup celery, diced or celery root, peeled
½ cup parsnip, diced
8 cups chicken or vegetable stock
½ cup green bell pepper, diced
1 cup greens (Swiss chard or tatsoi) including stems, chopped
1 cup okra, stems removed, sliced
1 cup Roma tomatoes, peeled, seeded, and diced
2 (8oz.) cans tomato sauce
1 bay leaf
¾ cup cooked white medium-grained rice
1½ cups cooked chicken or raw shrimp, peeled or use both chicken and
    shrimp, ¾ cup of each
1½ tsp. dried thyme
2 cloves garlic, minced
2 tsp. Cajun seasoning (or according to taste)
Chopped fresh parsley for garnish

Prepare all vegetables according to ingredient list, keeping items separate. This can be done one day in advance. If using fresh shrimp, prepare the day you are making the soup.

Heat oil in a stockpot; add onions, carrots, celery, and parsnip. Sauté until onions are translucent. Add stock and bring to a boil. Add remaining ingredients except chicken and shrimp; simmer until vegetables are tender. Add chicken and shrimp and simmer 3 minutes longer. Remove bay leaf. Serve sprinkled with chopped parsley. Makes 12 servings.

Ellen Bloecher, Private Chef

Fried Okra

2 cups okra, sliced
1 egg, beaten
1 cup all-purpose flour
1 tsp. salt
¼ tsp. paprika
⅛ tsp. black pepper
Vegetable oil for frying

In a medium bowl whisk together flour, salt, paprika, and pepper. Dip okra slices in beaten egg and then press into flour mixture to coat both sides. Fry slices in a heated oiled skillet until the bottoms are golden brown. Turn and fry the other side until golden brown. Makes 4–6 servings.

Whole Baby Okra and Tomatoes

A recipe for those who dislike the gooiness of okra

2 cups whole small okra
2 tbsp. butter or margarine
1 medium onion, chopped
2 cloves garlic, minced
1 bay leaf
2 cups tomatoes, chopped
1 tsp. salt
¼ tsp. black pepper
½ tsp. paprika

Wipe the okra clean with a towel and trim the stems. In a large saucepan, heat the butter or margarine and add the onion and garlic. Sauté until soft, about 3 minutes. Add the bay leaf, tomatoes, salt, pepper, and paprika. Cover and bring to a boil; reduce heat. Simmer for 30 minutes or until the okra is tender. Remove bay leaf. Serve with rice. Makes 6 servings.

OKRA

Pickled Okra

4 lbs. okra
1 quart water
1 quart white vinegar
1 cup sugar
½ cup canning salt (non-iodized)
3 tbsp. whole pickling spices
6 cloves garlic, peeled
1½ tsp. dried hot pepper, crushed

Wipe okra clean rather than washing in water because okra becomes gooey when wet.

In a large stainless steel kettle, mix together water, vinegar, sugar, and salt and bring to a boil. Tie pickling spices in a thin white cloth and boil in vinegar mixture for 10 minutes; remove and discard spice bag.

Place a clove of garlic in each sterilized pint jar along with ¼ tsp. dried crushed hot pepper. Pack each jar with whole okra as tightly as you can, filling to ¾-inch from the top. Pour boiling vinegar mixture over the okra, filling each jar to ½-inch from the top. Run a plastic knife down the side to remove bubbles. Adjust clean hot lids and process in boiling-water bath for 10 minutes. Remove and cool. Wait 2 weeks for flavors to develop. Makes 6 pints.

Onions

WHEN AVAILABLE

May–November

SOME VARIETIES

Scallions, yellow, white, red, leeks, and shallots

PREPARING ONIONS

Peel outer paper, trim tip, and root ends. Rinse with water and chop. Sauté in butter or oil until soft. Microwave in 2 tbsp. water, butter or oil until soft, stirring once. Shallots have a wonderful flavor—a cross between onions and garlic, only better!

Sauté time: 3–5 minutes

Blanch time: 4–6 minutes (slices)

Yields: 1 lb. fresh equals two 4 inch onions or 3 cups chopped; 1 lb. fresh leeks equals 3 cups chopped; 1 lb. fresh shallots or scallions equals 4 cups chopped

Nutrition: 1 cup raw equals 65 calories and contains potassium.

Roasting an Onion
A flavorful fat free alternative for sauteed onions

Preheat oven to 450 degrees. Put an unpeeled whole onion on a foil lined cookie sheet and bake for 45 to 60 minutes, or until onion is tender. Turn once halfway through the baking. Cool, peel, and chop.

Shallot Marinade for Vegetables

This marinade may be used for any fresh garden vegetables, such as asparagus, broccoli, cauliflower, Brussels sprouts, carrots, green beans, wax beans, peppers, etc., or a combination of these and other vegetables. The vegetables marinate best if they are blanched for a minute or so in boiling water, then rinsed in cold water and drained before adding the marinade.

¾ cup salad oil
½ cup red wine vinegar
2 tbsp. lemon juice
3 tbsp. shallots, minced
2 tsp. fresh tarragon, chopped, or any other fresh herb
1 tsp. salt
1 tsp. sugar

Combine all ingredients in a jar and shake well. Pour over blanched vegetables and chill 2 hours or more before serving. Makes about 1½ cups.

HILLTOP PRODUCE FARM

ONIONS

Creamy Leek and Potato Soup

3 tbsp. butter
5 leeks, white part only, sliced thinly
1 small clove garlic, finely minced
2 potatoes, peeled and sliced thinly
2 (15 oz.) cans chicken broth
1 carrot, shredded
2 stalks celery, sliced thinly
3 tbsp. butter
3 tbsp. all-purpose flour
1 cup whole milk
Salt and black pepper to taste
Chopped fresh parsley for garnish (optional)

In a large skillet, sauté leeks in butter until soft.

In a heavy saucepan, cook potato, carrot, and celery in chicken broth until vegetables are tender. Purée leeks in a food processor and add to potato mixture.

Melt butter in a small skillet; add flour and cook, stirring occasionally, until mixture bubbles. Do not brown. Add to cooked potato mixture and stir until thickened. Add milk and cook just until warmed and thick. Serve sprinkled with chopped fresh parsley, if desired. Makes 4–6 servings.

Patty Brand

ONIONS

French Onion Soup

1 tbsp. all-purpose flour
1½ tsp. dried oregano
1½ tsp. dried thyme
1½ tsp. dried basil
⅛ tsp. black pepper
3 large onions, peeled and sliced
3 tbsp. butter
1 cup red wine (such as burgundy)
4 cups chicken stock
4 cups beef stock
Salt to taste
1 French bread or baguette
Butter
Freshly grated parmigiano-reggiano cheese
1 cup grated Swiss Gruyere cheese for topping

Combine flour, oregano, thyme, basil, and black pepper in a small bowl; set aside.

Melt butter in a large, heavy saucepan over medium heat. Add onions and sauté, stirring frequently for 15 to 20 minutes, or until onions are tender and caramelized to a brown color. Stir in dry seasonings mixture. Add wine. Stir well and simmer for 2 to 4 minutes.

Add chicken and beef stocks and salt to taste. Simmer over low heat for 30 minutes.

Meanwhile slice 8 rounds of French bread. Spread each with butter and place on a baking sheet. Sprinkle each with Parmesan cheese. Bake in 350 degree oven for 20 minutes, or until crisp and golden brown. Remove from oven and set aside.

When soup is ready, ladle into bowls. Top soup with a toast round and sprinkle with grated Gruyere cheese. Bake or broil just until cheese is melted and lightly browned. Makes 8 servings.

Crystal Bloecher

ONIONS

153

Leek and Vegetable Soup

A delicious soup and simple to make!

6 cups sliced leeks, including some green tops (about 2 large or
    4 small leeks)
2 cups potatoes, peeled and diced into ¼-inch cubes
1 cup diced carrot, ¼-inch slices
4 tbsp. margarine
4 cups vegetable broth
2 tbsp. soy sauce

In a large pot, sauté leeks, potatoes, and carrots in margarine for 2 minutes.
Add vegetable broth and soy sauce. Cover and bring to a boil. Reduce heat
and simmer, covered, for 30 minutes or until vegetables are tender. Makes 4
servings.

Evelyn Kaiser

Baked Onions

6 medium onions
2 tbsp. butter
¼ cup tomato juice
3 tbsp. honey
1 tsp. salt
¼ tsp. paprika

Preheat oven to 375 degrees. Peel onions, cut in half crosswise, and place in
a buttered 1-quart casserole.
    In a 6-inch skillet over low heat, melt the butter; add the remaining
ingredients, and stir until combined. Pour over onions, cover, and bake for
50 to 60 minutes or until onions are tender. Makes 6 servings.

Alice Pieper

ONIONS

Homemade Fried Onion Rings

3 large sweet onions, sliced ⅓-inch thick and separated
1 cup all-purpose flour
½ tsp. baking soda
½ tsp. salt
1 egg, beaten
1 cup lowfat milk
Vegetable oil for frying

Preheat oven to 300 degrees. In a medium bowl, combine flour, soda, salt, egg, and milk. Beat together until smooth.

In a large skillet, heat oil. Dip onions rings in batter and deep fry, a few at time, in 1-inch of oil for 4 to 5 minutes or until golden. Drain on paper towel. Keep the fried rings in a 300 degree oven while you make the rest. Makes 6–8 servings.

Onions Au Gratin

4 cups onions, sliced ¼-inch thick
2 tbsp. butter
2 tbsp. all-purpose flour
½ tsp. salt
⅛ tsp. black pepper
1 cup lowfat milk
¼ cup onion liquid
½ cup cheddar or aged Tilsit cheese, grated
½ cup buttered bread crumbs (1 slice day-old bread, reduced to crumbs in
    food processor, sautéed lightly in a skillet with 1 to 2 tsp. butter)

Preheat oven to 375 degrees. Cook onions in boiling water about 15 minutes or until tender. Drain and save ¼ cup liquid. Place onions in a buttered baking dish. Melt butter, add flour, salt, and pepper. Gradually add milk, stirring until thickened. Add onion liquid and the cheese; stir until cheese melts. Pour over onions in dish. Top with buttered crumbs. Bake for 20 minutes. Makes 6 servings.

Hazel Dial

ONIONS

Onion Pie (with optional crusts)

One 9-inch baked pastry shell, not pricked, or optional crust from below

Filling:
3 cups onions, sliced
3 tbsp. butter or margarine
3 eggs, beaten
1 cup lowfat milk, scalded
1 tsp. salt
2 cups cheddar cheese, grated

Preheat oven to 375 degrees. In a medium saucepan, sauté onions in butter or margarine until clear and then pour in crust. In a bowl, combine eggs, milk, and salt. Pour over onions. Sprinkle with cheese. Bake for 30 minutes. Makes 6 servings.

Crust #1: Easy Biscuit Crust

In a hurry?

2½ cups biscuit mix
⅔ cup lowfat milk

In a mixing bowl, combine all ingredients to make dough. Knead 10 times, roll out and press into a 9-inch pie plate. Do not prebake.

Crust #2: Quick Cracker Crust

1½ cups crushed soda crackers
5 tbsp. butter, melted

In a mixing bowl, combine all ingredients. Press into a 9-inch pie plate. Do not prebake.

Soy "Hamburger" Stuffed Onions

3 quarts water for cooking
6 medium onions
1 (14oz.) pkg. beef-flavored soy hamburger or ground hamburger
2 cloves garlic, minced
1 tbsp. ketchup
½ cup cooked rice
½ tsp. Worcestershire sauce
1½ tsp. salt
½ tsp. black pepper
¼ cup grated Parmesan cheese

Preheat oven to 350. Peel onions and parboil in 3 quarts boiling water for 20 minutes. While onions are cooking, brown hamburger or soy hamburger in a large skillet. Add the garlic and cook 2 more minutes, stirring. Remove from heat. Add ketchup, rice, Worcestershire sauce, salt, pepper, and Parmesan cheese, and mix well. Remove the partially cooked onions from the water with a slotted spoon. Drain the onions in a colander. Cut a slice from the top of each onion and scoop out interiors leaving a ¼-inch thick shell. Save the interiors for soup.

Stuff each onion with the hamburger mixture. Place in a greased baking dish and bake for 40 minutes or until tender. Makes 6 servings.

LENGSFELD'S ORGANIC GARDENS

ONIONS

Moist Onion Stuffing
Great for stuffing squash or green peppers

1½ cups onion, chopped
¼ cup margarine or butter
2 tsp. dried basil
1 tsp. dried oregano
½ tsp. dried thyme
1 tsp. dried sage
1 tsp. salt
Dash black pepper
1 tsp. Worcestershire sauce
1½ cups chicken broth or water
8 cups unseasoned dry bread cubes

In a large skillet, sauté onion in margarine or butter until softened. Add seasonings. Add water or stock and then bread cubes. Stir until evenly moistened and heated through. Makes 8–10 servings.

Onion Marmalade
This condiment goes well with roast turkey, beef or pork and grilled meats

2 lbs. onion
2 tbsp. butter
1 tsp. salt
1 tsp. black pepper
½ cup sugar
½ cup red wine vinegar
1 cup white wine
2 tbsp. grenadine syrup

Peel onions, cut in half, and then slice. Melt butter in a 10-inch skillet. Add onions, salt, pepper, and sugar. Cook, covered, over medium heat, stirring occasionally, until moisture evaporates and onions are soft, about 25 minutes. Add vinegar, wine, and grenadine. Continue cooking, uncovered and stirring occasionally, until liquid evaporates, about 30 minutes. Remove from heat and spoon into pint jar; cover, cool completely and store in refrigerator. Makes 1 pint.

HILLTOP PRODUCE FARM

ONIONS

Parsnips and Rutabagas

WHEN AVAILABLE

Spring–parsnips   *Fall*–parsnips and rutabagas

PREPARING PARSNIPS

Wash, trim end, and scrub. Slice into ¼-inch rounds, strips or chunks. Cook until tender, which will be quickly. Microwave in a covered dish with 2 tbsp. water. Try including parsnips along with potatoes and carrots for your next roast.

Blanch time: 6–8 minutes

Steam time: 7–9 minutes

Microwave time: 4–6 minutes

PREPARING RUTABAGAS

Wash and peel or scrub. Cut into ½-inch cubes. Cook until tender. Microwave in a dish with 2 tbsp. water. Stir once halfway through.

Blanch time: 18–20 minutes

Steam time: 20 minutes

Microwave time: 12 minutes

Yields: PARSNIPS—1 lb. fresh equals eight 6-inch parsnips or 3 cups sliced. RUTABAGAS—1 lb. fresh equals half of a 6-inch rutabaga or 3 cups sliced.

Nutrition: PARSNIPS—1 cup cooked has 126 calories and contains potassium, calcium and magnesium. RUTABAGAS—1 cup cooked has 66 calories and contains Vitamin A and potassium.

Parsnip Stew

2 tbsp. vegetable oil
1 medium onion, chopped
2 cloves garlic, chopped
2 stalks celery, chopped
3 cups parsnips, diced ½-inch cubes
1 large potato, diced ½-inch cubes
1 carrot, diced ½-inch cubes
3 tbsp. shoyu or soy sauce
2 tbsp. lemon juice
2 tsp. dried basil
3–4 cups vegetable bouillon broth

In a large pot, heat oil. Sauté onion, garlic, and celery until soft. Add remaining ingredients. Cover and bring to a boil; reduce heat. Simmer over low heat for about 1 hour. Makes 4 servings.

Evelyn Kaiser

Glazed Parsnips

6 medium parsnips, sliced
3 tbsp. butter
1 tbsp. all-purpose flour
2 tbsp. cider vinegar
2 tbsp. apple cider
3 tbsp. brown sugar
½ tsp. salt

Steam parsnip slices until tender, about 10 minutes. In a medium saucepan, melt butter. Add flour and cook for 1 minute, stirring. Add cider vinegar, brown sugar, and salt. Bring to a boil; reduce heat. Stir over medium heat for a few minutes. Add parsnips and cook, spooning liquid over parsnips to glaze. Makes 6 servings.

PARSNIPS AND RUTABAGAS

Root Soup

1 large onion, coarsely chopped
2 tbsp. olive oil
3–4 large cloves garlic, chopped
1 cup parsnips, diced
1 cup rutabaga, diced
1 cup carrots, diced
1 cup potato, diced
2 bay leaves
1 tsp. salt
¼ tsp. black pepper
Water or vegetable broth to cover

In a large pot, brown onion in olive oil. Add garlic and cook 2 minutes. Add remaining ingredients and enough water to cover vegetables. Cover and bring to a boil; reduce heat. Simmer for 1 hour or until vegetables are soft.

Remove bay leaves. Process half of the soup in a blender. Pour back into remaining soup. Mix and heat through. Taste and adjust seasonings. Makes 8 servings.

Carol Neumann

Parsnip and Carrot Skillet

2 cups parsnips, sliced
2 cups carrots, peeled and sliced
3 tbsp. canola oil
1 medium onion, chopped
1 clove garlic, minced
2 tbsp. soy sauce

Steam parsnip and carrot slices until just tender, about 10 minutes. In a large skillet, heat oil. Sauté onion and garlic over medium heat until soft, about 3 minutes. Stir in the soy sauce. Add the cooked parsnip and carrot slices and mix well. Cook the mixture, stirring now and then, over low-medium heat. The longer the vegetables are cooked, the more caramelized they become. Makes 8 servings.

LENGSFELD'S ORGANIC GARDENS

PARSNIPS AND RUTABAGAS

Parsnip Cheese Pie

One 9-inch pastry crust

Filling:
2 cups parsnips, peeled and sliced ¼-inch thick
1 cup carrots, peeled and sliced ¼-inch thick

White sauce:
3 tbsp. butter or margarine
3 tbsp. all-purpose flour
1 cup lowfat milk, warm
1 tsp. salt
¾ cup Swiss cheese, grated

Preheat oven to 450 degrees. Line a 9-inch pie plate with pastry crust. Flute edges, prick bottom with a fork and place a pie weight in the crust. (Dried beans wrapped in foil works well). Bake for 10 minutes. Remove and set aside.

Reduce heat to 350 degrees. Steam parsnips and carrots until tender, about 10 minutes. Melt butter or margarine in a medium saucepan. Add flour and cook over medium heat, stirring constantly, for 2 minutes. Add warm milk, all at once, and bring to a boil, stirring. Reduce heat and continue to cook and stir over low heat until thickened. Stir in salt.

Put vegetables in pie crust. Pour white sauce over vegetables and spread evenly. Top with grated cheese and return to oven. Bake at 350 degrees for 5 to 10 minutes or until cheese is melted. Makes 6 servings.

Mashed Rutabaga

1 large rutabaga, about 2 lbs.
2 tbsp. margarine or butter
Salt and black pepper
2 tbsp. lowfat milk

Peel rutabaga and cut into 1-inch cubes. Cook, covered, in boiling water until tender, about 20 to 25 minutes. Drain. Mash with a potato masher. Add margarine or butter, salt and pepper to taste. Stir in milk.

Peas

WHEN AVAILABLE

May–August

SOME VARIETIES

Shelling, sugar snap, snow or flat

PREPARING PEAS

SHELLING PEAS—Wash, snap off stem, and pull down the thread, open the pod and pop out the peas. EDIBLE POD SUGAR SNAPS—Wash, pull down threads on both sides. Serve whole or cut in 1-inch pieces. SNOW OR FLAT PEAS—Wash and remove blossom end. Pull down threads on both sides. Serve whole or cut in 1-inch pieces. Eat raw or cook until bright green and tender-crisp. Microwave in a covered dish with 2 tbsp. of water.

Blanch time: 8–10 minutes (shelled) 2–4 minutes (snow peas)

Steam time: 10–12 minutes (shelled) 2–4 minutes (snow peas)

Microwave time: 6–8 minutes (shelled) 2–4 minutes (snow peas)

Yields: 1 lb. fresh peas equals 4–5 cups whole pods or 1¼ cups shelled peas.

Nutrition: 1 cup cooked has 110 calories and contains phosphorous, potassium and Vitamins A and C.

Marinated Sugar Snap Peas

The black sesame seeds stick to everything, making it look very exotic

3 cups fresh, cleaned sugar snap peas
⅛ cup sesame oil
2 tsp. cranberry and black peppercorn vinegar
2 tbsp. black sesame seeds

Blanch peas 1 minute in boiling water. Rinse with cold water and drain. Put cooked peas in a large bowl and add remaining ingredients. Serve on a bed of fresh greens. Makes 6 servings.

Laurie McCann

Fresh Pea and Cheese Salad

2 cups shelled peas, cooked
1 cup cheddar cheese, cubed
2 hard cooked eggs, chopped
¼ cup green onions, chopped
1 radish, sliced (optional)
2 tbsp. pimento pepper, diced
½ cup mayonnaise
¼ tsp. salt
⅛ tsp. black pepper

In a covered saucepan, cook peas in boiling water until tender, about 5 to 7 minutes. In a large bowl, combine mayonnaise, salt and pepper. Add remaining ingredients and mix well. Chill. Makes 6 servings.

Chicken Salad Hoisin

1 cucumber, unpeeled
8 oz. fresh peapods
1 cup bean sprouts
4 cups fresh spinach, torn into bite-size pieces
2 cups cold shredded cooked chicken

Dressing:
3 tbsp. hoisin sauce
¼ cup rice wine vinegar
2 tsp. sugar
2 tsp. soy sauce
1 tbsp. sesame oil
2 tsp. sesame seeds (optional)
Cashews or sliced almonds (optional)

Slice cucumber into rounds, then into thin strips. Plunge pea pods into boiling water for one minute. Drain and chill in cold water to preserve the bright color and crispness. Rinse bean sprouts, drain. Combine spinach, vegetables, and chicken in salad bowl.

In a separate small bowl, mix dressing ingredients. Pour over salad before serving. Sprinkle with nuts. Makes 4 servings.

Sue Zelickson, Editor
Minnesota Heritage Cookbook Volume II: Look What's Cooking Now!
AMERICAN CANCER SOCIETY

Creamed Peas over Biscuits

2½ cups fresh sugar snap peas, washed and stringed
1 cup cooked tempeh or turkey, ½-inch pieces
8 biscuits

White sauce:
8 tbsp. butter or margarine
8 tbsp. all-purpose flour
3½ cups lowfat milk, warm
2½ tsp. salt
Slice peas into thirds and steam until tender, about 3 to 5 minutes.

In a saucepan melt butter or margarine. Stir in flour and cook over low heat, stirring constantly for 2 minutes. Add warm milk all at once, and bring to a boil, continuing to stir. Reduce heat and cook, stirring until sauce thickens. Stir in salt, cooked peas and tempeh or turkey pieces. Mix well. Place 2 biscuits on a plate per person, split in half and spoon pea mixture on split biscuits. Makes 4 servings.

LENGSFELD'S ORGANIC GARDENS

Morel and Fresh Pea Ragout

Serve this with meat or hearty fish dishes. It is especially good with lamb

2 tbsp. unsalted butter
1 clove garlic, minced
1 shallot, minced
½ cup dry red wine
3 cups fresh morel mushrooms, chopped (may use fully reconstituted dried
    morels if fresh are not available)
½ cup rich chicken stock
2 tbsp. fresh herbs, minced (thyme is best, but sage, rosemary or chives
    work also)
¼ cup grated Parmesan cheese
Salt and freshly-ground black pepper

Melt butter in skillet; cook garlic and shallots until soft. Do not brown. Add
red wine and morels; cook 5 minutes. Add stock, herbs, and peas; cook until
liquid is almost gone. Add salt and pepper to taste. Mix in Parmesan cheese.
Makes 4 servings.

Philip Dorwart, Executive Chef
TABLE OF CONTENTS, MINNEAPOLIS

Fried Rice

2 cups snow peas, sugar snaps or fresh shelled peas
4 tbsp. canola oil
4 eggs, beaten
1 tsp. sesame oil
⅓ cup onions or scallions, minced
½ cup mushrooms, sliced
1 cup diced, cooked tempeh or cooked chicken pieces
2½ cups cooked rice
3 tbsp. shoyu sauce or soy sauce

In a medium saucepan, blanch peas until tender. Rinse under cold water.

In a large frying pan, heat 2 tbsp. of the oil and pour in the eggs. Tip the pan to form a thin sheet of egg. Fry lightly on one side, then flip and cook the other side for 1 minute. Remove, cool, and slice into thin strips.

Heat remaining 2 tbsp. oil plus sesame oil and fry the onions or scallions, mushrooms and tempeh until onions are soft. Add remaining ingredients, including egg and cook until hot. Makes 4 servings.

Peas and Kohlrabi with Tempeh

1 cup kohlrabi, peeled and sliced
2 cups whole sugar snaps peas, strings removed
1 (8oz.) pkg. tempeh, diced into ½-inch cubes
2 tbsp. canola oil
1 small onion, chopped
1 clove garlic, minced
3 tbsp. soy sauce

Steam kohlrabi slices until tender-crisp, about 4 minutes. Add whole pea pods to kohlrabi slices and continue to steam both until the vegetables are tender, about 5 more minutes. While vegetables are steaming, heat 1 tbsp. oil in a large skillet. Add tempeh cubes and fry until golden on all sides, turning when needed. Pour cubes into a bowl and set aside. In the same large skillet, heat the remaining oil and sauté the chopped onion and garlic until soft. Stir in soy sauce. Add the cooked vegetables and tempeh cubes. Mix well and heat through. Serve with rice or potatoes. Makes 6–8 servings.

Evelyn Kaiser

Peppers

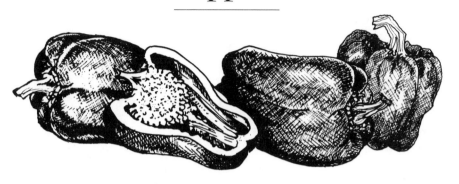

August–Frost

From mild to hot: Sweet bell, Hungarian wax, Italian sweet, Sweet banana, Anaheim Chili, Poblano, Hot Hungarian, Serrano, jalapeño, cayenne, Habanera

PREPARING PEPPERS

Wash, slice off stem end, remove seed and white membrane, and slice or chop. Consider wearing gloves when chopping hot peppers because the juice can be irritating. Be careful not to touch your eyes or mouth after chopping hot peppers. Sweet peppers may be eaten raw or add any pepper to cooked dishes.

Roasting peppers: Place under a broiler, over coals or hold over the flame of a gas stove. Turn until the skin becomes charred and blistered on all sides. Place peppers in a paper bag for 10 minutes to steam and loosen skin. Peel skins, slice open, remove stem, and scrape out seeds. The roasted peppers can be frozen or used right away.

Yields: 1 lb. fresh equals 2 medium peppers or 3 cups diced.

Nutrition: 1 whole raw has 15 calories and are an excellent source of Vitamins A and C.

Marinated Roasted Red Peppers

6 red bell peppers
3 tbsp. olive oil
¼ cup red wine vinegar
¼ tsp. salt
2 tsp. garlic, minced
¼ tsp. dried basil
¼ tsp. dried thyme
¼ tsp. dried rosemary
¼ tsp. dried marjoram
¼ tsp. dried oregano

Preheat grill or oven to 450 degrees. Roast peppers over hot coals, under broiler, or over a gas flame until charred on all sides. Put peppers in a paper bag to steam for 10 minutes. Peel loosened skins. Remove seeds and stems. Slice peppers into ¼-inch thick slices.

In a large bowl combine marinade ingredients and mix well. Add the pepper slices and toss to coat. Cover and marinate in the refrigerator for at least 30 minutes. Makes 10 servings.

PEPPERS

Green Pepper and Tomato Salad
Great in pita bread

2 large green bell peppers, sliced
1 large ripe tomato, diced
1 small cucumber, sliced
2 tbsp. olive oil
2 tbsp. fresh lemon juice
½ tsp. honey
¼ cup parsley, chopped
¼ tsp. salt
Dash black pepper

Put chopped vegetables in a large bowl. In a small bowl mix oil, lemon juice, honey, parsley, salt, and pepper. Pour over vegetables and toss to coat. Makes 3–4 servings.

Evelyn Kaiser

PEPPERS

Pepper Basil Casserole with Chevre

½ cup olive oil
1 tbsp. garlic, minced
¼ cup yellow onion, finely chopped
¼ red bell pepper, finely julienned
¼ green pepper, finely julienned
1½ tbsp. sun dried tomatoes, drained and finely chopped
3 tbsp. fresh basil leaves, chopped coarsely
3 oz. fresh chevre (goat cheese)
2 oz. Parmesan cheese, grated
Kosher or sea salt
Tabasco sauce
Freshly ground black pepper

Heat olive oil over medium heat and sauté onions without browning for 2 minutes. Add garlic and sauté 1 minute. Add peppers and cook until just tender-crisp. Remove from heat and stir in tomatoes. Allow to cool to room temperature.

Heat oven to 400 degrees. Stir basil and cheese into sautéed mixture. Season to taste with salt, Tabasco sauce and pepper. Pour into two individual baking dishes. Bake until bubbly. Add more Parmesan cheese on top, if desired.

Note from Ken: Play with the ingredient quantities until you get it just how you like it.

Ken Goff, Executive Chef
DAKOTA BAR AND GRILL, ST. PAUL

PEPPERS

Baked Barley-Stuffed Peppers

A Romanian recipe from my mother

12 peppers
3 tbsp. vegetable oil
2 medium onions, chopped
2 cups uncooked pearled barley
1 cup uncooked rice
4 stalks celery, chopped
3 tsp. salt
1 tsp. black pepper
¼ cup fresh parsley, chopped
¼ cup fresh dill, chopped
1 cup potato, diced
½ cup carrot, shredded
1 egg, beaten
All-purpose flour
2 cups tomatoes, diced

Preheat oven to 350 degrees. Cut tops off peppers and remove seeds. In a large skillet heat oil. Sauté onion until soft. Add barley and rice and sauté until brown. Add remaining ingredients and mix well. Stuff peppers with mixture. Sprinkle the tops of each pepper with a little bit of flour and press in. This keeps the stuffing from leaking.

Place peppers in a greased baking dish and pour tomatoes over all. Bake for 1 hour or until vegetables are tender. Makes 12 servings.

Connie Korolchuk

Stuffed Whole Anaheim Peppers

6–8 whole Anaheim peppers, stems removed and deseeded

Rice and bean stuffing:
1 tbsp. vegetable oil
1 small onion, chopped
2 cloves garlic, minced
1 cup cooked rice
1 cup cooked black beans
1 tsp. ground cumin
½ tsp. ground coriander
½ tsp. ground cardamom
½ tsp. salt
½ cup tomato, crushed
¾ cup pepper-jack cheese, grated
2 tbsp. water
Salsa
Pepper Jack cheese for garnish

Preheat oven to 350 degrees. In a medium saucepan, heat oil. Sauté onion and garlic until soft, about 3 minutes. Stir in cooked rice and beans, cumin, coriander, cardamom, salt, and crushed tomato. Remove from heat, cover, and set aside. When cooled, mix in the grated cheese.

Stuff peppers from the top, pushing stuffing all the way to the bottom. Use your fingers or a long spoon to do this. Another way is to stuff them is to slit the peppers lengthwise and fill through side opening. Place the stuffed peppers side by side in an 8x8 greased pan, along with 2 tbsp. water. Top with salsa. Cover and bake for 20 minutes. Remove, cover, and sprinkle with more cheese. Bake for 20 more minutes, or until peppers are tender. Makes 6–8 servings.

Merry Reimler & Joe Kaiser

PEPPERS

174

Chicken and Corn-Stuffed Chile Relleños

1 tbsp. olive oil
4 medium onions, chopped
8 poblano chili peppers
4 whole chicken breasts, grilled and cut in small pieces
3 cups Monterey Jack cheese, grated
3 cups cooked corn kernels
2 jalapeño peppers, minced
2 cups yellow cornmeal
3 tbsp. olive oil
Salsa

In a skillet, heat 1 tbsp. of olive oil. Sauté onion until soft. Set aside.

Preheat grill. Char the poblanos over hot grill, cool in paper bag, and remove skin. Slit each poblano and remove seeds but not the stem.

Preheat oven to 350 degrees. In a large bowl, combine all the stuffing ingredients and fill peppers. Roll in cornmeal, coating evenly. Coat a roasting pan with 1 tbsp. olive oil. Place peppers in pan and sprinkle with remaining 2 tbsp. olive oil. Bake for 20 minutes, until cornmeal coating is crisp. Serve with salsa. Makes 8 servings.

Green Chili Tomato Salsa

6 cups long green chilies, chopped, seeded
6 cups tomatoes, peeled, cored, chopped
1½ cups onions, chopped
2 jalapeño peppers, seeded, finely chopped
12 cloves garlic, finely chopped
3 cups white vinegar or bottled lemon juice
1 tsp. ground cumin
1 tbsp. dried oregano leaves
1 tbsp. canning salt

Combine all ingredients in a large saucepan and heat, stirring frequently, until mixture boils. Reduce heat and simmer for 20 minutes, stirring occasionally. Ladle hot salsa into sterilized pint jars, leaving ½ inch headroom. Adjust clean hot lids and process in boiling-water bath for 15 minutes. Remove and cool. Makes 6 pints.

UNIVERSITY OF WISCONSIN EXTENSION

PEPPERS

Pepper Relish

12 red peppers
12 green peppers
12 onions
2 cups white vinegar
2 cups sugar
3 tbsp. canning salt

Chop peppers and onions. In a large stainless steel kettle, boil peppers and onions in water and let stand 5 minutes. Drain; add vinegar, sugar, salt, and boil mixture for 5 minutes. Pour into hot pint jars, leaving ½-inch headroom. Adjust clean hot lids. Process for 10 minutes in boiling-water bath. Remove and cool. Makes about 6 pints.

Katherine Wojnar

Pepper Jelly

Can be served with assorted crackers or pour one jar over a block of cream cheese

6½ cups sugar
1½ cup cider vinegar
1 cup orange bell pepper, finely diced
1 cup red bell pepper, finely diced
1 cup yellow bell pepper, finely diced
½ cup jalapeño pepper, finely diced
½ tsp. canning salt
6 oz. liquid fruit pectin
4–5 sprigs of fresh rosemary (optional)

In a large saucepan, bring sugar, vinegar, peppers, and salt to a boil. Reduce heat and simmer for 10 minutes. Bring to a boil again, add pectin and boil for 1 minute, stirring constantly. Remove from heat and skim. Ladle boiling mixture into hot sterilized pint jars. Add an optional rosemary sprig to each jar. Adjust clean hot lids. Cool. Store in refrigerator. Makes 4–5 pints.

Pat Williams

PEPPERS

Pickled Green Peppers

4 quarts green bell peppers
1 jalapeño pepper
4 cups white vinegar
4 cups water
1 cup sugar
6 tbsp. canning salt
6 cloves garlic, peeled
6 heads fresh dill (optional)

Wash peppers thoroughly. Remove core, seeds and stems. Slice into desired sized strips.

In a large stainless steel kettle, mix vinegar, water, and sugar. Bring to a boil. It should not boil a long time.

In each sterilized hot pint jar put in 1 tbsp. salt, 1 clove garlic and some of the hot pepper strips. Pack each jar tightly with bell pepper strips. Place optional dill head on top. Pour hot vinegar mixture over the peppers to ½-inch of jar rim. Adjust clean hot lids and process in boiling-water bath for 10 minutes. Remove and cool. Makes 6 pints.

Pat Jordan

PEPPERS

Potatoes

June–Frost

SOME VARIETIES

Baking, red skinned, yellow fleshed, blue fleshed, fingerling, and orange and white fleshed sweet potatoes

PREPARING POTATOES

Wash and peel if desired. Cook small baby potatoes whole. Cut large potatoes into quarters and cook until tender. Microwave in a covered dish with 2 tbsp. of water. Whole unpeeled potatoes should be pierced in several places with a knife. Turn once halfway through. Bake directly on oven rack, at 400 degrees, after being pierced in several places with a knife.

Boiling time: 20 minutes (whole) 10 minutes (sliced)

Steam time: 30 minutes (whole) 15 minutes (sliced)

Microwave time: 5–8 minutes (whole) 3–5 minutes (sliced)

Bake time: 40–60 minutes

Yields: 1lb. fresh equals three 4-inch potatoes or 2 cups diced.

Nutrition: 1 potato, boiled, has about 105 calories. It is an excellent source of potassium and Vitamin C.

German Hot Potato Salad (Warmer Kartoffelsalat)

*This recipe came originally from the Spatenhaus Restaurant in Munich, Germany,
and I have been using it for almost forty years*

2 lbs. small German yellow potatoes
1 tsp. salt
½ cup bacon, diced
½ cup onion, minced
2 tsp. all-purpose flour
4 tsp. sugar
½ tsp. salt, or to taste
¼ cup white vinegar
¼ tsp. black pepper
½ cup water
¼ cup onion, minced
2 tbsp. fresh parsley, minced
1 tsp. whole celery seed
½ cup radishes, sliced

Cook unpeeled potatoes in boiling water in a covered saucepan with 1 tsp.
salt, until fork tender (about 20 minutes). Then drain, peel,, and cut into ¼-
inch slices. In a small skillet, fry bacon until crisp; remove from pan and
drain. Retain 1 to 2 tbsp. of the bacon drippings in the skillet; add the
onion and sauté until tender (do not brown). Meanwhile, in a small bowl,
mix flour, sugar, ½-tsp. salt, and pepper; stir in vinegar and water until
smooth. Add to skillet; then simmer, stirring until slightly thickened. Pour
dressing over potatoes. Add remaining onion, parsley, celery seed, radishes, and bacon. Serve lightly tossed and garnished with celery leaves. Makes
4 servings.

Ulrich Bloecher

Roasted Potato, Garlic and Red-Pepper Salad

6 garlic cloves, unpeeled
3 lbs. small boiling potatoes (white, red or fingerling)
2 red bell peppers
3½ tbsp. extra virgin olive oil, divided use
3 tbsp. balsamic vinegar, divided use
½ cup small fresh basil leaves

To roast vegetables: Preheat oven to 450 degrees. Wrap garlic cloves together in foil. Cut potatoes in half. Cut bell peppers into ½-inch pieces. In large bowl toss potatoes, bell peppers, and 3 tbsp. oil with salt and pepper to taste. Arrange potatoes and bell peppers in 1 layer in 2 large shallow baking pans. Roast in middle and lower thirds of oven (simultaneously, roast wrapped garlic on either rack), stirring occasionally and switching position of pans halfway through roasting time, for 35 minutes, or until potatoes are tender and golden brown.

    To make salad: In bowl, immediately toss potatoes and peppers with 2 tbsp. vinegar. Cool. Remove garlic from foil. Squeeze bulb into a small bowl. Using fork, mash garlic with ½ tbsp. oil and 1 tbsp. vinegar. Toss together with potatoes and peppers. Add salt and pepper to taste. Just before serving, add basil. Serve at room temperature. Makes 6 servings.

Parsley New Potatoes

This is the way my Austrian great-grandmother made new potatoes for family gatherings, and, for a long time, the only way I knew they were ever made. They are still my very favorite

1½ lbs. new potatoes
¼ cup butter or margarine
¼ cup fresh parsley, chopped
Salt and black pepper to taste

Cook potatoes in their skins until tender. Drain well. Add butter or margarine and chopped parsley immediately, while potatoes are still very hot. Cover tightly and allow to stand a few minutes before serving, until butter is melted and parsley has softened slightly. Add salt and pepper to taste. Makes 4 servings.

Ann Fox

New Potato Salad

4 cups whole small new potatoes, unpeeled
½ cup green onions, chopped including tops
1 cup radishes, sliced thinly
3 hard cooked eggs, chopped coarsely

Dressing:
1 cup mayonnaise
1 tbsp. white vinegar
1 tsp. sugar
1½ tsp. Dijon mustard
1 tsp. salt
½ tsp. black pepper

In a large pot, boil whole potatoes for 20 to 25 minutes until just tender. Drain well. Peel or leave skins on. Larger potatoes may be cut in halves or quarters and baby potatoes may be left whole. In a large bowl mix mayonnaise, vinegar, sugar, mustard, sugar, salt, and pepper. Add potatoes, onions, radishes, and eggs. Toss lightly to mix. Cover and chill. Makes 8 servings.

Potato Leek Soup

4 tbsp. unsalted butter
1 large or 2 medium sliced leeks, white part only
4 cups chicken broth
4 cups potatoes, peeled and diced
1 cup heavy cream
1 cup milk, whole or 2%
Salt and white pepper to taste
2 tbsp. chopped parsley, optional

Clean and thinly slice leeks. Melt butter in large, heavy soup pot; add leeks and sauté slowly until glassy—do not brown. Add chicken broth and potatoes. Bring to a boil and simmer, covered, until potatoes are soft, stirring frequently. Remove from heat. Mash or purée. Add cream, milk, salt, and white pepper and parsley, if desired. Reheat—do not boil and serve. Makes 8 servings.

HILLTOP PRODUCE FARM

POTATOES

Jansson's Temptation

This is a traditional Swedish recipe

5 large potatoes
1 large yellow onion
1 large leek, white part only
1½ cups heavy cream
½ lb. sweet anchovies with juice
¼-cup dry bread crumbs
¼ cup unsalted butter, room temperature
Ground white pepper
Salt

Heat oven to 325 degrees. Peel potatoes and cover with cold water. Peel and trim leeks and onions. Cut them into ¼-inch slices. In a skillet over medium heat, melt 1 tbsp. butter and sauté leeks and onions until soft, making sure they don't brown. Julienne potatoes into ⅜-inch sticks. Put into cream to prevent them from turning black. Cut anchovies lengthwise to match the size of the potatoes. Reserve the juice for later. Butter an ovenproof 9x13-inch pan with fresh butter. Layer potatoes, onions and leeks, and anchovies two times, finishing the top layer with potatoes. Add juice from anchovies to cream, and add a good amount of pepper to taste and salt, if needed. Pour the cream over the temptation until layers are almost covered. Bake in oven for about 10 minutes. Remove from oven and sprinkle a thin layer of bread crumbs and fresh butter on top. Bake for another 20 to 30 minutes, until potato is cooked and golden brown. Makes 10–12 servings.

Roger Johnsson, Chef,
AQUAVIT RESTAURANT, MINNEAPOLIS

POTATOES

Potatoes Italian Style

6 medium potatoes
1 red pepper
1 green pepper
2 large white onions
⅓ cup olive oil
⅓ cup vinegar
1 clove garlic
Salt and black pepper to taste

Preheat oven to 400 degrees. Oil a 9x11-inch baking dish. Peel potatoes and slice as thin as possible. Core and seed peppers and slice in narrow rings. Slice onions and break into rings. Arrange potatoes, peppers, and onions in baking dish. Add the oil, vinegar, garlic, salt, and pepper. Toss as you would a salad and bake in 400-degree oven for one hour. Turn occasionally with a spatula. Makes 6 servings.

Mary Broeker

Creamed New Potatoes and Peas

2 cups whole small new potatoes, unpeeled
2 cups sliced sugar snap or shelled fresh peas

Cream sauce:
5 tbsp. butter or margarine
5 tbsp. all-purpose flour
2½ cups lowfat milk, warm
1½ tsp. salt
Black pepper

Boil potatoes in water until tender, about 30 minutes. Drain. Steam peas until tender, about 5 minutes. Make white sauce. In a medium saucepan, melt butter or margarine. Stir in flour and cook over low-medium heat for 2 minutes, stirring constantly. Add warm milk, all at once, and bring to a boil, stirring. Reduce heat and stir until sauce thickens. Stir in salt. Pour over the mixed potatoes and peas. Makes 6 servings.

German Potato Pancakes

5 large yellow potatoes
2 medium onions
2 tsp. lemon juice
1 large egg, lightly beaten
Salt and black pepper to taste
Vegetable oil for frying

Peel and grate potatoes and onions separately. Mix grated potatoes with lemon juice and drain liquid off through a sieve. Now mix potatoes and onions together and add egg. Season with salt and pepper to taste. In a large skillet, heat ⅛-inch of oil over medium heat until hot. Place about ¼ cup of batter in heated pan, spreading batter to make a flat pancake. Fry golden brown on both sides. May be able to fry three pancakes simultaneously, depending on the size of the skillet. Drain pancakes on a plate lined with paper towels. Continue as above until all of the batter is used, adding oil as needed. Serve hot with applesauce. Makes 4 servings.

Ulrich Bloecher

Parsley Potato Dumplings

6 medium yellow variety potatoes, peeled and grated coarsely
4 slices white bread, crusts trimmed
½ tsp. salt
1 medium onion, peeled and coarsely grated
2 tbsp. fresh parsley, finely minced
2 eggs, beaten
¼ cup all-purpose flour
2 quarts boiling water

Squeeze grated potatoes in a wire sieve to remove as much water as possible. Soak bread in water and squeeze out. Mix bread, salt, onion, parsley, potatoes, and eggs. Shape into balls about 1½ inches in diameter. Roll balls in flour and lower into boiling water. Boil, covered, for 12 minutes. Remove to a serving dish with slotted spoon. Makes 6 servings.

Crystal Bloecher

POTATOES

Café Loup's Mashed Potatoes with Shallots, Goat Cheese, and Herbs

2 tsp. olive oil
¾ cup shallots, peeled and chopped (about 4 large)
2½ lbs. Yukon Gold or red skin potatoes, scrubbed but unpeeled
6 to 8 oz. soft goat cheese, crumbled
1 cup milk (1% or 2% works fine), heated until warm
¾ tsp. salt or to taste
Freshly ground white or black pepper
1 tbsp. each chopped fresh thyme, chives, and parsley, or 1 tsp. dried
    crushed rosemary (see note)
Sprigs of fresh herbs for garnish (optional)

Heat oil in medium, heavy skillet over medium-high heat. When hot, add shallots and sauté, stirring, until softened and light golden, 4 to 5 minutes. Remove from heat and set aside. Bring large pan of water to boil. Add potatoes and cook until tender, 30 to 40 minutes, depending on size of potatoes. Drain. When cool enough to handle, peel potatoes. Purée potatoes in food mill or mash with wooden spoon or masher. Do not use food processor; it will make potatoes gluey. Stir in shallots, cheese, and warm milk. Add salt and pepper to taste. Serve immediately or transfer mixture to buttered baking dish for later use. Potatoes can be prepared a day ahead to this point. Cover and refrigerate. Reheat in microwave on high power several minutes, depending on oven, until hot. Or reheat in covered baking dish at 350 degrees 15 to 25 minutes. Stir in herbs and check seasonings again. Serve hot in dish, garnished with bundle of fresh herbs.

Note: fresh basil, rosemary or tarragon all make good additions. Makes 6 servings.

Betty Rosbottom, Director
LA BELLE POMME COOKING SCHOOL

Scalloped Potatoes with Carrots

2 tbsp. margarine
1 medium onion, minced
3 tbsp. all-purpose flour
1 tsp. salt
Dash black pepper
1½ cups lowfat milk, warm
4 medium potatoes (about 1¼ lbs.), thinly sliced
2 carrots, sliced thin
Paprika for garnish

Preheat oven to 375 degrees. In 2-quart saucepan, heat margarine. Add onion and sauté over low-medium heat until soft. Stir in flour, salt, and pepper until blended. Gradually stir in milk, stirring constantly until mixture thickens. In a greased 2-quart casserole, arrange half the potatoes and carrots in a layer, pour half the sauce on top, repeat. Sprinkle with paprika. Bake, covered, 45 minutes. Uncover and bake 15 minutes or until tender. Makes 6 servings.

Evelyn Kaiser

Lefse (Norwegian)

3 cups yellow potatoes, diced and hot
¼ cup butter
¼ cup light cream
1 tsp. salt
2 cups all-purpose flour, plus extra flour

Peel and cook potatoes until done; put through a ricer or mash thoroughly. Add butter, cream, and salt. Chill. Add 1 cup flour to ½ of the potato mixture. Form a log about 1½ inches in diameter. Cut off 1-inch pieces and, on a floured board, roll each very thinly into a circle. Bake on a very hot griddle, turning to lightly brown on both sides. Stack baked lefse under a damp towel to prevent drying out. Repeat with the second half of the potato mixture. Lefse is best eaten fresh, but it may be frozen until it is needed. Makes about 20 lefse.

HILLTOP PRODUCE FARM

Maple Roasted Sweet Potato Slices

Substitute any root vegetable or winter squash for the sweet potato

Sweet potatoes (about 3 large)
2 tsp. olive oil
½ tsp. coarse (kosher) salt
¼ cup pure maple syrup
1 tbsp. cider vinegar
1 tsp. fresh thyme leaves (or ½ tsp. dried)

Preheat oven to 425 degrees. Cut squash or sweet potatoes (peeled or unpeeled) into slices, ¾ to 1 inch wide. Oil or line a large jelly-roll pan or baking sheet with parchment paper. Toss the slices with 1 tsp. of olive oil (more if needed) and the salt in a large bowl. Put slices on pan in a single layer and place in oven. Roast, turning once, until fork-tender and lightly browned, about 25 minutes. Meanwhile, whisk together the maple syrup, vinegar and remaining 1 tsp. oil. Brush this glaze lightly over the roasted slices. You may need more or less of this mixture depending on how much squash you've used. Return to oven and continue roasting until they are caramelized, about 10 minutes. Remove from oven, sprinkle with thyme and serve.

Mary Broeker

Sweet Potato Casserole

This is a very forgiving recipe. It's never been made the same way twice

6–8 sweet potatoes
¼ cup lowfat milk or yogurt
2 tbsp. butter
Salt
Ground cinnamon
Ground cloves
Ground allspice
Black pepper
Other seasonings to taste

Wash and bake the sweet potatoes. Scrape the meat of the potatoes into a dish. Mash and blend with butter and milk. Plain yogurt can be substituted for the butter and milk if you want a lowfat dish. Season to taste with salt, a small amount of ground clove, cinnamon, lots of allspice, and a generous amount of black pepper. This is the kind of recipe that varies from year to year and begs for experimentation and lots of cooks. Everybody should grab a spoon, sample it, and offer advice. You can add jalapeño peppers. You can add onions, shaved as thin as possible and layered into the potatoes. You can sprinkle freshly-grated Parmesan cheese over the top. But you should never top it with marshmallows. Grease a soufflé dish. Layer the potatoes into the dish. You can alternate layers with mashed white potatoes for a surprise. Onions should be layered, not mixed. The dish can be refrigerated and baked the next day at 350 degrees for 45 minutes to an hour.

Lynne Rossetto Kasper

Sweet Potato and Pecan Pie with Bourbon Cream

1 unbaked pastry for a 9-inch pie

Filling:
1 egg
1½ cups sweet potato, cooked and mashed
¼ cup sugar
2 tbsp. unsalted butter, softened
1 tsp. vanilla
¼ tsp. ground cinnamon
⅛ tsp. each ground nutmeg and allspice

Pecan Topping:
2 eggs
½ cup sugar
½ cup dark corn syrup
2 tbsp. unsalted butter, melted
1 tsp. vanilla
Dash ground cinnamon
1 cup pecan halves

Bourbon Cream Topping:
½ cup heavy whipping cream, chilled
2 tbsp. sugar
1 tbsp. bourbon

Preheat oven to 350 degrees.

To make filling: With a hand mixer, in a medium bowl, beat egg until frothy. Add sweet potato, sugar, butter, cinnamon, nutmeg, and allspice. Beat at medium speed until smooth.

To make pecan topping: With a hand mixer, in a medium bowl, beat eggs until frothy. Add sugar, corn syrup, butter, vanilla, and cinnamon; blend well. Stir in pecans.

Spread filling in pie shell. Pour pecan topping over filling. Bake 60 to 70 minutes, until set and knife inserted comes out clean. Cool completely.

To make bourbon cream topping: Whip cold cream, adding sugar gradually, until peaks stand up. Add bourbon while continuing to whip 30 seconds longer. Serve immediately on pie wedges. Makes 8 servings.

Aurore Miller

POTATOES

Radishes

May–June

SOME VARIETIES

Red, white, and daikon

PREPARING RADISHES

Wash and trim off the tops and tap root. Leave whole or slice. Eat raw or cook. Radishes will lose some of their sharp flavor when cooked. Microwave in a covered dish with 2 tbsp. water.

Blanch Time: 5–7 minutes (whole)

Steam Time: 7–10 minutes (whole)

Microwave Time: 3–5 minutes (whole)

Yields: 1 lb. fresh equals 3 cups whole radishes.

Nutrition: 4 raw radishes have 5 calories and contain small amounts of potassium and vitamin C.

Radish Flowers

Using a sharp paring knife, start at the root end of the radish and carve 6–8 thin slices down to about ⅛-inch from the stem end without cutting all the way through. Do not detach petals. Place carved radishes in a bowl of cold water and in a few hours the petals will open.

Marinated Radish and Spinach Salad

1½–2 cups radishes, sliced
¼ cup white wine vinegar
¼ cup olive oil
1 tsp. dried oregano
1 tsp. dried basil
½ tsp. salt
½ cup green onions, sliced
8 cups spinach, torn

In a large bowl, combine vinegar, oil, oregano, basil, and salt. Add green onions and radishes. Cover and marinate in the refrigerator for 1 to 24 hours. Just before serving, toss with spinach. Makes 4 servings.

Pea and Radish Stir-fry

Radishes make a great homegrown substitute for water chestnuts

2 tbsp. vegetable oil
2 cups radishes, sliced
2 cups snow peas, strings removed
½ cup green onions, sliced
1 clove garlic, minced
2 tbsp. soy sauce
1 tsp. cornstarch

In a medium pan, heat oil and stir-fry radishes, snow peas, green onions, and garlic for 5 minutes. In a small bowl, mix soy sauce and cornstarch. Add to vegetables and stir until mixture thickens. Cover and simmer on low until vegetables are tender, about 5 minutes. Makes 4 servings.

Evelyn Kaiser

RADISHES

191

Radish and Lettuce Slaw

2 cups radishes, sliced
4 cups lettuce, torn
2 tbsp. green onions, chopped
1 cup mayonnaise
1 tbsp. dry mustard
1 tbsp. white vinegar
1 tbsp. sugar
1 tbsp. fresh dill weed, chopped
¼ tsp. black pepper
⅛ tsp. garlic powder

In a large bowl, combine mayonnaise, mustard, vinegar, sugar, dill weed, pepper, and garlic powder. Mix well. Add vegetables and coat well. Makes 4 servings.

Cream of Radish Soup
The color of this soup is pink!

4–6 cups radishes, sliced
1 cup onion, chopped
2 tbsp. butter or margarine
3 tbsp. all-purpose flour
2 tbsp. butter or margarine
3 cups lowfat milk, warm
2 tsp. salt
¼ tsp. black pepper
1 tsp. ground nutmeg

In a skillet, sauté onions and radishes in 2 tbsp. butter or margarine until both are limp. Put vegetables in blender and process until smooth. In a medium pot, melt 2 tbsp. butter or margarine, stir in flour, and cook over low heat, stirring constantly, for 2 minutes. Add milk all at once, and bring to a boil, stirring. Reduce heat and stir until thickened. Add vegetables, salt, pepper, and parsley. Makes 6 servings.

Creamed Whole Radishes

The radishes will lose some of their sharp flavor when cooked

2 cups whole radishes, washed and ends trimmed
3 tbsp. butter or margarine
3 tbsp. all-purpose flour
1–1½ cups warm lowfat milk, less for a thinner sauce and more for a
    thicker one
1 tsp. salt

Small radishes may be cooked whole and larger radishes may be sliced in
halves or quarters. Blanch in boiling water, until tender, about 7 to 10 minutes. In a medium saucepan, melt butter or margarine. Stir in flour and cook
over low heat, stirring constantly, for 2 minutes. Add warm milk all at once,
and bring to a boil, stirring. Reduce heat and stir until sauce thickens. Stir in
salt. Pour over the cooked radishes. Makes 4 servings.

LENGSFELD'S ORGANIC GARDENS

RADISHES

Spinach

May–June and September–November

PREPARING SPINACH

Wash and remove stems. Leave whole or chop. Eat raw or cook until wilted. Microwave in a covered dish with 2 tbsp. water. Remember to squeeze out excess liquid before using cooked and chopped spinach.

Blanch Time: 2–4 minutes

Steam Time: 3–5 minutes

Microwave Time: 4–5 minutes

Yields: 1 lb. fresh equals 8 cups washed; trimmed spinach leaves equals 1½ cups cooked.

Nutrition: 1 cup, cooked has 40 calories and contains substantial amounts of calcium, potassium and vitamins A and C.

Spinach Salad

1½ lbs. fresh spinach, washed and drained dry
3 hard boiled eggs, sliced
8 oz. fresh mushrooms, washed and sliced
8 oz. fresh bean sprouts
1 red onion, sliced thinly
½ lb. bacon, cooked, drained, and crumbled

Dressing:
½ cup salad oil
½ cup sugar
¼ cup ketchup
¼ cup red wine vinegar

Combine dressing ingredients in a saucepan. Bring to a boil and remove from heat. Cool to room temperature. Meanwhile assemble remaining ingredients, except bacon, in a large salad bowl. When ready to serve, pour dressing over salad and sprinkle bacon over the top. Toss to coat and serve. Makes 4 servings.

Kim Pinkham

SPINACH

Dancing Winds Spinach Salad with Feta

4 slices of bacon
2 tbsp. olive oil or bacon drippings
½ cup white vinegar
1 tsp. fresh basil, chopped
1 tsp. fresh rosemary, chopped
1 tsp. fresh thyme, chopped
1 tsp. fresh parsley, chopped
1 small red onion, chopped
8–10 fresh mushrooms, sliced
¼ lb. spinach greens, washed and stems trimmed
¼–½ lb. Low-salt plain or tomato-basil feta

In a skillet, fry bacon until crisp. Drain on paper towels. Crumble and set aside. Pour off fat, reserving 2 tbsp. of bacon drippings, if desired. In the same skillet, heat olive oil or reserved bacon drippings. Add vinegar, chopped herbs, onion, and mushrooms. Cook and stir over medium heat until tender. Remove from heat and set aside. Tear spinach into bite-size pieces and put in a large bowl. Pour hot dressing over greens and toss. Crumble feta cheese over salad. Serve at once. Makes 4 servings.

Mary Doerr

Spicy Spinach Soup

1½ lbs. fresh spinach, about 1–2 large bunches
2 quarts vegetable or chicken stock, unsalted
6 tbsp. unsalted butter or canola oil
1 large sweet yellow onion (Spanish, Bermuda, etc.), peeled and coarsely
    chopped or 1–2 bunches of green onions, cleaned and chopped, whites
    and greens
2–3 cloves garlic, minced
1 tsp. each ground cumin, cardamom, and cayenne
4–6 tbsp. all-purpose flour
Zest and juice of 1 lemon, zest blanched and juice at room temperature
½–¾ cup half and half, or unflavored soy milk, warmed
Sea salt and freshly-ground white pepper to taste
½ lb. fresh spinach leaves, julienne for garnish

SPINACH

Remove the stems and any bruised spots from the spinach. Wash the leaves 2 or 3 times in cold water, depending on how dirty the spinach is. Shake leaves to remove excess moisture, place in a colander, and set aside. Heat the stock in a large saucepan. Melt the butter, or heat the oil, in a large soup pot over medium heat. Add the chopped onions, and sauté until transparent. Add the minced garlic and sauté for 1 to 2 minutes. Increase the heat to high and add the spices, stirring to evenly coat the onions and garlic. Sauté for about 1 minute, taking care not to burn the spices. Lower the heat to medium, and add the flour a bit at a time, using only as much as the butter or oil will absorb. Cook, stirring as needed, for 2 to 3 minutes to remove the raw taste from the flour. Add 3 cups of the warmed stock, stirring or whisking constantly. Allow this mixture to simmer for 10 minutes. Stir or whisk in 3 more cups of the warmed stock. Add the washed spinach leaves, and allow the soup to simmer for 10 more minutes, adding additional stock if the soup seems to be too thick. Purée the soup in batches in a blender, or in the pot with a stick blender. Blanche the lemon zest in boiling water for 30 seconds, and cool in ice water for 30 seconds. Pat dry and add to the soup with the room temperature* lemon juice, while stirring constantly.* Heat the cream or soy milk until warm and add to the soup, stirring constantly. Season with sea salt and freshly-ground white pepper to taste. Thin with additional stock if necessary. Julienne spinach leaves for garnish; pat dry if they are excessively wet. Bring a small pot of water to a boil. Make an ice water bath and place close to the sink. Place a colander in the sink. Add a pinch of salt to the boiling water. Place the spinach in the boiling water for *no longer than 15 seconds, and immediately* drain the spinach and place it in the ice water bath. This will stop the cooking and fix the bright green color. Drain the blanched spinach, and pat dry with paper toweling. Either stir into the whole pot of soup, or reserve for top garnishing individual servings. Makes 6–8 servings.

*It is important that the lemon juice be at room temperature, or warm if possible, and that you stir constantly while adding so the acid doesn't break the soup.

B. J. Carpenter & Mary Ryan, Cooking Instructors
COOKS OF CROCUS HILL, ST. PAUL

Creamed Spinach

Serve over noodles, rice or potatoes

6–8 cups washed spinach, stems trimmed

Cream Sauce:
3 tbsp. butter or margarine
3 tbsp. all-purpose flour
1–1½ cups warm lowfat milk, less for a thinner sauce and more for a
    thicker one
½ tsp. salt
¼ tsp. ground nutmeg

Chop spinach coarsely and steam until wilted, about 3 to 5 minutes. Squeeze
out excess water. Set aside. In a medium saucepan, sauté onion in butter or
margarine, over very low heat, until onion becomes transparent. Stir in flour
and cook 2 minutes, stirring constantly. Add milk all at once, and bring to a
boil, stirring. Reduce heat and stir until sauce thickens. Stir in salt and nutmeg. Add spinach and mix well. Serve alone as a side dish or over noodles,
rice, or potatoes. Makes 4 servings.

LENGSFELD'S ORGANIC GARDENS

Spinach Balls in Sauce

2 lbs. fresh spinach
1 medium onion, finely chopped
2 cloves garlic, minced
2 tbsp. olive oil
½ cup fresh parsley, chopped
¼ cup melted butter
1 cup dry seasoned bread crumbs
1 cup grated Parmesan cheese
½ tsp. salt
1 tsp. dried basil
¼ tsp. black pepper
4 eggs, slightly beaten
Spaghetti sauce

SPINACH

Preheat oven to 350 degrees. Sauté onion and garlic in 2 tbsp. olive oil until tender. Add parsley and cook 3 minutes, stirring. Remove from heat. In a bowl, combine butter, bread crumbs, Parmesan, salt, basil, pepper, and eggs. Add onion mixture and mix well. With lightly floured hands, shape into 1-inch balls. Sauté balls in 1 tbsp. olive oil until brown on all sides. Place in a baking dish, cover with spaghetti sauce, and sprinkle with Parmesan cheese. Bake for 15 to 20 minutes until warmed through. Makes 8 servings.

Carol Neumann

Risotto Agli Spinachi (Spinach Risotto)
from a recipe by Guiliano Bugialli, Florence, Italy, 1982

1 tbsp. olive oil
1 tbsp. sweet butter (unsalted)
1 lb. fresh spinach, finely chopped
Salt to taste
Freshly ground black pepper
Freshly grated nutmeg
3 cups chicken broth
3 tbsp. sweet butter (unsalted)
2 cups raw arborio rice
1 cup heavy cream
½ cup parmigiano-reggiano cheese, grated
1 lb. Italian plum tomatoes, chopped coarsely
Small mint leaves for garnish

Heat oil in large sauté pan. Add spinach. Season to taste with salt and fresh-ly-ground black pepper and nutmeg. Cook until wilted and soft. Set aside. In a separate pot, bring chicken broth to a boil and hold at a simmer. In a heavy pot, over medium heat, melt 3 tbsp. butter. Add rice and sauté for 4 minutes, stirring. Add sautéed spinach and stir 3 minutes. Then add ¼ cup of hot chicken broth, stirring and cooking until absorbed. Then add another ¼ cup broth, cooking and stirring until absorbed; continue until all broth is incorporated. Then slowly add cream while stirring. Season to taste with salt and pepper and more nutmeg, if desired. Remove from heat and stir in parmi-giano-reggiano cheese. Serve surrounded by chopped tomatoes, garnished with small mint leaves.

Susan Dietrich, Pastry Chef
PRAIRIE SWEETS

SPINACH

Sautéed Spinach and Portobello Salad

½ lb. Portobello mushrooms, sliced
Olive oil (your favorite type)
1 clove garlic, peeled and finely chopped
¼ cup lemon juice (fresh is best)
1 tsp. dried rosemary
Salt and black pepper to taste
1 lb. spinach, washed
2–3 shallots, thinly sliced

Make dressing by mixing garlic, lemon juice, ⅓ cup olive oil, rosemary, and salt and pepper. Heat 2 tbsp. olive oil in sauté pan until quite hot; add portobello slices in one layer and cook until browned on first side; turn and cook on other side. Add oil as needed. Total cooking time will be about 5 minutes. Remove to large plate and sprinkle with dressing. Cook any remaining portobello slices and sprinkle with dressing. Just before serving salads, tear spinach into serving-sized pieces and rinse. Heat sauté pan to medium. Add about one third of the spinach with the water clinging to it, sprinkle with a dash of salt, and stir. Remove from pan just as it begins to wilt and change color, about 30 seconds. Don't overcook! Remove spinach to individual serving plates with a slotted spoon. Repeat with remaining spinach in manageable batches. Divide sliced shallots and portobello slices over spinach. Sprinkle with remaining dressing and serve immediately. Makes 4 servings.

Anne Boyd & Hal Jabolner

SPINACH

Spinach Lasagna

8 lasagna noodles
2 large bunches spinach, washed and trimmed
2 tbsp. vegetable oil
1 medium onion, chopped
2 garlic cloves, minced
1 (8 oz.) can no-salt-added tomato paste
1 cup water
1 tsp. honey
¾ tsp. dried basil, crushed
¾ tsp. dried oregano, crushed
Freshly ground black pepper
2 cups lowfat cottage or part-skim ricotta cheese
1 cup part-skim mozzarella cheese, grated
1 cup Parmesan cheese, freshly grated

To prepare noodles: Cook lasagna noodles in boiling water until tender. Drain and set aside.

To prepare spinach: Place spinach in steamer over medium heat. Cook for 2 minutes. Drain well and set aside.

To prepare sauce: In medium skillet, heat oil. Sauté onion until soft. Add garlic. Sauté a few minutes more. Stir in tomato sauce, tomato paste, water, honey, basil, oregano, and pepper. Reduce heat. Simmer for 20 minutes, stirring occasionally. Preheat oven to 350 degrees.

To assemble: Lay 4 noodles on bottom of nonstick, sprayed, 9x13-inch baking pan. Layer spinach, cottage or ricotta cheese, and mozzarella cheese evenly over noodles. Top with half of sauce mixture. Cover with remaining noodles and sauce. Sprinkle with Parmesan. Bake, covered, for 20 to 25 minutes, or until lasagna is heated through and cheeses are melted.
Makes 8 servings.

Spinach Noodle Roll-Ups

4 lasagna noodles
1¼ lbs. fresh spinach, washed, stems trimmed and chopped

Filling:
8 oz. feta cheese, crumbled
¼ cup grated Romano or Parmesan cheese
1 tsp. salt
Spaghetti sauce and grated mozzarella cheese

Preheat oven to 375 degrees. Cook noodles according to directions on package. Rinse noodles under cold water to cool quickly. Drain. Lay noodles in a single layer on a piece of waxed paper and set aside. Steam spinach until tender, about 3 to 5 minutes. Squeeze out excess water. Set aside. In a medium bowl, combine chopped spinach, feta cheese, Romano cheese, and salt. Press ¼ of the filling on each of the noodles and roll up. (These may be stored or frozen.) To heat, place seam side down in a lightly greased baking dish. Flatten slightly with the palm of your hand. Top with spaghetti sauce and mozzarella. Bake for 10 to 15 minutes or microwave for 1½ minutes or until heated through and cheese is melted. Makes 4 roll-ups.

LENGSFELD'S ORGANIC GARDENS

Easy Spanakopita Pie

1–1½ lbs. fresh spinach
½ tsp. salt
8 oz. feta cheese, crumbled
2 eggs, beaten
2 9-inch pie crusts

Preheat oven to 400 degrees. Wash and dry spinach and chop it fine. Put spinach in a large bowl and sprinkle with salt. Squeeze to wilt it. Crumble in feta cheese, add eggs, mix well and set aside. Place one pastry crust on a cookie sheet and spread filling evenly on it within an inch of the edge. Place top crust on top and seal edges well. With a fork, poke holes all over the top. Bake on the bottom rack of the oven, at 400 degrees, for 45 to 50 minutes, until golden brown. Makes 6 servings.

LENGSFELD'S ORGANIC GARDENS

SPINACH

Spinach Pie with Cheese Crust

¾ lb. muenster cheese from a deli, have it sliced ⅛-inch thick or a little less
2 lbs. spinach, cooked, drained well and chopped
3 eggs beaten
1 cup lowfat cottage cheese
⅓ cup grated Parmesan cheese
1 small onion, finely chopped
1 tsp. fresh dill, chopped
Salt and black pepper to taste
⅛ tsp. garlic, crush with salt

Preheat oven to 350 degrees. Line a 10-inch pie plate with muenster, going all the way up the sides. in a mixing bowl, combine all remaining ingredients and pour into the muenster crust. Bake for 45 minutes or until center is firm. Allow to set a few minutes to firm up before slicing. Makes 6 servings.

Kim Pinkham

Spinach Cheese Muffins

2 cups all-purpose flour
1½ tsp. baking powder
½ tsp. baking soda
¼ tsp. ground nutmeg
1 tbsp. sugar
½ tsp. salt
½ lb. fresh spinach, washed, steamed, and squeezed dry
1 cup buttermilk
2 tbsp. melted butter
¼ cup Parmesan cheese
¼ cup Swiss cheese, grated
1 egg, beaten

Preheat oven to 400 degrees. In a medium bowl, whisk together dry ingredients. Chop spinach. In another bowl combine spinach, buttermilk, butter, Parmesan cheese, and the beaten egg. Make a well in the dry ingredients and pour in spinach mixture. Stir briefly until just combined. Spoon batter into 12 greased muffin tins. Sprinkle with Swiss cheese. Bake at 400 degrees for 25 minutes. Cool for 5 minutes before turning them out. Makes 12 muffins.

SPINACH

Summer Squash and Zucchini

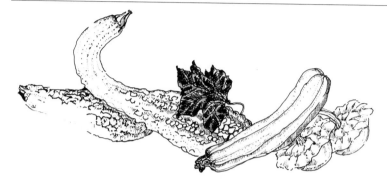

WHEN AVAILABLE
June–Frost

SOME VARIETIES
Green and gold zucchini, straight neck and crookneck squash, green and yellow patty pan, and round zucchini

PREPARING SUMMER SQUASH
Wash and trim stem end. Peeling is not required. Larger sizes can be sliced and diced, while tender young ones can be served whole. Eat raw or cook until tender. Microwave in a covered dish with 2 tbsp. Water. Salting grated zucchini removes excess moisture. Use about ½ tsp. salt for every 3 cups grated squash. Drain in a colander for 30 minutes, rinse, and squeeze out water. All varieties of squash and zucchini can be used interchangeably in recipes. They are wonderful additions to stir-frys and casseroles.

Blanch Time: 4–6 minutes

Steam Time: 5–7 minutes

Microwave Time: 3–4 minutes

Yields: 1 lb. fresh equals 4 medium summer squash, 3 cups sliced or diced or 3½ cups grated.

Nutrition: 1 cup cooked has 30 calories and contains potassium, calcium, and vitamins A and C.

Marinated Zucchini Salad

⅔ cups white wine vinegar
⅓ cup vegetable oil
1 small clove garlic, minced or crushed
½ tsp. salt
¼ tsp. freshly-ground black pepper
2 zucchini, 10–12 inches, stem end removed and sliced in ⅛-inch circles
3 small to medium-sized tomatoes, cored and sliced in ¼-inch slices
2 green onions, cut in ¼-inch diagonal slices (greens included)
1 small green pepper, cored, seeds removed, and sliced in ¼-inch circles
1 tbsp. chopped fresh parsley

For the vinaigrette, whisk together vinegar, oil, garlic, salt, and pepper in small bowl. Arrange sliced vegetables in a flat-bottomed plate with a raised edge or a flat baking dish. Pour vinaigrette over vegetables and stir lightly to coat. Chill up to 1 hour. Makes 6 servings.

HILLTOP PRODUCE FARM

Zucchini Salad

This salad is especially good with grilled meats

6 zucchini, 6–8 inch, ends removed, coarsely grated (not peeled)
1 tsp. salt
3 tbsp. sour cream
3 tbsp. mayonnaise
1 clove garlic, peeled and pushed through a garlic press or thoroughly
    crushed with salt
1 tsp. Dijon mustard
4–6 large leaves Boston lettuce
4–6 medium tomatoes, cut in wedges
Freshly cracked black pepper

Mix grated zucchini with salt and drain for at least an hour in a colander. Squeeze out excess moisture. Mix with sour cream, mayonnaise, garlic, and mustard. Chill 1 to 2 hours. Plate lettuce leaves and arrange tomato wedges in a circle. Spoon zucchini salad into the center of each tomato circle. Sprinkle with freshly cracked black pepper. Makes 4–6 servings.

HILLTOP PRODUCE FARM

Zucchini Soup with Fresh Peas

1 medium-sized yellow onion
2 lbs. zucchini, about 4 medium-sized
½–1 tsp. each fresh chervil, basil, tarragon, parsley and chives
1–2 tbsp. canola oil, or unsalted butter
1 tbsp. all-purpose flour
6 cups unsalted chicken, turkey or vegetable stock
1 cup fresh peas, blanched with cooking water saved
Sea salt and freshly-ground white pepper to taste
½ cup sour cream, for garnish
2–3 tbsp. mixed fresh chervil, basil, tarragon, parsley and chives

*Use all or any combination of the above herbs as is your personal preference

Peel the onion, dice, and set aside. Wash the zucchini, cut into small to medium-sized pieces and set aside. Wash the herbs, mince, and set aside. Place the oil, or butter, in a stock or soup pot and heat over medium setting. Add the onions and cook until soft. Add the zucchini and cook for another 3 to 5 minutes, stirring once or twice to evenly coat all pieces. Increase the heat to high, add the minced herbs. Mix well and cook for an additional 1 to 2 minutes, taking care not to burn the herbs. Mix in the flour to coat, and cook another 1 to 2 minutes to make a light roux. While the vegetables and herbs are sautéeing, heat the stock in another pot until warm. Slowly add the warmed stock to the vegetables, stirring until mixture is slightly thickened. Reduce heat to simmer and continue cooking for 20 minutes. While the soup is cooking, blanch the peas in boiling water for 2 minutes. Drain, reserving some of the liquid for use in thinning the soup if necessary. Add half of the peas to the soup. Place ⅓ of the soup in a blender and blend briefly for a textured consistency, or for several minutes for a smooth consistency. Remove to a serving bowl or large pan, and continue with the rest. Stir the soup, and thin with reserved water if needed. Stir in remaining peas. Serve hot or cold, garnished with sour cream and minced herbs. Makes 6 servings.

B. J. Carpenter & Mary Ryan Cooking Instructors
COOKS OF CROCUS HILL, ST. PAUL

Crispy Southern Fried Zucchini

2 medium zucchini
½ cup all-purpose flour
1 tsp. salt
2 tsp. paprika
¼ tsp. black pepper
Vegetable oil for frying

Slice zucchini into 1-inch slices. In a medium bowl, combine flour, salt, paprika, and pepper. Press slices into flour mixture. In a skillet, heat oil and fry slices over medium heat until golden brown on both sides, about 3 minutes a side. Makes 4 servings.

Summer Squash Frittata

3 cups shredded summer squash, any kind
2 tbsp. butter or oil
1 onion, chopped finely
1 sweet banana pepper, seeded and chopped
1 fresh tomato, chopped
4 eggs, beaten
1½ tsp. seasoned salt
¾ cup mozzarella cheese, grated (optional)

In a large skillet, heat oil. Sauté squash, onions, and peppers until tender. Add tomato. Stir in eggs and seasoned salt. Cover and cook over low heat until eggs are almost set. Sprinkle with optional mozzarella cheese. Cook slowly until cheese is melted and eggs are set. Use a spatula to slide frittata out of pan and onto a serving plate. Cut in wedges and serve. Makes 4 servings.

Ann DesLauriers

Zucchini Bean and Cheese Burritos

The zucchini inside these will surprise them!

2 6-inch zucchini
4 wheat tortillas
1 cup seasoned refried beans
1 cup cheddar cheese, grated
1 cup salsa

Trim the stems of zucchini and cut each one in half lengthwise. Steam zucchini halves, cut side down, until tender, about 6 minutes. They may also be microwaved in a covered dish, with 2 tbsp. water, until tender, about 3 minutes. On each tortilla spread ¼ cup of beans. Place a zucchini half, cut side up, on top of the beans. Sprinkle with ¼ cup cheese and fold up. Place burritos seam side down in a greased baking dish. Top with salsa and more cheese. Broil for 5 minutes or until cheese is melted. May also be cooked in the microwave, in a covered dish, for 2 minutes, or until cheese is melted. Makes 4 servings.

Evelyn Kaiser

Fast Zucchini Italian

Here's another way to use those ever-abundant zucchini!

Zucchini
Spaghetti sauce or salsa
Mozzarella or cheddar cheese, grated

Cut zucchini in half lengthwise. Steam for 6 minutes or microwave in a covered dish with 2 tbsp. water until tender, about 3 minutes. Drain excess water from dish. Turn zucchini cut side up. Spread with spaghetti sauce and sprinkle with cheese. Broil or microwave until cheese is melted. A southwestern version of this can be made by substituting salsa for the spaghetti sauce and cheddar cheese for the mozzarella.

LENGSFELD'S ORGANIC GARDENS

Pasta Primavera

This pasta primavera recipe should help lighten your zucchini load, too. Remember that the smaller size squash work best. Also, cook the pasta only until al dente—cooked through, but still firm.

12 oz. linguine or fettucine
2 tbsp. olive oil
¼ cup light cream
1 lb. zucchini
½ bunch broccoli, about ½ lb.
½ lb. green beans
¼ cup vegetable oil
6 shallots or 4 scallions, white part only
2 cloves garlic, minced
¼ cup fresh parsley, chopped
2 tbsp. fresh basil, chopped; or 2 tsp. dried, crushed; or 1 tsp. pesto sauce
1 tsp. salt and black pepper
½ cup freshly grated Parmesan cheese

To prepare pasta: Cook pasta until al dente. Drain. Transfer to warm bowl. Toss with 2 tbsp. oil and ¼ cup light cream.

To steam vegetables: Meanwhile, wash and trim zucchini, broccoli, and green beans. Chop into small pieces. Heat ¼ cup oil in skillet. Add vegetables. Stir to coat with oil. Add shallots and garlic. Cover. Steam over high heat for 5 minutes. Uncover. Add basil and parsley. Stir well. Cook slightly longer, until vegetables are just crunchy.

To serve: Add vegetables to pasta. Toss well. Add salt and pepper to taste. Toss again. Serve. Pass around grated Parmesan cheese. Makes 4 servings.

Garden Delight

This recipe is open-ended in that it allows you to vary your ingredients and their amounts as you like. The final dish is delicious, and it's a good way to use those summer garden vegetables.

Preheat oven to 350 degrees. In a buttered shallow glass baking dish (such as a 9x13-inch dish) layer the following vegetables in the order given:
1. Sliced zucchini
2. Halved, peeled tomatoes
3. Finely chopped onion
4. Finely chopped green pepper
5. Garlic salt and black pepper to taste
6. Plenty of grated cheddar or Parmesan cheese or both
7. On top, place cocktail rye bread squares, which have been cut twice, diagonally into triangles
8. Pour ¼ cup melted butter (more or less, depending on your vegetable volume) over all

Bake, covered, at 350 degrees for 30 to 45 minutes or until vegetables are tender. Uncover and bake 10 minutes longer. Makes about 12 servings.

Kim Pinkham

Pattypan Squash Stuffed with Spinach and Cheese

6 3-inch Pattypan squash
½ lb. spinach, washed and stemmed
½ cup scallions, thinly sliced
2 tbsp. butter
⅔ cup cottage cheese
Freshly grated nutmeg to taste
Cayenne pepper to taste
3 tbsp. freshly grated Parmesan cheese
1–2 tbsp. stale bread crumbs
Oil for brushing the shells

Preheat oven to 350 degrees. Steam squash, covered, for 10 minutes; rinse with cold water and dry. Cut off stem end of each squash and scoop out the pulp, leaving a ¼-inch shell. Sprinkle shells with salt and let drain, inverted, for 30 minutes. Chop reserved pulp. Steam spinach for 2 to 3 minutes; drain, squeeze dry and chop. Cook scallions in butter until soft; add squash pulp and cook, stirring, until liquid is evaporated. Add spinach and stir one minute. Add cottage cheese, nutmeg, cayenne, salt and pepper to taste, and cook, stirring, for 1 minute. Remove from heat and add the Parmesan. Sprinkle insides of squash shells with bread crumbs and mound the filling inside of the shells. Place on an oiled baking sheet after brushing the outsides lightly with oil. Bake at 350 degrees for 30 to 40 minutes. Serve warm. Makes 4–6 servings.

Crystal Bloecher

Mock Apple Pie

1 9-inch double pie crust
6 cups zucchini, peeled and cut into thin slices
¼ cup water
2 tbsp. fresh lemon juice
½ cup white sugar
½ cup light brown sugar, packed
3 tbsp. all-purpose flour
2 tsp. ground cinnamon
¼ tsp. ground nutmeg

Preheat oven to 350 degrees. Line a 9-inch pie plate with bottom crust. In a medium saucepan, cook zucchini slices in water until tender. Drain well. Toss with lemon juice. Set aside.

In a large bowl, combine sugars, flour, cinnamon and nutmeg. Add cooked zucchini and combine well. Pour into bottom crust, place on top crust, pinch edges to seal and poke a few holes with a knife to allow steam to escape. Bake for 45 minutes or until golden brown. Makes 8 servings.

Ken Epstein

SUMMER SQUASH AND ZUCCHINI

Vegetable Lasagna with Basil-Garlic Béchamel

6–8 fresh pasta sheets, purchase at one of the local Italian specialty stores or homemade or if you are using dried lasagna noodles, par-cook and briefly place in ice water bath to halt cooking, drain and pat dry.
1 cup Parmesan, Asiago or dry jack cheese, or a combination
3 medium zucchini
3 medium summer squash
4–6 large vine-ripened tomatoes
2 tbsp. all-purpose flour seasoned with salt and black pepper
4–6 tbsp. olive oil

Basil-Garlic Béchamel:
6 cloves garlic
1 generous bunch of fresh basil
2 tbsp. olive oil
1 quart whole milk
4 tbsp. unsalted butter
4 tbsp. all-purpose flour
Salt and freshly cracked black pepper, to taste

If making pasta, prepare dough, cover with a towel and set aside to rest at room temperature. If using commercially-made fresh pasta, set sheets out and cover with a cloth.

Grate cheese and set aside.

Wash squashes, remove stems, and slice into ½ to ¾-inch diagonal slices. Lay out paper or cotton toweling, lightly sprinkle the surface with salt. Place squash slices on top of toweling in a single layer. Lightly salt the tops of the squash, cover with another layer of toweling and press down on the squash. Pat dry with toweling and set aside. Heat 2 to 3 tbsp. of olive oil in a 7-inch sauté pan over high. When the oil begins to ripple, add squash and quickly sauté until cut surfaces of squash begin to brown. Remove from pan with a slotted spoon, and set on paper toweling to drain. Remove pan from heat, reserving oil.

Slice tomatoes into ½-inch slices, and lightly dredge in seasoned flour; set aside. Heat remaining 2–3 tbsp. of olive oil in the sauté pan. Place only as many floured tomato slices as will fit comfortably in the pan, leaving room to turn. Quickly sauté over high heat, browning flour. Remove to a

plate, and repeat with remaining tomatoes. Add more olive oil if needed between browning, allowing it to heat before placing more tomato slices in the pan.

Make basil bechámel: Peel and mince garlic cloves. Remove basil leaves from stem and julienne. Heat 2 tbsp. of olive oil in a small sauté pan. Add minced garlic and quickly cook over high heat until garlic opens up, about 1 to 2 minutes. Add julienned basil, sauté briefly, just until the basil turns bright green, and remove from heat. Set aside. Heat the quart of milk in a separate saucepan, or in the microwave. Do not boil. Melt 4 tbsp. of butter over medium heat in a small saucepan. Add 4 tbsp. of flour, and cook over medium until all the flour is incorporated, and the roux is bubbling and smells nutty. Slowly whisk in the heated milk, stirring in to incorporate all the roux. Scrape the sides and bottom of pan to loosen any remaining roux, and whisk in. Lower the heat and allow the béchamel to thicken, 5 to 10 minutes. Remove from heat, whisk to smooth, and stir sautéed garlic and basil. Season with salt and pepper to taste. Set aside.

Assemble lasagna: Preheat oven to 375 degrees. If using fresh pasta sheets, briefly plunge into salted, boiling water, then an ice water bath and drain. Handle quickly and carefully so the sheets don't tear. Lay pasta sheets flat on a towel-covered surface and pat dry with toweling. Cover to keep from drying out. Brush the bottom and sides of a 9x13 baking dish with olive oil. Spoon ½-cup béchamel over the bottom of the pan spreading to cover. Lay enough pieces of pasta in the baking dish so that they completely cover the bottom and hang over the edges. Later these flaps will be folded over the top of the lasagna. Spread another ½-cup of béchamel over the top of the pasta. Layer ¼ of the sautéed zucchini and summer squash on the top of the béchamel, top this with a layer of sautéed tomato slices, another ¼-cup of the béchamel and sprinkle with grated cheese. Continue in this fashion making 4 layers in all. Finish by laying several strips of pasta lenthwise down the middle, folding the hanging edges over the top, spreading remaining béchamel and grated cheese evenly over the top.

Loosely cover the top with aluminum foil and bake for 15 minutes in the center of the preheated oven. Remove the foil, turn pan in oven, and continue baking until top is puffed and browned, about 25 minutes. Let lasagna rest a few minutes before cutting.

B. J. Carpenter & Mary Ryan, Cooking Instructors
COOKS OF CROCUS HILL, ST. PAUL

SUMMER SQUASH AND ZUCCHINI

Stuffed Zucchini Deluxe

4 12-inch zucchini
1 cup fresh bread crumbs
¼ cup onion, chopped
1 medium tomato, peeled and chopped
½ tsp. salt
¼ tsp. black pepper
2 tbsp. melted butter
8 oz. cheddar cheese, grated
6 slices crisply cooked bacon, crumbled

Preheat oven to 350 degrees. Trim ends of zucchini. Cook, covered, in boiling salted water 5 to 8 minutes; drain well. Cut in half lengthwise; scoop out center; chop scooped center. Combine chopped zucchini, bread crumbs, onion, tomato, seasoning, and butter; toss lightly. Fill each shell; place in baking dish. Top with grated cheddar cheese. Bake at 350 degrees for 25 to 30 minutes. Makes 8 servings.

Crystal Bloecher

Zucchini Jelly

2 (3oz.) boxes orange or lemon gelatin
½ cup lemon juice
6 cups zucchini, grated
5½ cups sugar
1 8-oz. can crushed pineapple, undrained

In a small bowl, dissolve gelatin in the lemon juice. Set aside.

In a medium saucepan, mix zucchini, sugar, and pineapple. Bring to a boil and cook 10 minutes over low-medium heat, stirring constantly. Add gelatin mixture and boil for 2 more minutes, continuing to stir. Remove from heat and ladle hot mixture into sterilized hot pint jars to ½ inch of rim of jars. Adjust clean hot lids and cool. Store in refrigerator. Makes 3–4 pints.

Diane Heintz

Zucchini Pancakes

A much-requested summer treat!

2 eggs, beaten
¾ cup grated Parmesan cheese
2 tsp. Spike seasoning
½ tsp. salt
¼ tsp. garlic powder
1 cup biscuit mix
3 cups zucchini, grated
2–3 tbsp. vegetable oil, for frying

Shred zucchini in a shredder and set aside. In a large bowl, combine beaten egg, Parmesan cheese, Spike seasoning, salt, garlic powder, and biscuit mix. Mix well. Add shredded zucchini and stir until mixture becomes smooth. Heat oil in a skillet and drop dough by spoonfuls into the oiled skillet. Fry until golden, about 3 minutes. Turn with a spatula and fry until golden. Makes 6 pancakes.

Duane Lengsfeld

Zucchini Relish

10 cups zucchini, grated
4 large onions, chopped
5 tbsp. salt
4½ cups sugar
2 tbsp. corn starch
2 tbsp. celery seed
2 tbsp. dry mustard
1 tsp. turmeric
1 tbsp. ginger
1½ cups white vinegar
2 cups green peppers, chopped
2 cups red peppers, chopped

In a stainless steel bowl, combine zucchini, onions, and salt. Let stand overnight; drain well. In a stainless steel kettle, combine sugar, corn starch, celery seed, mustard, turmeric, ginger, and vinegar. Cook over medium heat until fairly thick. Add zucchini mixture and peppers. Boil until thick, about ½ hour, stirring frequently. Fill sterilized hot pint jars, leaving ½-inch headroom. Adjust clean hot lids. Process in boiling-water bath for 15 minutes. Remove and cool. Makes 10 pints.

Zucchini Cookies

3½ cups all-purpose flour
2 tsp. baking powder
2 tsp. baking soda
1 tsp. ground cinnamon
½ tsp. salt
¾ cup butter
1½ cup sugar
1 egg, beaten
1 tsp. vanilla
1½ cups zucchini, grated
1 cup walnuts, chopped
1 cup chocolate chips

Preheat oven to 350 degrees. In a medium bowl, whisk together flour, baking powder, baking soda, cinnamon, and salt.

In a separate large bowl, cream together butter and sugar. Add beaten egg and vanilla. Beat until light and fluffy. Add the flour mixture and mix until just combined. Stir in grated zucchini, nuts and chocolate chips. Mix well.

Drop by rounded tsp. fulls onto greased baking sheets. Bake for 12 to 15 minutes or until the edges begin to brown. Makes about 2 dozen.

Nancy Jordan

Zucchini Bread

3 cups all-purpose flour
1 tsp. baking soda
½ tsp. baking powder
¼ tsp. salt
2 tsp. ground cinnamon
3 eggs, beaten
1 cup vegetable oil
2 cups sugar
1 tsp. vanilla
2 cups zucchini, grated
1 cup nuts, chopped (optional)

Preheat oven to 350 degrees. In a medium bowl, whisk together flour, baking soda, baking powder, salt, and cinnamon.

In a separate large bowl, beat eggs until fluffy. Beat in oil, sugar, and vanilla. Add flour mixture and stir until just combined. Add grated zucchini and optional nuts. Mix well. Pour equal amounts of batter into two greased and floured 8x4x2-inch baking pans. Bake for 1 hour or until a toothpick inserted near the center comes out clean. Makes 2 loaves.

Marilyn Heschke

Mock Apple Squares
People can't believe these are not apples!

Crust Mix:
4 cups all-purpose flour
2 cups sugar
2 sticks butter or margarine

Filling:
7 cups zucchini, peeled and sliced into ¼-inch pieces
⅔ cup fresh lemon juice
1 cup sugar
½ tsp. ground cinnamon
¼ tsp. ground nutmeg
½ cup crust mix
1 tsp. ground cinnamon

Preheat oven to 350 degrees. In a large bowl, combine flour and sugar. Cut in butter or margarine until mixture resembles coarse crumbs. Set aside.

In a large saucepan, combine zucchini and lemon juice. Bring to a boil; reduce heat. Cover and simmer until tender, about 7 minutes. Remove from heat. Stir in cinnamon, nutmeg and ½ cup of the crust mix, set aside to cool.

In a greased 9x13 cake pan, press half of the remaining crust mix into bottom of pan. Spread cooled filling over bottom crust. Add 1 tsp. cinnamon to remaining crust mix and sprinkle on filling. Bake for 30 to 40 minutes or until topping is lightly browned. Makes 12 servings.

Ann DesLauriers

Zucchini Cake

3½ cups all-purpose flour
2 tsp. baking soda
1 tsp. baking powder
1 tsp. salt
3 tsp. ground cinnamon
4 eggs
1½ cups canola oil
2 cups sugar
3 cups zucchini, shredded
1 cup pecans, chopped, (optional)

Preheat oven to 350 degrees. In a medium bowl, whisk together flour, baking soda, baking powder, salt, and cinnamon.

In a separate large bowl, beat eggs until fluffy. Beat in oil and sugar. Add flour mixture and beat until well mixed. Add shredded zucchini and optional chopped pecans. Stir 250 strokes. Pour into greased and floured 9x13 cake pan. Bake 1 hour or until a toothpick inserted near center comes out clean. Cool and frost if desired.

Cream Cheese Frosting:
3 oz. cream cheese, softened
¼ cup margarine, softened
1 tsp. vanilla
2–2½ cups powdered sugar, sifted

In a medium bowl, beat together cream cheese, margarine, and vanilla until light and fluffy. Gradually beat in 1 cup powdered sugar. Beat well. Beat in enough remaining sugar to make frosting spreading consistency. Makes enough to frost the top of a 9x13 cake. Makes 12 servings.

Janet Marshall

Chocolate Zucchini Cake

½ cup margarine
1½ cups sugar
1 tsp. vanilla
½ cup vegetable oil
2 eggs, beaten
½ cup sour milk (or ½ cup lowfat milk and ½ tsp. white vinegar or
   lemon juice)
½ tsp. salt
1 tsp. baking soda
½ tsp. baking powder
¼ cup cocoa, sifted
½ tsp. ground cinnamon
2⅓ cups all-purpose flour
2 cups zucchini, peeled and shredded

Topping:
1 cup chocolate chips
1 cup light brown sugar, packed

Preheat oven to 350 degrees. In a large bowl, beat together margarine and sugar until light and fluffy. Beat in vanilla, oil, eggs, and sour milk until well mixed. Stir in salt, baking soda, baking powder, cocoa, cinnamon, and flour. Beat until just combined. Add zucchini and mix well. Pour into a greased and floured 9x13 cake pan. Sprinkle chocolate chips and brown sugar over unbaked cake. Bake for 40 to 45 minutes or until a toothpick comes out clean. Makes 12 servings.

COSTA FARMS

Tomatoes

SOME VARIETIES

Heirloom, red, purple, yellow, orange, red and yellow cherry, red and yellow pear, Roma, and tomatillos

PREPARING TOMATOES

Wash and slice. Eat raw or cook. A very ripe tomato will peel quite easily. Otherwise, blanch for 3–5 minutes or until skin just begins to split, dip in cold water and skins will slip right off.

Yields: 1 lb. fresh equals two 4-inch tomatoes, 1½ cups diced or 1 cup puréed.

Nutrition: 1 raw tomato has 25 calories, contains potassium and are an excellent source of vitamins A and C.

Marinated Tomatoes

This recipe was taken from the St. Paul Pioneer Press *in 1990, with the comment,*
"Judy Leahy makes this salad with tomatoes purchased at the Farmers' Market"

6–8 tomatoes, peeled and quartered or sliced (use both yellow and
    red tomatoes)
¼ cup fresh basil leaves, chopped
6 green onions, thinly sliced
¼ cup fresh parsley, chopped

Dressing:
3 tbsp. red wine vinegar
1 tsp. balsamic vinegar
½ tsp. salt
2–3 dashes Tobasco sauce
¼ tsp. dry mustard
1 clove garlic, crushed
½ cup olive oil

Arrange tomatoes, slices overlapping or wedges in a single layer, on a serving dish. Sprinkle with basil leaves, onions, and parsley. Combine the
dressing ingredients in a jar with a tight cover; shake to mix. Pour over the
tomatoes and allow to marinate at least 2 hours before serving. Makes 6–8
servings.

BLT Stuffed Cherry Tomatoes

20–25 cherry tomatoes
1 lb. bacon, cooked, drained, and crumbled
½ cup Miracle Whip
⅓ cup red onion, finely chopped
3 tbsp. Parmesan cheese
2 tbsp. fresh parsley, chopped

Cut a thin slice off each tomato top. Scoop out and discard pulp. Invert the
tomatoes on a paper towel to drain. In a small bowl, combine all remaining
ingredients; mix well. Spoon into tomatoes, refrigerate for several hours.
Makes 20–25 appetizer servings.

Mary Gerdesmeier

TOMATOES

Tabouli Stuffed Tomatoes

1 cup plus 2 tbsp. bulgur wheat or 1 (10oz.) pkg. plain couscous
2 cups boiling water
7 large vine-ripened tomatoes
1 bunch green onions, finely chopped
1 bunch of mint, leaves only, finely chopped; reserve 6 sprigs for garnish
1 bunch Italian parsley, finely chopped; reserve 6 sprigs for garnish
1 large or 2 small-to-medium lemons
6 tbsp. extra virgin olive oil or sesame oil
Kosher salt and freshly-ground black pepper, to taste

Place the bulgur in a large metal or ceramic bowl, and cover with the boiling water (or follow the directions on the package), and allow to stand for several minutes. Taste for tenderness, and when satisfied, drain off any excess moisture through a fine sieve or strainer. Remove any additional moisture from the bowl, and return the drained bulgur to it.

Wash and dry tomatoes. Remove the cores and discard. Cut the top quarter of 6 of the tomatoes off, and set aside, reserving the seventh tomato for chopping. Carefully scoop out the insides of the tomato, and place on a cutting board with the cored tomato tops. Trim the bottoms so the tomatoes will sit level, taking care not to puncture tomato shell. Add the trimmings to the scooped tomato flesh. Finely chop the tomato flesh and trimmings along with the reserved whole tomato, and add to the bulgur.

Clean the green onions, and finely chop. Add all (white and greens) to the bulgur. Mince the mint and parsley leaves, remembering to reserve 6 sprigs of each for garnish. Add the minced herbs to bulgur.

Remove long strips of zest from one of the lemons, and reserve for garnish. Roll the lemons with your hand or the flat side of a chef's knife to elicit more juice. Juice the lemons into a small bowl, removing seeds. Whisk in the olive or sesame oil, and add salt and pepper to taste. Pour over bulgur mixture, and toss to blend. Blanch the lemon zest in boiling water for 30 seconds, drain under cold water, and pat dry. Fill tomato shells with tabouli, and garnish with mint and parsley sprigs and lemon zest. Makes 6 servings.

B. J. Carpenter & Mary Ryan, Cooking Instructors
COOKS OF CROCUS HILL, ST. PAUL

Gazpacho

6 tomatoes, (3 cups) peeled and chopped
½ cup onions, finely chopped
1 cucumber, peeled, seeded, and diced
1 green pepper, chopped
1 small clove garlic, minced
1 tbsp. fresh basil, chopped
2½ cups chicken broth or tomato juice
⅓ cup red wine vinegar
¼ cup olive oil

Combine all in a large bowl and chill. You may also process in a blender, if desired. Makes 4–6 servings.

Fresh Tomato Soup

4 large red, ripe tomatoes (1¾ lb.)
2 large yellow onions
2 tbsp. olive oil
1 tbsp. garlic, minced
3½ cups beef or chicken stock
Salt and black pepper to taste
¼ tsp. hot red pepper flakes
¼ cup fresh basil, chopped
¼ cup fresh Italian parsley, finely chopped

Peel and core the tomatoes, then dice. Peel and dice the onions. Heat oil in a large saucepan; add onions. Cook, stirring often, to prevent sticking or browning, 5 minutes, until the onions are translucent. Add garlic and cook one minute more. Add tomatoes and cook, stirring often, 10 minutes. Add stock, salt, pepper, red pepper, basil, and parsley. Cook, stirring occasionally, about 20 minutes. Serve hot. Makes 6 servings.

Crystal Bloecher

TOMATOES

Chili with Sweet Corn

Fresh tomatoes and corn make this the best ever!

1 large onion, chopped
2 cloves garlic, chopped
4 tbsp. vegetable oil
2 green peppers, chopped
1 tbsp. chili powder
1 tbsp. ground cumin
8 cups fresh tomatoes, chopped
2 cups raw or cooked corn kernels
2 cups cooked kidney or black beans
1 tbsp. salt
2 tsp. dried oregano

In a large pot, heat oil and sauté onion until soft. Add garlic, green pepper, and spices, and sauté for 3 more minutes. Add tomatoes, corn, beans, salt, and oregano. Cover and simmer for 30 minutes. Taste and adjust spices. Makes 8 servings.

LENGSFELD'S ORGANIC GARDENS

TOMATOES

Tomato Vegetable Juice

8 qts. tomatoes
8 stalks celery (includes leaves)
¼ cup parsley, minced
3 small onions
1 leek
½ tsp. ground allspice
1 tbsp. Worcester sauce
1 lemon, sliced thin
1 cup carrots, finely chopped
1 cup green pepper, finely chopped
Dash of sugar
Dash of dried basil
1½ tsp. salt
Freshly ground black pepper

Cut tomatoes in quarters. Chop vegetables. In a large pot, cook all for 30 minutes. Put through sieve and add seasonings. Cover and chill. Makes 6 quarts.

Mona Cordes

Cherry Tomato Pasta

1 pint cherry tomatoes, red and yellow mixed
2 tbsp. olive oil
2 tbsp. fresh chives, chopped
1 tbsp. fresh basil, chopped
1 tbsp. fresh thyme, chopped
1 lb. pasta, cooked and drained (mafalda, bow ties, radiatore, gnocchi, or
    shells work well)
Salt and black pepper
Parmesan cheese

Halve the cherry tomatoes. Heat oil in skillet. Add the tomatoes and herbs and toss for 1 minute until well coated. Toss in hot pasta. Season with salt and pepper. Garnish with Parmesan cheese. Makes 4 servings.

Robin Chan

TOMATOES

Italian Style Stuffed, Baked Tomatoes

6 large vine-ripened tomatoes
Sea salt
½ cup short grain or quick cooking rice
Extra virgin olive oil
4 tbsp. Parmesan cheese, freshly grated
1 medium clove garlic, minced
3–4 anchovy fillets, finely chopped
4 tsp. capers, finely chopped
2–3 sprigs Italian parsley, leaves only, finely chopped
2–3 sprigs basil, leaves only, finely chopped
Freshly ground black pepper, to taste

Preheat oven to 325 degrees. Wash and dry tomatoes. Slice off the tops and reserve. Trim a bit of the tomato from the bottom, if necessary, so the tomatoes will sit level. Pour or gently squeeze the juice into a medium-sized bowl. Remove the seeds and discard. Scrap any excess flesh from the inside of the tomato, taking care not to break the walls of the tomatoes. Place the tomato flesh on a cutting board and finely chop. Place in a bowl with the tomato juice. Sprinkle the insides of the tomato shells with sea salt, and set aside.

Add the remaining ingredients to the tomato juice and flesh, and mix well. Taste, and add more pepper and salt if desired. Do this last taking the saltiness of the cheese, anchovies, and capers into account.

Fill tomato shells half full, to allow the rice to swell during baking. Lightly oil a shallow baking dish, and place the filled tomatoes in it so they stand upright. Brush the top edges of the tomatoes with olive oil, and cover with the reserved tops. Sprinkle with olive oil. Bake for 45 minutes to 1 hour, or until the tomatoes are tender but firm. Makes 6 servings.

B. J. Carpenter & Mary Ryan, Cooking Instructors
COOKS OF CROCUS HILL, ST. PAUL

Eggs in Tomato Cups with Dilled Hollandaise

Try making this with a combination of red, orange and yellow tomatoes

6 large firm tomatoes
6 large eggs
Butter
Salt and black pepper to taste

Dilled hollandaise:
3 egg yolks
1½ tsp. fresh lemon juice
1 tsp. fresh dill weed
¼ tsp. salt
Dash hot pepper sauce
6 tbsp. unsalted butter, melted

Preheat oven to 350 degrees. Halve tomatoes and hollow out. Drain upside-down. Place in oven proof custard cups. Gently break egg yolk into each tomato half. Dot with butter and season with salt and pepper. Bake 6 to 8 minutes for soft cooked, or 8 to 10 minutes for hard cooked eggs. Remove from custard cups and serve with dilled hollandaise.

To make the hollandaise: combine all ingredients except butter in a food processor. While running processor, add butter in a thin stream; process until thick. Makes 6 servings.

Doe Hauser-Stowell

Broiled Tomatoes with Garlic

A fine lowfat brunch dish or excellent as an accompaniment to grilled meat or fish

4 large ripe tomatoes, room temperature
Freshly ground black pepper
¼ cup toasted wheat germ
1 small clove garlic, minced
2 tbsp. fresh parsley, chopped
Olive oil, small amount
Lowfat Jarlsberg cheese

Preheat oven to 450 degrees. Wash and cut tomatoes in half crosswise; do not peel. Arrange halves cut side up on a greased baking dish and sprinkle with pepper.

In a small bowl or cup, combine wheat germ with garlic, parsley, and olive oil. Grate a small about of Jarlsberg into mixture and stir to combine.

Spoon mixture onto cut tomato halves and pat down lightly, covering all of tomato surface. Bake for 10 minutes or until topping is lightly browned and tomato is heated through. Makes 4 servings.

Carlen Arnett & Keith A. Parker

Tomato Pasta Pie with Goat Cheese

2 tsp. olive oil, divided
Cooking spray
2 cups onion, thinly sliced
½ cup red bell pepper (2x¼-inch) julienne cut
4 garlic cloves, minced
2 cups cherry tomatoes, quartered
¼ cup dry red wine
3 tbsp. pitted kalamata olives, chopped
2 tbsp. sun-dried tomato sprinkles
¼ tsp. black pepper
2 cups tomatoes, diced
6 cups hot cooked linguine (about 10 oz. uncooked pasta)
½ cup (2oz.) crumbled goat cheese (low-salt feta)

Heat 1 tsp. oil in a nonstick skillet coated with cooking spray over medium heat. Add onion and sauté 3 minutes. Add bell pepper and garlic; sauté 5 minutes. Add cherry tomato; sauté 2 minutes. Add wine, olives, tomato sprinkles, pepper, and diced tomatoes; reduce heat and simmer 5 minutes. Combine tomato mixture and pasta in a bowl; toss to coat.

Preheat oven to 350 degrees. Wipe skillet with paper towels; recoat with cooking spray and 1 tsp. oil. Arrange cheese in skillet; top with pasta mixture. Cover in foil coated with cooking spray, pressing firmly to pack. Wrap handle of skillet with foil; bake at 350 degrees for 30 minutes. Place a large plate upside down on top of skillet; invert onto plate. Cut into 6 wedges. Makes 6 servings.

DANCING WINDS FARM

Mary's Spanish Rice

The bright flavors of the fresh summer vegetables are the secret to what makes this taste so good!

1 large onion, chopped
2 cloves garlic, minced
3 tbsp. butter or margarine
1 green or red bell pepper, chopped
1 cup uncooked basmati rice
4 cups ripe tomatoes, chopped
2 tsp. salt
¼ tsp. black pepper

In a heavy pot, heat butter or margarine, and sauté onion until soft, about 3 minutes. Add garlic, peppers, and rice. Fry over medium heat until rice is browned, stirring frequently. Stir in the tomatoes and salt. Cover and bring to a boil; reduce heat. No extra water is needed since the rice will absorb the tomato juice. Cook over very low heat for about 1 hour or until all the tomato juice is absorbed by the rice. Makes 6 servings.

Mary Lengsfeld

TOMATOES

Joe's Fresh Salsa

4–5 cloves garlic, minced
1 medium onion, chopped
7 hot peppers, (jalapeños or hot banana) chopped
2 handfuls of fresh cilantro, chopped
6 medium tomatoes, chopped
Salt to taste

Combine everything, except the tomatoes, in a blender or food processor. Cover and process just until coarse and chunky in texture. Pour into a bowl. Put tomatoes in blender or food processor. Cover and process until somewhat chunky. Add to vegetable mixture and mix well. Add salt to taste. Makes 6 servings.

Joe Kaiser

Costa's Totally Hot Salsa

4 medium onions
12 cloves garlic, peeled
6 red or yellow sweet bell peppers
6 Italian fry peppers
1 pair plastic gloves
24 hot peppers, your choice: jalepeño, habañero, hot banana, cayenne
   or poblano
25 large Roma tomatoes, peeled
1½ cups red wine vinegar
¼ cup canning salt

Chop onions and garlic, bell peppers, and Italian peppers to desired size. Wear plastic gloves to chop hot peppers.

In a large stainless steel kettle, combine all ingredients. Cover and bring to a boil; reduce heat. Simmer for 30 minutes. Ladle boiling salsa into clean hot sterilized pint or quart jars, leaving ½-inch headroom for pints and 1 inch headroom for quarts. Adjust clean hot lids. Process pints for 10 minutes and quarts for 20 minutes. Remove and cool. Makes 10 pints or 5 quarts.

COSTA FARM: "THE PEPPER PEOPLE"

TOMATOES

Tomato Jam

3 cups tomatoes, peeled and crushed
3 cups sugar
Cinnamon stick (optional)
1 pkg. orange gelatin

In a large stainless steel saucepan, bring tomatoes and sugar to a boil. Add cinnamon stick, if desired and boil for 15 minutes, stirring constantly. Gradually stir in gelatin. Remove from heat. Remove cinnamon stick, if needed. Ladle hot mixture into hot sterilized jars leaving ½-inch headroom. Adjust clean hot lids. Cool. Store in refrigerator. Makes about 4 cups

   Variation: Yellow tomato jam: Substitute yellow for red tomatoes and lemon for orange gelatin.

Nancy Jordan

Ev's Thick and Rich Roma Tomato Salsa

1 peck ripe Roma tomatoes (about 14 lbs.)
6 medium onions
5–25 cloves garlic
½–3 cups sliced jalapeño peppers (warning: use 3 cups only if spontaneous
   combustion is desired!)
2–3 cups white vinegar
2 tbsp. canning salt

In small batches, blanch tomatoes in a large pot of boiling water until their skins just begin to split, then dunk in cold water. Peel and halve tomatoes. Put in a large heavy-bottomed stainless steel pot. Crush tomatoes with a potato masher. Bring to a boil and cook thirty minutes, uncovered, over medium heat. Stir occasionally to prevent scorching. Peel and chop onions. Stir into the bubbling tomatoes. Peel and mince garlic. Add to the mixture. Partially cover the pot and cook over low heat until desired thickness is reached, anywhere from fifteen minutes to four hours. Add vinegar and salt to taste. This will thin it a bit. Add sliced jalapeño peppers and simmer, covered, for ten minutes. Turn off heat. The jalapeños will retain a bright color and have a pleasant crunchiness.

   For canning, ladle boiling hot salsa into hot pint jars, leaving ½-inch headroom. Adjust clean hot lids and process in a boiling-water bath for fifteen minutes. Remove and cool. Makes about 12–15 pints.

LENGSFELD'S ORGANIC GARDENS

TOMATOES

Lengsfeld's Best Roma Tomato Sauce

Good and thick for pasta, pizza, and lasagna

4 tbsp. olive oil
1 red onion, chopped
3 whole cloves garlic
½ cup carrots, grated and finely chopped
1 green pepper, chopped
¼ cup fresh parsley, finely chopped
3 bay leaves
1 tsp. dried oregano, or 1 tbsp. fresh, chopped
2 tsp. dried thyme, or 2 tbsp. fresh, chopped
4 tsp. dried basil, or 4 tbsp. fresh, chopped
4 cups ripe Roma tomatoes, peeled and crushed
1 (12oz.) can tomato paste
4 tsp. salt
½ tsp. black pepper
2 tsp. honey

In a large saucepan, heat oil. Sauté onion and garlic cloves until soft. Crush garlic cloves with a fork. Add carrot, green pepper, parsley, bay leaves, and herbs. Stir well, then add the tomatoes, tomato paste, and seasonings. Taste and adjust seasonings. Bring to a boil, reduce heat and cook, covered, over medium heat at least 30 minutes, longer if a thicker sauce is desired. Remove bay leaves and add honey. Makes 6 cups.

LENGSFELD'S ORGANIC GARDENS

Lemon–Tomato Butter

2 lemons, peeled, quartered, and seeded
14 large yellow tomatoes, cut into chunks
2 cups sugar
¼ tsp. salt
½ cup honey
½ cup light corn syrup

TOMATOES

Grind lemon quarters in a food processor or a blender.

Combine ground lemons with tomatoes in a large saucepan and bring to a boil. Lower heat and simmer until the tomatoes are soft, then remove from heat. When the mixture cools enough to handle, run it through a food mill or sieve.

Measure 9 cups of the purée into a large saucepan. Stir in the sugar, salt, honey, and corn syrup. Slowly bring the mixture to a boil, then simmer over low heat until it thickens enough to round up in a spoon, stirring frequently so the butter doesn't stick. Ladle the mixture into jars, leaving ¼-inch of headroom and then process the jars, 10 minutes, in a boiling-water bath.

Jim Trenter

Uncooked Tomato Relish

This delicious relish does not need to be canned—it keeps in the refrigerator!

18 medium tomatoes
2 stalks celery
2 green peppers
2 sweet red peppers
4 medium onions
½ cup finely ground horseradish (freshly-ground is best!)
⅓ cup salt
2½ cups sugar
½ tsp. black pepper
½ tsp. ground cloves
2 tsp. ground cinnamon
3 tbsp. whole mustard seed
3 cups white vinegar

Scald tomatoes in boiling water, rinse under cold water. Peel and core tomatoes; then chop them in small pieces. They will make about 3 quarts. Put celery, peppers, and onions through the food chopper, using a coarse grind. Combine vegetables and salt. Let stand overnight, covered in the refrigerator. Drain thoroughly in a strainer, at least ½ hour. Add sugar, spices, mustard seed, and vinegar. Mix well. Pack in sterile jars and cover with clean hot lids. Store in the refrigerator. Makes 4 quarts.

Hazel Dial

TOMATOES

J. M.'s Chili Sauce

1 gallon (16 cups) ripe tomatoes, chopped and peeled
6 large onions, ground
3 hot peppers, chopped
1 tbsp. canning or kosher salt
1 tbsp. celery seed
1 tbsp. ground allspice
1 tbsp. whole mustard seed
1 tbsp. ground cloves
1 tbsp. ground cinnamon
1 tbsp. black pepper
3 cups vinegar (white or cider)
4 cups sugar

Put tomatoes, onions, and peppers into a large heavy-bottomed saucepan; cook 20 minutes. If there is too much liquid, scoop out and discard some. Add other ingredients; cook ¾ to 1 hour, stirring occasionally, until thickened. Pour into sterilized pint jars. Adjust clean hot lids. Process 10 minutes in a boiling-water bath. Remove and cool. Makes about 8–10 pints.

Doe Hauser-Stowell

Meatless Spaghetti Sauce
Suitable for canning

10 quarts tomatoes, peeled and chopped (about 30 lbs.)
1 cup onions, chopped
1 cup green sweet peppers, chopped
1 cup celery, chopped
¼ cup fresh parsley, chopped (optional)
1 lb. fresh mushrooms (optional)
2–4 cloves garlic, minced
4 tbsp. canning salt
¼ cup sugar
1 tbsp. sweet basil, crushed
1 tbsp. dried oregano

Seasonings in this recipe may be altered according to your tastes.

Combine all ingredients in a large kettle. Heat rapidly to simmering and simmer until thickened, about 1½ hours. Stir frequently to prevent sticking. Bring to a boil and pack into clean hot sterilized quart jars, leaving 1-inch headroom. Adjust clean hot lids. Process in a boiling-water bath for 20 minutes. Remove and cool. Makes about 10 quarts.

UNIVERSITY OF WISCONSIN EXTENSION

Tomato Ketchup

4 quarts fully ripe tomatoes, chopped (10–12 lbs.)
2 medium onions, chopped (1 cup)
1 red sweet pepper, seeded and chopped (¾ cup)
1 tsp. whole mustard seed
1½ tbsp. whole celery seed
½ tsp. whole allspice
2 tsp. whole cloves
1 bay leaf
1 3-inch cinnamon stick
1½ cups firmly packed light brown sugar
1 tbsp. canning salt
1 tbsp. paprika
1½ cups cider vinegar (5% acetic acid)

Wash all vegetables. Core tomatoes, but do not peel. Chop coarsely with a knife, or in a blender or food processor.

Cook vigorously until quite thick, about 45 minutes, stirring frequently. Blend and press through a wire strainer. Place in a large kettle and bring to a boil. Boil gently without covering until the volume is reduce by about half. Stir often.

Tie spices loosely in a cheesecloth bag and add to purée. Add brown sugar, salt, and paprika. Continue cooking over medium heat until very thick (about 1½ to 2 hours). As mixture thickens, stir often and reduce heat to prevent scorching. Add vinegar during the last 10 to 15 minutes of cooking. Remove spice bag and discard. Pour into clean hot pint canning jars, leaving ½-inch headroom. Adjust clean hot lids. Process 10 minutes in boiling-water bath. Makes 8–10 pints.

TOMATOES

Smoky Tomato Ketchup

Hot, spicy and addictive–great as dip for oven fried potatoes

5 lbs. ripe tomatoes, coarsely chopped
1 large onion, finely chopped
1 large poblano chili, finely chopped
2 jalapeño chilies, coarsely chopped
2 dried or canned chipotle chilies, chopped
½ cup cider vinegar
1 cup brown sugar (packed)
1 tsp. celery seed
1½ tsp. mustard seed
¼ tsp. cayenne pepper
1 tsp. black pepper
1½ tsp. salt

Combine all ingredients in a large nonreactive pot and bring to a boil over medium heat. Reduce heat and simmer 1½ hours, stirring occasionally until vegetables are soft and sauce is reduced by ¼.

Purée in food processor or food mill. Leave as is or strain through a sieve into a clean pot. Bring to a boil over medium-low heat and simmer, partially covered to prevent splatters, for 1 to 3 hours or until quite thick and dark brownish red.

Store in refrigerator in a glass jar for up to 1 month. Freeze for longer storage, or can. Makes 3–4 pints.

Mary Broeker

Fried Green Tomatoes

1 egg, beaten
2 tbsp. lowfat milk
¾ cup cornmeal, or all-purpose flour
3 tbsp. Parmesan cheese (optional)
¾ tsp. dried Italian seasoning
¼ tsp. salt
⅛ tsp. black pepper
4 medium-large green tomatoes, cut into ½-inch thick slices
4 tbsp. vegetable oil for frying

In a shallow bowl combine egg and milk. In another shallow bowl combine cornmeal, optional Parmesan cheese, Italian seasoning, salt, and pepper. Dip tomatoes in egg mixture and then into cornmeal fixture.

In a 10-inch skillet, heat oil over medium heat. Fry tomatoes in a single layer until golden brown on one side. Turn and cook other side. Repeat with remaining slices. Makes about 15 slices.

Tomato Soup Cake

2 cups all-purpose flour
2 tsp. baking powder
1 tsp. baking soda
½ tsp. salt
2 tsp. ground cinnamon
½ tsp. ground cloves
½ tsp. ground nutmeg
½ cup butter or margarine
1 cup sugar
2 eggs, beaten
1 cup tomato soup or 1½ cups fresh tomatoes, peeled and diced
½ cup dates, chopped (optional)
½ cup pecans, chopped (optional)

Preheat oven to 350 degrees. In a medium bowl, whisk together flour, baking powder, baking soda, salt, cinnamon, cloves, and nutmeg.

In a separate bowl, cream together butter or margarine and add sugar. Add beaten eggs and beat until light and fluffy. Add tomato soup or diced tomatoes and optional dates and pecans. Mix well. Pour into a greased and floured 9x13 cake pan. Bake for 30 minutes or until a toothpick, inserted near center, comes out clean.

TOMATOES

Green Tomato Pie

Pastry for one 9-inch, 2 crust pie
4 cups green tomatoes, thinly sliced
1 cup brown sugar
½ tsp. ground cinnamon
½ tsp. salt
½ tsp. ground nutmeg
½ tsp. ground cloves
2 tbsp. all-purpose flour
4 tbsp. fresh lemon juice
2 tbsp. butter or margarine

Preheat oven to 425 degrees. Line a 9-inch pie pan with the bottom crust. In a medium bowl, mix sugar, cinnamon, salt, nutmeg, cloves, and flour.

In a separate bowl, toss tomato slices with lemon juice. Add sugar mixture to tomatoes and mix well. Pour into bottom crust. Dot with butter or margarine. Cover with top crust, seal and crimp edges. Cut 4 to 5 slits in top crust. Bake at 425 degrees for 30 minutes. Reduce heat to 350 degrees and bake for an additional 30 minutes.

Green Tomato Relish

This relish is wonderful with roast beef, hamburgers, and hot dogs.
It's a good way to use the end of the season tomatoes and peppers from the garden

1 peck green tomatoes (8 quarts)
1 cup canning salt
1 medium head green cabbage
6 green peppers, seeded and cut in large strips
5 red peppers, seeded and cut in large strips
6 medium onions, peeled
3 quarts white vinegar
8 cups sugar
2 tbsp. whole celery seed
2 tbsp. whole mustard seed
1 tbsp. whole cloves, tied in cheese cloth bag

TOMATOES

Grind tomatoes in a food processor, using medium grind. Mix tomatoes with salt and let drain overnight.

Next morning grind cabbage, peppers, and onions. Mix all vegetables, including tomatoes, in a large, heavy-bottomed stainless steel pot. Add vinegar, sugar, celery seed, mustard seed, and cloves. Boil until onions are tender, about 20 minutes. Pour in hot sterilized pint jars, leaving ½-inch headroom. Adjust clean hot lids and process in a boiling-water bath for 10 minutes. Remove and cool. Makes about 16 pints.

Hazel Dial

Green Tomato Pickles

6 cups firm green tomatoes, sliced
6 medium onions, peeled and sliced
1 green pepper, seeded and sliced
½ cup canning salt
4 cups cold water
2 cups white vinegar
2½ cups sugar
2 cups water
1 tbsp. whole mustard seed
6 pieces cinnamon stick
12 whole cloves
6 whole allspice

Combine vegetables and salt. Pour cold water over them and let stand 2 hours. Drain well. In a large stainless steel pot, boil together vinegar, sugar, 2 cups water, and spices. Cook 2 minutes. Add drained vegetables and bring to a boil; cook 2 minutes. Pack vegetables into sterilized pint jars; pour cooking syrup over them, leaving ½-inch headroom; adjust clean hot lids and seal. Process 10 minutes in boiling-water bath. Remove and cool. Makes about 6 pints.

Ann Berg

TOMATOES

White Chili with Tomatillos

2 whole chicken breasts, skinned and diced
2 tbsp. vegetable oil
3 shallots or 1 onion, diced
3 cloves garlic, minced
½ cup fresh green chilies, diced
1 (14½ oz.) can chicken broth
1 lb. tomatillos, husks removed, chopped (about 10)
½ tsp. ground cumin
1 tbsp. fresh cilantro, chopped (½ tsp. dried coriander)
1 tsp. fresh oregano, chopped (½ tsp. dried oregano)
Juice of 1 lime
2 (15 oz.) cans white beans, drained and rinsed
Salt and black pepper to taste
Optional condiments: chopped red onion, grated cheddar cheese, chopped
    avocado, sour cream

Sauté diced chicken in oil in skillet over medium heat until cooked; remove
and set aside. Add shallots or onions, garlic, and diced chiles; sauté until
slightly browned. Add chicken broth, tomatillos, and spices; bring to a boil
and simmer 25 minutes. Add lime juice and beans. Heat thoroughly. Salt and
pepper to taste. May add optional condiments if desired. Makes 6 servings.

HILLTOP PRODUCE FARM

TOMATOES

Tomatillo Green Salsa

5 cups chopped tomatillos or green tomatoes
1½ cups long green chilies, seeded and chopped
½ cup jalapeño peppers, seeded and finely chopped
4 cups onion, chopped
1 cup bottled lemon juice
6 cloves garlic, finely chopped
1 tbsp. ground cumin
3 tbsp. dried oregano leaves
1 tbsp. canning salt
1 tsp. black pepper

Combine all ingredients in a large saucepan. Stir frequently over high heat until mixture begins to boil, then reduce heat and simmer for 20 minutes, stirring occasionally. Ladle hot salsa into clean, hot pint jars, leaving ½-inch headroom. Adjust clean hot lids and process in a boiling-water bath for 15 minutes. Remove and cool. Makes 5 pints.

Winter Squash and Pumpkins

WHEN AVAILABLE

September–November

SOME VARIETIES

Acorn, buttercup, butternut, delicata, hubbard, red kuri, spaghetti, sweet mama, sweet dumpling, and pie pumpkins

PREPARING SQUASH AND PUMPKIN

Wash, cut in half, and scoop out seeds. Bake halves whole or cut into 1-inch cubes and steam or boil. Cook until tender. To bake, place halves, cut side down, in a baking dish and bake at 350 degrees. Microwave in a covered dish, cut side down, with 2 tbsp. of water.

Blanch time: 10–12 minutes, 1-inch cubes

Steam time: 12–15 minutes, 1-inch cubes

Microwave time: 10–14 minutes, 1 half

Bake time: 45–60 minutes, 2–4 halves

Yields: PUMPKIN—An 8 lb. whole pumpkin equals 4 lbs. flesh; 1 lb. raw pumpkin equals 3 cups sliced, diced or grated or 2 cups cooked and puréed. WINTER SQUASH—1 lb. fresh equals one 6-inch acorn squash, 3 cups peeled and diced or 2 cups cooked and mashed.

Roasted Acorn Squash Soup

1 acorn squash
Salt to taste
2 tbsp. butter
¼ cup celery, chopped
¼ cup carrot, chopped
2 tbsp. yellow onion, chopped
2 cups chicken broth
¼ cup whipping cream
1½ tsp. fresh lemon juice
Pepper to taste

Preheat oven to 300 degrees. Cut squash in half and scrape out seeds. Place on a jelly roll pan, cut side down. Bake about 1 hour and 15 minutes, until completely soft.

In a medium saucepan, melt butter. Add celery, carrot, and onion; Cook slowly about 5 minutes until soft. Scrape flesh from squash and add to pan along with chicken broth. Heat to a boil. Reduce heat, cover, and simmer slowly 20 to 30 minutes, until the carrot and celery are tender.

Purée soup in a food processor or blender. Return to pan and add cream, lemon juice, salt, and pepper. Heat. Garnish soup with roasted pumpkin seeds. Makes six 1-cup servings.

THE GOOD EARTH RESTAURANT

WINTER SQUASH AND PUMPKINS

Spaghetti Squash Fettucine

1 spaghetti squash
2 tbsp. water

Filling:
1½ cups sour cream
3–4 cloves garlic, minced
3 tsp. dried oregano
Salt and pepper to taste
Parmesan and Romano cheese

Preheat oven to 350 degrees. Cut squash in half and scoop out seeds. Place squash halves, cut sides down, in a covered baking dish with 2 tbsp. water. Bake for 1 hour or until tender.

In a large bowl, mix sour cream, garlic, and oregano. Scrape out cooked squash; reserving shells. Add cooked squash to sour cream mixture and mix well. Scoop back into reserved squash shells. Grate Parmesan and Romano cheese on top. Broil for about 15 minutes until lightly browned. Makes 2 servings.

Carol Neumann

Turkey and Vegetable Stuffed Squash

2 medium winter squash, each about 2 lbs.
¼ lb. ground turkey
1 cup onions, chopped
1 cup whole-kernel corn, cooked
½ cup carrots, shredded
¼ tsp. ground cumin
¾ cup vegetable cocktail juice
½ cup green chilies, chopped
⅛ tsp. freshly-ground black pepper
¾ cup instant rice, uncooked
¾ cup cheddar cheese, grated (optional)

To prepare squash: Cut squash in half lengthwise. Scoop out seeds. In 5-quart Dutch oven, bring 1-inch of water to a boil. Place 2 squash halves, cut side down, in boiling water. Reduce heat to low. Simmer, covered, for 10 minutes, or until squash is tender. Remove to platter. Repeat with remaining squash halves.

To make filling: Into 3-quart saucepan over medium-low heat, crumble ground turkey. Immediately add onion, corn, carrots, and cumin. Cook, stirring constantly, until turkey begins to give off liquid. Increase heat to medium-high. Continue cooking until turkey is browned and onions are tender. Stir in vegetable juice cocktail, chilies, and pepper. Heat to a boil. Stir in instant rice. Remove from heat. Cover and let stand for 5 minutes. Stir in optional cheddar cheese.

To fill squash: Spoon mixture into the warm squash halves. If necessary, scoop out some of the cooked squash from the narrow end of vegetable. Makes 4 servings.

Orange Honeyed Squash

3 small acorn or sweet dumpling squash

Sauce:
¼ cup honey
2 tbsp. frozen orange juice concentrate
1 tsp. salt
2 tbsp. butter or margarine
⅛ tsp. ground nutmeg (optional)

Preheat oven to 400 degrees. Cut the squash in half and scoop out seeds. Place halves in an ungreased baking dish. In a small bowl, stir together honey, orange juice concentrate, and salt. Fill each half with ¼ of the sauce along with ½ tbsp. butter or margarine. Sprinkle with optional nutmeg. Cover and bake for 30 minutes. Then uncover and bake for an additional 30 minutes or until tender. Makes 6 servings.

Joan Jordan

Butternut Squash and Blue Cheese Tart with Baby Arugula

1 9-inch pie crust (family favorite or frozen), prebaked in a 9-inch tart pan
1½ lbs. butternut squash
1 jalapeño pepper
¼ cup chives, minced
4 oz. blue cheese, preferably a good Gorgonzola, broken into ¼-inch
    crumbles
1 tsp. kosher salt
¼ tsp. black pepper
½ cup golden raisins
½ cup pinenuts
A couple of handfuls of baby Arugula
Parmesan cheese
High quality extra virgin olive oil

Preheat oven to 350 degrees. Roast squash in oven until tender, approximately 60 minutes. Allow to cool and scrape out soft flesh into bowl. Mash squash pulp with a potato masher until smooth. Add jalapeño, chives, blue cheese, salt, and pepper; mix to combine. Turn squash mixture out into the prebaked pie shell and spread evenly. Top with pine nuts and raisins. Bake for about 10 minutes, until pine nuts begin to brown.

Serve warm topped with baby Arugula, shavings of Parmesan cheese, and drizzle of extra virgin olive oil.

Christopher Stevens, Chef
TABLE OF CONTENTS, ST. PAUL

Flaky Squash Biscuits

Delicate, sweet, and vibrant in color, these tender biscuits pair well with winter stews and soups. For dairy-free biscuits, substitute margarine and soy milk for the butter and milk.

2 cups unbleached white flour or 1 cup unbleached and 1 cup whole-
    wheat flour
3 tsp. baking powder
½ tsp. salt
⅓ cup cold butter
1 cup puréed squash (delicata, pumpkin or butternut)
2 tsp. honey
1–4 tbsp. lowfat milk

Preheat oven to 400 degrees. In a large mixing bowl, stir together flour, baking powder, and salt. Cut butter into small pieces and work into flour mixture with a pastry cutter until it's the size of small peas.

Mix honey into puréed squash, then stir into flour mixture. Add enough milk to make a soft dough. Turn out dough onto a lightly floured surface. With your hands, flatten it out to about a ½-inch thickness. Fold the dough in half as you would close a book. Rotate dough 90 degrees, pat it out, and fold it again. Repeat this twice, dusting with flour as necessary to prevent the dough from sticking to your fingers. Work quickly to prevent the butter from becoming overly soft. After the last folding, roll out dough to about ½-inch thickness. Cut into 1½-inch rounds. To shape the biscuits, form your thumb and first finger into a "C" shape. Hold the biscuit upright in this "C" with your fingers curled around the cut edges. Rotate and gently squeeze the biscuit to give it more height.

Note: Shaping makes a marked difference in the lightness of the biscuits. If you simply cut them and place them on a baking sheet, they'll still work, but they won't be as good.

Place the biscuits closely together in a 9-inch square baking pan. Bake until puffed and very lightly browned, 18 to 20 minutes. Serve piping hot. Makes 20–24 biscuits.

Parmesan Onion Squash Bake

4 tbsp. vegetable oil
4 tbsp. unsalted butter or margarine
5 onions, thinly sliced
2 tbsp. sugar
4 tbsp. balsamic vinegar
2 lbs. butternut or other orange flesh squash, peeled, seeded and thinly sliced
Salt and black pepper to taste
3 tbsp. grated Parmesan

Melt butter and oil in sauté pan. Add onion; sauté 10 minutes. Add brown sugar and stir until sugar melts. Add balsamic vinegar; mix to combine.

Preheat oven to 350 degrees. Transfer onion mixture to 9x13-inch baking dish; arrange sliced squash on top. Season with salt and pepper. Cover pan with foil. Bake until squash is almost tender, about 30 minutes. Increase oven temperature to 400 degrees. Uncover squash; bake until tender, about 10 minutes. Sprinkle with Parmesan; bake until cheese melts, about 10 minutes. Makes 4 servings.

Squash Cake

This is our favorite winter snack cake!

4 eggs
1 cup salad oil
2 cups sugar
1¾ cups cooked squash, mashed
2 cups all-purpose flour
2 tsp. baking powder
1 tsp. baking soda
½ tsp. salt
3 tsp. ground cinnamon
½ tsp. ground ginger
¼ tsp. ground cloves
¼ tsp. ground nutmeg
1 cup chopped pecans (optional)

Preheat oven to 350 degrees. In a medium bowl, beat eggs well. Add oil, sugar, and squash. Beat until smooth and well mixed.

In a separate medium bowl, whisk together dry ingredients and spices. Add to squash mixture along with optional nuts. Mix with electric mixer on high speed for 2 minutes. Pour into a 9x13 greased and floured cake pan. Bake for 30 minutes or until toothpick, inserted near center, comes out clean.

LENGSFELD'S ORGANIC GARDENS

Pumpkin Soup

1 onion, chopped
2 tbsp. butter
2 cans chicken broth
2 cups potatoes, peeled and diced
2 cups cooked pumpkin
2 cups whole or 2% milk
½ tsp. ground nutmeg
Salt and black pepper
1 cup sour cream
3 strips bacon, cooked, drained, crumbled
Fresh parsley, chopped

Melt butter in a large heavy saucepan. Add onion and sauté until soft. Add broth and potatoes; cook until potatoes are tender. Mash or purée. Return to saucepan and add pumpkin. Heat. Add milk, nutmeg, salt, and pepper to taste. Garnish with sour cream, bacon, and parsley. Makes 6 servings.

HILLTOP PRODUCE FARM

WINTER SQUASH AND PUMPKINS

Dinner in a Pumpkin

Stuff with turkey stuffing or with this seasoned rice stuffing

1 medium pie pumpkin
2 cups water
1 vegetable or chicken bouillon cube
½ cup wild rice
½ cup brown rice
½ tsp. salt
1 medium onion, chopped
3 tbsp. vegetable oil
1 clove garlic, minced
1 red pepper, chopped
1 stalk celery, chopped
1 tsp. dried sage
½ tsp. dried marjoram
¼ tsp. dried thyme
1½ cups cooked garbanzo beans
1 cup cooked corn kernels
Salt and black pepper to taste

Preheat oven to 350 degrees. Cut top off pumpkin and scoop out seeds. Brush the cut surfaces with oil. Bake in oven until tender.

While pumpkin is baking, bring water and bouillon cube to a boil. Add wild rice, brown rice and salt. Cook, uncovered, until all the water is absorbed and the wild rice is tender, about 45 minutes.

In a skillet, heat oil. Sauté onion until soft. Add garlic, celery, and pepper and sauté over low heat for 3 minutes. Add spices and mix well. Combine onion mixture with garbanzo beans and corn and season to taste with salt and pepper.

Spoon the stuffing in the pumpkin. Return to oven for 10 to 15 minutes or until everything is heated through. Makes 6 servings.

WINTER SQUASH AND PUMPKINS

Pumpkin Butter

8 cups pumpkin, cooked and puréed or mashed
8 cups brown sugar
Grated rind of 4 lemons
Juice from 4 lemons
1¼ tsp. ground cinnamon
½ tsp. ground ginger

In a heavy pot or kettle, combine all ingredients. Cook over low heat for about 1 hour, stirring frequently to prevent scorching. When mixture is very thick, yet easily spreadable, spoon into hot, sterilized pint jars, leaving ½-inch headroom. Adjust clean hot lids. Cool. Store in refrigerator. Makes 6 pints.

Pumpkin Muffins

1 cup boiling water
½ cup raisins
1 cup shortening
1 cup sugar
1 egg
1 cup fresh or canned pumpkin (not pie filling)
1 tsp. vanilla
1 tsp. ground cinnamon
1 tsp. salt
½ tsp. ground nutmeg
2 cups all-purpose flour
1 tsp. baking powder
1 tsp. baking soda
1 cup chopped nuts

Preheat oven to 350 degrees. Pour boiling water over raisins in small bowl. Set aside. In large bowl, cream shortening and sugar. Beat in egg, pumpkin, vanilla, cinnamon, salt, and nutmeg. Combine flour, baking powder, and soda. Beat into pumpkin mixture until smooth. Drain raisins. Stir in nuts and raisins. Fill greased muffin tins ⅔ full. Bake for 20 minutes. Makes 12–15 muffins.

Buttery Pumpkin Bread

4 large eggs, at room temperature
3 cups granulated sugar
1 cup canola oil
⅔ cup water
2 cups cooked sugar pumpkin, mashed
3½ cups all-purpose flour
2 tsp. baking soda
1 tbsp. cinnamon
1½ tsp. ground nutmeg, freshly grated if possible
1½ tsp. salt
2 cups raisins
1 cup walnut pieces
4 tbsp. unsalted butter, softened

Preheat oven to 350 degrees. Beat eggs until light. Gradually mix in sugar. Beat until well blended. Add oil and mix until smooth. Add water and mix until smooth. Add mashed pumpkin and mix until smooth. Sift the flour, soda, cinnamon, nutmeg, and salt together. Add to the liquid ingredients in three parts. Mix well after each addition. Add raisins and nuts. Grease or oil four 1-pound loaf pans. Divide the batter evenly among the pans. Bake for 1 hour, rotating and turning the pans after 30 minutes. During the final 15 minutes of baking time, spread 1 tbsp. butter on the top of each loaf and finish baking. Remove from oven and allow to cool slightly before removing from pans. Makes 4 1-pound loaves.

B. J. Carpenter & Mary Ryan, Cooking Instructors
COOKS OF CROCUS HILL, ST. PAUL

WINTER SQUASH AND PUMPKINS

Spiced Pumpkin Bread

2 eggs, at room temperature
1¼ cups light brown sugar, firmly packed
½ cup vegetable oil
1 cup pumpkin purée
¼ cup brandy (orange juice works well as an alternative)
1¼ cups all-purpose flour
1 tsp. baking soda
½ tsp. baking powder
½ tsp. ground cinnamon
¼ tsp. ground cardamom
¼ tsp. ground cloves
¼ tsp. salt
½ cup crystallized ginger, finely chopped
Whole pieces of crystallized ginger, sliced thinly for garnish

Pumpkin Purée: Peel, seed and cut 1 lb. pumpkin into chunks. Steam or boil pumpkin for 15 to 20 minutes until tender. Drain thoroughly. Purée in food processor or blender until smooth and strain through a fine mesh sieve.

Preheat oven to 350 degrees. In a medium bowl, combine eggs, brown sugar, and vegetable oil and beat for 4 minutes. Beat in pumpkin and brandy or orange juice. In a separate bowl sift together flour, soda, baking powder, cinnamon, cardamom, cloves, and salt. Add dry ingredients to pumpkin mixture and mix well. Stir in chopped, crystallized ginger. Spoon batter into a greased 9x5x3-inch loaf pan. Carefully place sliced ginger on top. Place in preheated oven and bake for 50 minutes or until toothpick comes out clean. Cool pan for 5 minutes. Turn loaf out on wire rack to finish cooling. If desired, top with marscapone or whipped cream. Wrap in aluminum foil to preserve moistness. Makes 1 loaf.

GOLDEN FIG EPICUREAN DELIGHTS

WINTER SQUASH AND PUMPKINS

Pumpkin Pie Squares

Crust:
1 cup all-purpose flour
½ cup quick-cooking oats
½ cup brown sugar
½ cup unsalted butter

Filling:
4 cups pumpkin, cooked and mashed
1 (13-oz.) can evaporated milk
3 eggs, beaten
¾ cup sugar
½ tsp. salt
1 tsp. ground cinnamon
½ tsp. ground ginger
¼ tsp. ground cloves

Topping:
½ cup pecans, chopped
¼ cup brown sugar
2 tbsp. unsalted butter

Preheat oven to 350 degrees. Combine flour, oats, and ½ cup brown sugar in a mixing bowl. Cut in butter until mixture is crumbly. Press into ungreased 9x13-inch baking dish. Bake for 15 minutes. Cool 1 minute before adding filling. For the filling, combine beaten eggs in a mixing bowl with milk, pumpkin, ¾ cup sugar, salt, cinnamon, ginger, and cloves. Pour over pre-baked crust. Bake for 20 minutes.

To make topping: Mix pecans, ¼ cup brown sugar and 2 tbsp. unsalted butter until crumbly. Sprinkle carefully over pumpkin and return to oven for another 15 to 20 minutes. Allow to cool; cut in squares to serve. Makes 24 squares.

Mrs. Charles Harrington

Fresh Pumpkin Pie

The small pie pumpkins are especially meaty and sweet!

1 small pie pumpkin, about 4 lbs., stem removed
1 10-inch pastry for single-crust pie
½ cup white sugar
¼ cup brown sugar
½ tsp. salt
1½ tsp. ground cinnamon
½ tsp. ground ginger
¼ tsp. ground cloves
2 eggs
1¾ cups pumpkin (extra pumpkin can be frozen), cooked and mashed
1 cup milk or evaporated milk

Preheat oven to 350 degrees. To prepare the pumpkin, wash and cut in half. Scoop out seeds and place cut side down in a baking dish with a small amount of water. Cover and bake until tender, about 1 hour. Scrape out meat and mash. If pumpkin is too mushy, cook in a saucepan over low heat, stirring, to evaporate excess water. Line a 10-inch pie plate with pastry. In a small bowl, combine sugars, salt, cinnamon, ginger, and cloves. In a large bowl, beat eggs. Stir in pumpkin and sugar mixture. Gradually stir in milk. Pour filling into pastry-lined pie plate. Increase oven temperature to 425 degrees and bake for 15 minutes. Reduce heat to 350 degrees and bake for 40 to 50 minutes or until a knife inserted near center comes out clean. Cool on a wire rack. Makes 8 servings.

Pumpkin Roll with Cream Cheese Filling

For the roll:
¾ cup sifted all-purpose flour
1 tsp. baking powder
2 tsp. ground cinnamon
½ tsp. ground ginger
½ tsp. ground nutmeg
⅛ tsp. ground allspice
½ tsp. salt
3 eggs, slightly beaten
1 cup sugar
⅔ cup pumpkin, cooked
1 cup walnuts or pecans, chopped

For the filling:
1 cup sifted confectioners' sugar
1 (8-oz.) package cream cheese, softened
6 tbsp. unsalted butter, softened
1 tsp. vanilla

Preheat oven to 375 degrees. Grease a 15x10x1-inch jellyroll pan. Line with wax paper; grease and flour the wax paper.

To make the roll: Sift flour, baking powder, cinnamon, ginger, nutmeg, allspice, and salt. Beat eggs and sugar in a large bowl until thick and fluffy; beat in pumpkin. Stir in sifted dry ingredients all at once. Pour into prepared pan; spread evenly with rubber spatula. Sprinkle with nuts. Bake in preheated oven for 15 minutes or until center springs back when lightly touched with fingertip. Loosen cake around edges with a knife. Invert onto clean damp towel dusted with confectioners' sugar; peel off wax paper. Trim ¼-inch from all sides. Roll up cake and towel together from the short side. Place seam side down on wire rack; cool completely.

To make the filling: Beat together sifted confectioners' sugar, cream cheese, butter, and vanilla until smooth. Unroll cake. Spread with cream cheese filling. Reroll cake and place seam side down on plate. Refrigerate until ready to serve. Makes 10 servings.

Brigitte Bloecher

Pumpkin Bars

This recipe can easily be cut in half for one pan of bars, or make two and freeze one for later.

2 cups all-purpose flour
2 tsp. baking powder
½ tsp. salt
1 tsp. soda
2 cups sugar
2 tsp. ground cinnamon
4 eggs, beaten
2 cups cooked, puréed pumpkin or squash
1 cup corn oil
1 cup chopped nuts

Frosting:
1 (3-oz.) package cream cheese
¾ stick (⅓ cup) butter
1 tsp. cream
1 tsp. vanilla
1¾ cup powdered sugar

Preheat oven to 350 degrees. Grease and flour 2 9x13-inch baking pans. Combine flour with baking powder, salt, soda, sugar, and cinnamon. Add the eggs, pumpkin, and corn oil, blend well, and stir in nuts. Divide batter between 2 greased pans. Bake for 20 to 25 minutes. To make frosting, cream the cream cheese and butter well and blend in cream and vanilla, then the powdered sugar. Frost cooled bars. Makes two 9x13-inch pans.

Mary Broeker

Spicy Pumpkin Pickles

8 cups pumpkin, peeled and cubed
2½ cups white vinegar
2½ cups sugar
4 cinnamon sticks
1½ tsp. canning salt
½ tsp. whole picking spices
1 tsp. ground cloves

Steam pumpkin cubes in steamer basket until just tender. Make sure the water never touches the pumpkin or it will become mushy. In a large stainless steel kettle, combine vinegar, sugar, cinnamon sticks, salt, pickling spices, and cloves. Bring to a boil, reduce heat, and simmer for 10 minutes. Add pumpkin cubes and simmer for 5 more minutes. Pack into hot, sterilized pint jars, leaving ½ inch headroom. Adjust clean hot lids. Process for 5 minutes in boiling-water bath. Remove and cool. Makes 4 pints.

Fruits

Apples

August–November

Yields: 1 lb. fresh equals 2–3 medium apples or 2¼ cups chopped.

Nutrition: 1 raw apple has 80 calories and contains some potassium, fiber, vitamins A and C.

Apples for Minnesota
MINNESOTA EXTENSION SERVICE
Emily Hoover, David Bedford, Shirley Munson and Doug Foulk

VARIETY	AVERAGE HARVEST DATES	FRUIT CHARACTERISTICS	USE
MANTET	August 6–13	Medium to small, round, bright red. Juicy sweet.	Fresh eating, pie, sauce.
ORIOLE	August 7–14	Orange-yellow, striped with red. Very good eating and cooking	Fresh eating, pie, sauce.
DUCHESS (of Oldenburg)	August 9–15	Above medium size, pale yellow skin striped with red. Tart, yellowish flesh, tender, juicy.	Pie, sauce.
STATE FAIR	August 18–24	Medium size, white flesh, round, smooth, bright red, glossy finish. Crisp, juicy, moderately acid.	Fresh eating, pie, sauce.
PAULA RED	August 25–September 1	Medium size, roundish, oblate, red color, heavy bloom. White flesh, firm, crisp, juicy, sub-acid.	Fresh eating, pie, sauce.
BEACON	August 17–24	Medium size, very attractive red. Sweet, aromatic flavor.	Fresh eating, sauce.
CHESNUT CRAB	September 3–11	Large crabapple, flesh crisp, firm. Highly flavored. An attractive blush yellowish orange.	Fresh eating.

APPLES

VARIETY	AVERAGE HARVEST DATES	FRUIT CHARACTERISTICS	USE
WEALTHY	September 8–16	Medium size, striped red. Somewhat tart in flavor.	Fresh eating, pie, sauce.
MINJON	September 9–17	Below medium size, very attractive red. Flesh often pink, somewhat tart.	Fresh eating, pie, sauce.
RED BARON	September 12–20	Medium size, attractive cherry red. Crisp, juicy, and sweet.	Fresh eating, sauce.
LAKELAND	September 17–25	Medium size, solid red color. Pleasant flavor. Slices hold shape when cooked.	Fresh eating, pie, sauce, baking.
SWEET SIXTEEN	September 19–27	Medium to large size, colored by stripes and solid wash of rosy red. High sugar, moderately acid, crisp, and fine texture.	Fresh eating, pie, sauce.
MCINTOSH	September 18–26	Medium size, nearly solid bright red. High quality for eating. Rich flavor, but soft when cooked.	Fresh eating, pie, sauce, baking.
HONEYCRISP	September 20–28	Red with mottled yellow background. Extremely crisp and juicy. Excellent, well-balanced, aromatic flavor.	Fresh eating, sauce, pies.
CORTLAND	September 25–October 3	Medium size, attractive red. White flesh similar to McIntosh. Holds flesh color well in salad. Aromatic flavor.	Fresh eating, pie, sauce, baking, salad.
NORTHWESTERN (Greening)	September 30	Very large size, attractive green or yellow.	Pie, sauce.

REDWELL	September 29–October 7	Large size, attractive red. Pleasant flavor, mildly acid.	Fresh eating, sauce, baking.
SPARTAN	September 29–October 5	Medium size, round, deep red. Flesh is white, firm, crisp and juicy.	Fresh eating, pie, sauce, baking.
PRAIRIE SPY	September 27–October 5	Large size, striped red. Mild flavor. Slices hold shape when cooked.	Fresh eating, pie, sauce, baking.
HARALSON	September 30–October 8	Medium size, striped red. Very popular, tart, crisp apple for eating and cooking.	Fresh eating, pie, sauce, baking, freezing.
HONEYGOLD	October 9–17	Medium to large size, golden to yellow green. Very crisp and juicy with an excellent, sweet flavor.	Fresh eating, pie, sauce, freezing.
RED DELICIOUS	October 11–20	Medium size, striped to solid red. Flavor sweet, low acid. Not recommended for cooking.	Fresh eating, salad.
REGENT	October 9–17	Attractive red-striped apple with well-balanced, excellent flavor. Flesh is crisp and juicy.	Fresh eating, pie, sauce, baking, freezing.
GOLDEN DELICIOUS	October 15	Medium size, attractive yellow. Flavor rich, high quality.	Fresh eating, pie, sauce, baking, salad.
FIRESIDE/CONNELL RED	October 8–18	Large size, attractive red. Flavor rich, high quality, sweet. Connell Red: Blush becoming very deep red. Fireside: Red streaked.	Fresh eating, baking, salad.
KEEPSAKE	October 11–19	Small to medium with irregular angular sides, red with scattered white dots. Light yellow, fine-textured flesh, firm and crisp. Store under humid conditions.	Fresh eating; after storage: pie, sauce.

APPLES

Apple, Parsnip and Carrot Coleslaw

4 carrots, shredded
3 parsnips, shredded
2 apples (Granny Smith or other more tart variety), peeled, cored, and
    chopped finely
¼ head red cabbage, shredded
1 small onion, sliced thinly
¼ cup golden raisins (optional)
2 tbsp. fresh parsley, chopped
½ cup mayonnaise (homemade is preferable)
1 tbsp. herbed vinegar
1 tbsp. sugar
Salt and black pepper to taste

Combine carrots, parsnips, apples, cabbage, onion, raisins, and parsley. Mix
well. In a separate dish, whisk together remaining ingredients. Fold mayonnaise mixture into cabbage mixture. Chill and serve. Makes 6–8 servings.

GOLDEN FIG EPICUREAN DELIGHTS

September Waldorf Salad

2 cups apples, chopped
¼ cup red or green pepper, chopped
1 stalk celery, chopped
½ cup mayonnaise
¼ cup walnuts, chopped

In a bowl, combine all ingredients and mix well. Makes 4–5 servings.

APPLES

Minnesota Brie and Apple Soup

This is one of the signature dishes of Ken Goff, Executive Chef, Dakota Bar & Grill, St. Paul

4 tbsp. unsalted butter
1 cup yellow onion, chopped
¼ cup sliced leeks (white part only)
4 large tart apples, peeled and quartered
2 cups clear chicken broth
1 sprig fresh rosemary, about 1½ inches long (save a little for garnish)
¼ tsp. dried thyme
1 small bay leaf
1½ tsp. kosher salt
3 cups heavy cream (for a lighter soup, light cream or whole milk may be
    used; then use 4 potatoes instead of 3)
3 small potatoes, peeled and sliced ⅛-inch thick
8 oz. brie cheese, cut into pieces
Kosher salt and ground white pepper to taste

In a soup pot with a heavy bottom, melt the butter over high heat until it
bubbles. Add the onion, leek, and apple. Stir to coat them. Reduce heat to
medium and cook until onions are softened, about 8 minutes. Add the chick-
en stock, rosemary, thyme, bay leaf, and salt. Bring to a boil, reduce heat to
medium low and simmer until the vegetables are tender, about 15 minutes.
Remove bay leaf and rosemary. Meanwhile, in a separate heavy-bottomed
pot, combine the cream and potatoes. Cook slowly, stirring frequently, until
the potatoes are tender—takes about 12 minutes. Combine this with the
contents of the first pot. In a blender, purée in batches, adding pieces of
cheese while blending just long enough to incorporate. Add salt and white
pepper to taste. Garnish each bowl with slices of green apple and a sprig of
rosemary. Makes 6 servings.

Spiced Apple Rings

4 small apples, cored
2 cups cider or water (cider is better)
¼ cup brown sugar or sugar
2 sticks cinnamon

Peel apples, if desired. Cut each apple crosswise into ½-inch thick rings. In a medium saucepan, combine cider and sugar, add cinnamon sticks, and bring to a boil. Add apples and bring to boil again. Cover, reduce heat, and simmer for 15 minutes, spooning syrup over apples occasionally, or until apples are tender. Makes 6 servings.

Easy Applesauce

5 cups peeled, cored and sliced apples
½ cup water
¼ tsp. ground cinnamon (optional)
¼–¾ cup sugar or brown sugar (optional)

In a kettle, combine apples, water, and optional cinnamon. Cover and bring to a boil; reduce heat. Simmer for 20 minutes, or until apples are soft. Add more water if needed. Remove from heat. Mash with potato masher or process in blender to smooth consistency. Taste for sweetness and add sugar, if desired.

GROVE ORCHARD
NOVAK ORCHARD

APPLES

Cider Braised Chicken with Apples

½ cup all-purpose flour
1 tsp. salt
¼ tsp. black pepper
6 bone-in chicken breasts (about 3 lbs.)
1½ tbsp. vegetable oil
1 medium onion, sliced
1 large carrot, diced
1 large rib celery, slices
⅔ cup apple cider
½ cup chicken broth
2 tsp. fresh rosemary, chopped (or 1 tsp. dried)
1½ tsp. garlic, minced
3 medium, tart-sweet apples, such as Connell Red

Mix flour, salt and pepper in a paper or plastic bag. Add chicken and shake until coated. Reserve 2 tbsp. of the flour mixture. Heat oil in a large, deep skillet over medium heat. Add chicken, skin side down. Cook 5 to 7 minutes, turning once, until well browned. Remove to a plate. Add onion, carrot, and celery to drippings in skillet. Cook 3 to 4 minutes, stirring several times. Stir in garlic and cook 1 minute longer. Stir in cider, broth, and rosemary. Add chicken, skin side up. Bring to a boil, reduce heat, cover and simmer 25 to 30 minutes, until chicken is opaque in center. Remove to a serving platter and cover to keep warm. While chicken is cooking, halve, core, and peel apples. Cut in thick wedges. Skim off and discard excess fat from liquid in skillet. Add apples and cook over low heat until tender, about 7 minutes. Mix reserved 2 tbsp. flour with 2 tbsp. water or cider. Add to hot liquid in pan and stir until thick. Pour over chicken and serve with rice or wild rice. Makes 6 servings.

HILLTOP PRODUCE FARM

APPLES

Curried Pork in Apple Cider

3 tbsp. butter
4½-inch slices boneless pork loin (1 lb.)
1½ tbsp. curry powder
1 medium onion, chopped
2 cups fresh apple cider
½ tsp. salt or to taste
1 tbsp. corn starch (optional)

Melt butter in a large skillet. Coat both sides of meat slices generously with curry. Brown meat on both sides over medium heat in skillet; remove from skillet. Add onion to skillet and sauté until golden. Deglaze skillet with apple cider and reduce over low heat to about ½ the volume. Return meat to skillet with the cider reduction and simmer for 10 minutes. Add salt. If desired, thicken sauce with corn starch mixed with a little cider or water. Serve with rice or pasta. Makes 4 servings.

HILLTOP PRODUCE FARM

Snickers Apple Dessert

This is an easy dessert that kids will enjoy making

6 regular-size Snickers bars, cut in small, bite-size pieces
6 large apples, sliced (peeling optional)—any good eating apple may
    be used
1 cup cashew or other nuts (optional)
1 (8-oz.) container whipped topping

Mix all of the ingredients in a bowl. Refrigerate and serve cold. Makes 8 servings.

Reprinted from Linda's Favorite Apple Recipes
BOB'S BLUEBIRD ORCHARD

APPLES

Apple Crisp

6 cups apples, peeled, cored, and sliced
½ cup white sugar
1 tsp. ground cinnamon
1½ tbsp. kirsch liqueur (optional)

Topping:
1 cup all-purpose flour
½ cup brown sugar
½ cup butter, slightly softened
⅛ tsp. ground cinnamon (optional)
½ cup chopped walnuts (optional)

Preheat oven to 350 degrees. Grease an 8- or 9-inch square baking dish. Combine apples, sugar, and cinnamon in the greased baking dish; sprinkle with kirsch, if desired.

For the topping: in a mixing bowl, combine flour, brown sugar, and cinnamon, if desired. Work in slightly softened butter with a pastry blender. When mixture begins to form large crumbs, work in walnuts, if desired. Pour the topping evenly over the apples. Bake for 45 minutes or until topping is golden brown and apples are tender. Makes 4–6 servings.

Variations:
Maple Apple Crisp: substitute ¼ cup maple syrup for the white sugar.
Pumpkin Apple Crisp: substitute 3 cups uncooked, cubed pumpkin for half of the apples.

Rolling Hills Orchard and Grove Orchard eliminated cinnamon and substituted 2 tbsp. orange juice and 1½ tsp. grated orange rind, plus ½ cup flaked coconut.

Nan Gianoli
Greg Novak
Sue Christopher

APPLES

Austrian Apple Pancake

3 tbsp. butter
½ cup sugar
1 tsp. cinnamon
3 apples, peeled, cored, and sliced ¼-inch thick
1 tsp. vanilla
3 tbsp. all-purpose flour
3 eggs, separated
3 tbsp. milk

Preheat oven to 400 degrees. Melt butter in frying pan. Stir in sugar and cinnamon, then add apple slices and cook over low heat for 3 minutes until slices are well coated. Beat vanilla, flour, egg yolks, and milk together. In a separate bowl, beat egg whites until stiff, then gently fold egg yolk mixture in. Pour apple slices into 8½-inch buttered round cake pan. Pour batter over the apple slices and spread with a rubber spatula. Bake for 20 minutes, until the pancake is brown and puffy. Loosen sides. Place plate over cake pan and invert. Remove pan. Cut pancake into wedges and serve with maple syrup, ice cream or yogurt. Makes 4 servings.

MAPLE LEAF ORCHARD

Baked Apples with Goat Cheese

The marriage of savory and sweet ingredients in a dessert creates an intriguing combination. Use your favorite baking apples, tart or mellow, for this dish.

6 apples
10 oz. (1¼ cup) chevre (goat cheese)
½ cup firmly packed brown sugar
½ cup golden raisins or chopped dates
¼ cup slivered blanched almonds, toasted

APPLES

Preheat oven to 375 degrees. Using a small paring knife, remove the core from each apple to within about ½-inch of the bottom. Be careful not to cut all the way through to the bottom. Using a small spoon, scoop out a cavity in the center of the apple about 1½ inches in diameter and 2 inches deep. Set aside. In a small bowl, combine goat cheese and brown sugar and stir until smooth. Add raisins or dates and stir to combine. Spoon the mixture into the hollowed-out apples, dividing it evenly and mounding it so that it barely rises above the tops. Sprinkle the almonds evenly over the filling. Select a baking dish large enough to hold the apples snugly and line it with aluminum foil. Place the apples in the dish. Bake, uncovered, until the filling and almonds brown and the apples are very soft, as if about to collapse, about 45 minutes. Serve hot. Makes 6 servings.

DANCING WINDS FARM

Honey Baked Apples
Scrumptious!

6 large baking apples (Northern Spy if available)
6 tbsp. butter, softened
6 tbsp. honey (mild flavor)
1 tsp. ground cinnamon
Grated rind of lemon
1 cup sweet Marsala

Preheat oven to 375 degrees. Wash apples and dry. Core. In a small bowl, mix butter, honey, cinnamon, and lemon rind. Fill apple cavities with mixture. Pour Marsala in bottom of a 7 x11-inch baking pan. Place apples in pan. Drizzle honey on top of each. Bake for 30 minutes or until tender. Do not overcook. Serve with light cream. May be served hot or cold. Makes 6 servings.

BERNIE BRAND APIARY

APPLES

Apple Rosemary Bread Pudding

2 cups stale bread, crust removed and cubed
1 cup heavy cream
½ cup milk, whole or 2%
3 tart cooking apples, peeled and thinly sliced
2 tbsp. dried currants or raisins (optional)
1 tsp. lemon zest
1 tsp. orange zest
1 tbsp. corn meal
1 egg
¼ cup sugar
1 tsp. vanilla
1 tsp. ground nutmeg
½ tsp. salt

Topping:
3 tbsp. butter
1 tbsp. sugar
1 tsp. fresh rosemary, chopped

Combine milk, sugar, cream, and bread, soak for one hour. Preheat oven to 350 degrees. Grease 9-inch round baking dish. Combine apples, currants, zest, corn meal, nutmeg, and salt. Then add fruit mixture to soaked bread mixture. Beat together egg and vanilla and add to fruit mixture. Pour mixture into greased baking dish. Top with 3 tbsp. butter dots, sugar, and rosemary. Bake in oven until light golden brown and fruit is tender. Serve warm or at room temperature. Makes 6–8 servings.

Leah Henderson, Pastry Chef
D'AMICO CUCINA

Dutch Apple Cobbler

This is my favorite apple dessert!

6 apples (Fireside or Connell Red), cored, peeled, and thinly sliced

Batter:
1 cup all-purpose flour
2 tsp. baking powder
1 tbsp. butter
¼ cup sugar
Water to make a stiff dough

Syrup Topping:
1 cup sugar
1 tbsp. all-purpose flour
1½ tsp. ground cinnamon
1 cup boiling water

Preheat oven to 350 degrees. Grease a round 9-inch baking dish or soufflé dish. Put sliced apples in baking dish. Set aside. To make the batter, combine flour, baking powder, and sugar. Cut in the butter until mixture is fine crumbs. Add water, a bit at a time, stirring until a stiff dough is obtained. Spoon batter over apples and spread to cover. To make the topping, mix sugar, flour, and cinnamon in a bowl. Add boiling water, stirring until sugar is dissolved and mixture is slightly thickened. Pour syrup over batter. Bake for 30 minutes or until batter is golden brown. Serve hot with vanilla ice cream. Makes 6 servings.

Hazel Dial

APPLES

Apple Bread

1 cup sugar
½ cup butter or margarine
2 eggs, beaten
1 tbsp. buttermilk or sour milk
½ tsp. vanilla
2 cups all-purpose flour
1 tsp. soda
1 tsp. baking powder
¼ tsp. ground nutmeg
2 cups raw apples, peeled and chopped
½ cup walnuts, chopped

Preheat oven to 350 degrees. Grease and flour one bread pan. Cream together butter or margarine and sugar in a mixing bowl. Add eggs and beat well. Add buttermilk or sour milk and mix well. Add dry ingredients; mix just until blended. Add apples and walnuts and blend well. Pour into bread pan. Bake for one hour or until crust springs back when pressed with finger. Makes 1 large loaf.

Bette Herrick

Minnesota Apple Oatmeal Cookies

2½ cups all-purpose flour
1 cup quick oats (not instant)
½ tsp. salt
1 tsp. ground cinnamon
¼ tsp. ground cloves
1 cup dark brown sugar, packed
1½ sticks butter, softened
1 egg, slightly beaten
½ cup unsweetened applesauce
½ cup honey
1 cup fresh apple, peeled, and finely chopped
1 cup raisins (optional)
½ cup nuts, chopped

APPLES

Preheat oven to 300 degrees. In a medium bowl, combine flour, oats, salt, cinnamon, and cloves and set aside. In a separate bowl, cream sugar and butter together. Add egg, applesauce, and honey. Mix until smooth. Add flour mixture and remaining ingredients and mix until just combined. Dough will be soft. Drop by rounded tablespoonfuls onto ungreased baking sheet 1½ inches apart. Bake for 18 to 22 minutes or until edges are golden. Makes about 4 dozen cookies.

Ev's Fresh Apple Pie

Pastry for a 10-inch double-crust pie
7–8 cups apples, peeled, cored, and sliced
¾ cup sugar
1½ tbsp. all-purpose flour
½–1 tsp. ground cinnamon
2 tbsp. butter (optional)
Granulated sugar (optional)

Preheat oven to 375 degrees. Line a 10-inch pie plate with pastry for bottom crust. In a medium bowl, combine sugar, flour, and cinnamon. Add apples and toss. Pour filling in bottom crust of pie. Dot with butter, if desired. Place on top crust. Seal and flute edges and cut slits in top. Sprinkle top with sugar, if desired. Bake for 45 to 55 minutes, or until bubbly.

Variations:
Honey Apple Pie: substitute ¾ cup honey for sugar
Maple Apple Pie: substitute ¾ cup maple syrup mixed with 3 tbsp. cornstarch for sugar

GROVE ORCHARD

BERNIE BRAND APIARY

MAPLE LEAF ORCHARD

APPLES

Cinnamon-Apple Bars with Cream Cheese Frosting

This delicious recipe includes two possible toppings: a delicious cream cheese frosting, or, serve as a warm dessert by topping unfrosted squares with warm vanilla sauce.

2 large eggs, at room temperature
1 cup canola, or other light vegetable oil
2 cups granulated sugar, or 1⅓ cups granulated and ⅔ cup brown sugars
1 tsp. vanilla
2 cups all-purpose flour
1 tsp. baking soda
1 tsp. ground cinnamon
¼ tsp. salt
3 cups firm sweet apples, peeled and coarsely chopped
1 cup walnuts, coarsely chopped

Preheat oven to 350 degrees. Crack eggs into a mixing bowl large enough to hold all the ingredients, and beat until the yolks and whites are mixed. Wisk in oil, blending until smooth. Add sugars, and beat until light. Blend vanilla in, and set aside. Sift flour, soda, cinnamon, and salt together. Stir into the egg-sugar mixture, blending until smooth. Place nuts on a sided sheet pan, and roast in the preheated oven on the center rack for 5 minutes. Remove the nuts from oven and roughly chop. Peel, core, and chop apples. Mix the apples and walnuts into the batter. Lightly grease or oil a 9 x13-inch cake or sheet pan. Pour the batter into the pan and gently spread over the pan surface so it is even and level. Bake on the center rack for 40 to 45 minutes, or until the apples are tender and an inserted toothpick or cake tester comes out clean. Remove the pan from the oven, and place on a rack to cool. When the bars have completely cooled, frost with cream cheese frosting, cut and serve.

Quick Cream Cheese Frosting
2 (3-oz.) pkgs. of cream cheese at room temperature (don't use lowfat or
    Neufchatel-type cream cheeses, they won't work well)
3 tbsp. unsalted butter, at room temperature
1½ cups powdered sugar, sifted
1–2 tsp. whole milk or half and half

APPLES

Place the 2 packages or softened cream cheese in a medium-sized bowl. Beat with an electric hand mixer until smooth. Add softened butter, mixing until smooth. Add sifted powdered sugar in three parts, thoroughly mixing after each addition. Beat until smooth and fluffy, adding some or all of the milk or cream if needed. Evenly spread on the cooled bars. *Note:* the frosting can be made a day ahead and refrigerated. Bring to room temperature and beat to a spreading consistency before using. Makes 24–30 bars.

Vanilla Sauce:
½ cup unsalted butter
½ cup light cream (half and half)
1 cup granulated sugar
1½ tsp. real vanilla

Place all ingredients in the top of a double boiler and stir to blend. Cook over simmering water, stirring occasionally, until thick. Keep warm, and pour over individual servings of warm apple cake or bars.

B. J. Carpenter & Mary Ryan, Cooking Instructors
COOKS OF CROCUS HILL, ST. PAUL

Spiced Whole Crabapples

2½ lbs. crabapples
1½ tbsp. whole cloves
1½ tbsp. whole allspice
2 cinnamon sticks, broken
6 cups sugar
3 cups white vinegar
3 cups water

Wash crabapples. Do not peel. Run a large needle (the thicker the better) through each apple to prevent bursting. Tie cloves, allspice, and broken cinnamon sticks in a cheesecloth bag. Combine remaining ingredients in a large pot and add spice bag. Bring to a boil; boil 5 minutes. Add apples, reduce heat, and simmer until apples are tender. Remove spice bag. Pack apples into sterilized hot pint jars. Pour boiling syrup over apples, leaving ½-inch headroom. Adjust clean hot lids. Process for 15 minutes in boiling-water bath. Remove and cool. Makes 6 pints.

Kimberly Huggins

APPLES

277

Cinnamon Apple Coffee Cake

Batter:
1½ cups all-purpose flour
1 tsp. ground cinnamon
1 tsp. soda
½ tsp. salt
1 cup brown sugar
½ cup unsalted butter or margarine
1 egg, beaten
2 cups apples (any kind), peeled and finely chopped

Topping:
½ cup brown sugar
2 tbsp. unsalted butter or margarine
½ cup chopped walnuts or pecans
¼ cup flaked coconut

Preheat oven to 350 degrees. Grease an 8-inch square baking dish. Mix flour, cinnamon, soda, and salt in a bowl. In a large mixing bowl, cream butter or margarine and brown sugar; add beaten egg. Add flour mixture to creamed mixture. Blend in chopped apples. Spread in baking dish.

To make topping: Blend topping ingredients until crumbly. Sprinkle over cake batter and bake for 35 to 45 minutes, until toothpick inserted comes out clean. Makes 12 large servings.

Reprinted from Linda's Favorite Apple Recipes
BOB'S BLUEBIRD ORCHARD

APPLES

Snowy Glazed Apple Squares

3¾ cups sifted all-purpose flour
½ tsp. salt
1½ cups shortening (may use ½ butter and ½ shortening)
3 eggs, yolk and whites separated
Milk (may use whole or skim)
1½ cups corn flakes, crushed
1 cup sugar
1½ tsp. ground cinnamon
10 medium-sized tart apples (McIntosh or Haralson), peeled and sliced
    (about 6 cups)

Glaze:
1¼ cups sifted powdered sugar
3 tbsp. milk (whole or skim)
½ tsp. vanilla

For the dough, combine flour and salt in a bowl. Cut in shortening until mixture is uniform pea-sized crumbles. In a measuring cup, beat egg yolks with enough milk to make 1 cup. Add slowly to flour mixture, tossing with a fork, until dough forms a ball. Refrigerate while preparing apples. Preheat oven to 350 degrees. In a large bowl, combine sugar and cinnamon. Add sliced apples and stir to coat. Divide dough almost in half. Roll out larger portion on a floured board to fit a 10x15-inch jelly roll pan. Dough should cover bottom and sides of pan. Sprinkle dough evenly with crushed cornflakes. Spread apple mixture over corn flakes. Roll out remaining dough. Place on top; seal edges. Beat egg whites until foamy. Spread on top of crust. Bake for 1 hour or until golden brown. Cool slightly. To make the glaze, combine powdered sugar, milk, and vanilla. Drizzle on top of baked dessert. Makes 35 squares.

Esther Voelker

APPLES

Cinnamon Basil Apple Jelly

This jelly recipe is versatile—you can use any apple-compatible herb, such as mint or lemon balm

5 lbs. crabapples or other tart-sweet apple
5 cups water
2 cups chopped cinnamon basil,* packed, tied into a piece of cheesecloth
   (herb bag)
1 box Sure Jell fruit pectin
9 cups sugar

*You may use lemon basil, licorice basil, lemon balm, any of the mints or even rosemary (four 3-inch sprigs of rosemary for this amount of juice).

To make the juice: Wash apples, remove stems and blossom ends, cut into small pieces (need not peel or core) and put into large saucepan along with water. Bring to a boil and simmer, covered, 10 minutes. Crush the cooked apples and simmer 5 minutes longer. Place a sieve or colander with a triple thickness of cheesecloth over a large bowl or container. Pour apples into the cheesecloth and let drain overnight.

Next day, sterilize 10 ½-pint jars and lids. Measure 7 cups of juice into large heavy-bottomed saucepan. Add herb bag and pectin, plus ½ tsp. butter or margarine. Bring to a full boil, stirring constantly. Add sugar; bring to a full rolling boil and boil 1 minute, stirring constantly. Remove from heat, skim foam, and remove cheesecloth bag. Pour immediately into sterilized ½-pint jars, filling to ⅛-inch from top. Wipe drips from rims and threads of jars, cover with sterile lids and screw on bands tightly. Invert jars for 5 minutes, then turn upright. Cool and allow to gel completely before handling. Label jars with contents, date and store in a cool, dark place. Makes 10 ½-pint jars.

HILLTOP PRODUCE FARM

APPLES

Apple Ketchup

This condiment is excellent with roast pork and turkey

Fresh apples, any amount (see method), any variety

Wash, core, and cut apples in quarters. Steam with enough water to keep from scorching until soft, about 10 minutes. Run through a sieve or food mill. For each quart (4 cups) of pulp add the following:

1 cup sugar
1 tsp. black pepper
1 tsp. ground cloves
1 tsp. dry mustard
2 tsp. ground cinnamon
1 tbsp. salt
2 cups white vinegar

Simmer in a heavy saucepan until thick, about 2 to 3 hours or more, stirring frequently. Pour into sterile pint jars. Adjust clean hot lids. Process in boiling-water bath 10 minutes. Remove and cool.

HILLTOP PRODUCE FARM

From Scratch Apple Butter

15 cups apples, peeled, cored, and sliced
1 cup apple cider
2½–3 cups white or brown sugar
2 tsp. ground cinnamon
½ tsp. ground cloves
¼ tsp. ground nutmeg

In a large heavy-bottomed enameled kettle, cook apples and cider over medium heat until soft, stir to prevent sticking. Remove from heat and cool. Put through a food mill or sieve. Add ¼ cup sugar for every 1 cup pulp. Return to kettle, add spices, and bring to a boil. Cook over medium heat, stirring constantly, until desired thickness. Fill sterilized pint jars to ½-inch from top. Adjust clean hot lids. Process for 5 minutes in a boiling-water bath. Remove and cool. Makes 4 pints.

GROVE ORCHARD
NOVAK ORCHARD

APPLES

Apple-Bacon-Cheddar Bake

½ lb. bacon, fried crisp, drained and crumbled
1½ cups apples, peeled and sliced
1 tbsp. sugar
1 cup sharp cheddar cheese, shredded
1 cup all-purpose flour
1½ tsp. baking powder
¼ tsp. salt
1 cup milk, whole or skim
3 eggs

Preheat oven to 375 degrees. Grease a 9x9-inch pan. Mix flour, baking powder, and salt. In a separate bowl, mix sliced apples and sugar. Place slices by rows in greased pan. Cover apples with cheese; sprinkle with bacon. Beat remaining ingredients together. Using a ladle, pour the egg mixture evenly over the apples, cheese, and bacon. Bake for 25 to 35 minutes, until lightly browned.

Original recipe from The Griffin Inn, reprinted from *Wake Up & Smell the Coffee*, with kind permission of Laura Zahn, Down to Earth Publications, St. Paul, Minn.

APPLES

Blueberries

July–August

PREPARING BLUEBERRIES

Store in refrigerator until ready to use. Wash and spread berries out on a paper towel to absorb excess moisture.

Yield: 1 lb. fresh equals 3 cups blueberries.

Nutrition: 1 cup raw has 90 calories and contains potassium, some calcium, and vitamins A and C.

Blueberry Vinaigrette Salad

½ cup blueberry vinegar
¾ cup extra virgin olive oil
¾ pint fresh blueberries
½ cup fresh basil leaves
1 tbsp. water
1 tbsp. coarse ground mustard
Salt and black pepper to taste
4 cups fresh lettuce
1 cup fresh blueberries

Put blueberry vinegar in a blender and turn blender on slow speed. Slowly add ½ of the olive oil and blend until mixture begins to thicken. Add blueberries and basil leaves to mixture and blend for 2 minutes. Add remaining olive oil, water, mustard, and a pinch each of salt and pepper. In large bowl, toss vinaigrette with 4 cups fresh greens. Place 1 cup greens with vinaigrette on each plate. Place ¼ cup fresh berries on greens in the center of each plate. Makes 4 servings.

GOLDEN FIG EPICUREAN DELIGHTS

Blueberry Sauce

1½ cups fresh blueberries
¼ cup sugar
2 tsp. lemon juice

In 4-cup microwave-safe dish, combine blueberries, sugar, and lemon juice. Microwave on high for 4 to 6 minutes, or until mixture boils, stirring twice during cooking period. Serve warm over pancakes, yogurt, ice cream or waffles. Makes 1 cup.

BLUEBERRIES

Blueberry Curd

½ pint blueberries
¼ cup unsalted butter, diced
1¼ cups superfine sugar
3 large eggs, beaten

Combine blueberries with 1 tbsp. water in covered saucepan. Cook gently 10 minutes until very soft. Press through a sieve or use food mill. Place in double boiler, stir in butter and sugar, and heat gently over simmering water. Do not allow water to boil or bottom of pan to sit in the water. Heat, stirring, until sugar dissolves and butter melts. Strain eggs through fine sieve and continue to stir over simmering water until the curd thickens enough to coat back of spoon, about 30 to 40 minutes. Stir occasionally at first, then constantly the last 15 to 20 minutes so that the curd cooks evenly. *Water must not boil.* Pour curd into sterilized jars, process in boiling-water bath for 10 minutes. Store in a cool, dark place. Refrigerate after opening. This has a six month shelf life. Makes 3¼-pints.

Jim Trenter

Blueberry Muffins

These placed second at the Ramsey County Fair!

1½ cups all-purpose flour
3 tsp. baking powder
½ tsp. salt
½ cup sugar
1 egg, beaten
¼ cup vegetable oil
½ cup lowfat milk
1 cup fresh blueberries

Preheat oven to 400 degrees. In a medium bowl, whisk together flour, baking powder, salt, and sugar. In a large bowl, beat together egg, oil, and milk until well mixed. Add dry ingredients. Carefully fold in blueberries. Lightly grease muffin cups or line with paper bake cups; fill ½ full. Bake 20 minutes or until golden. Makes 12 prize-winning muffins.

BLUEBERRIES

Blueberry Cream Pie

Sour cream and a streusel topping make this pie different from the classic blueberry pie

1 cup dairy sour cream
5 tbsp. all-purpose flour
¾ cup sugar
1 tsp. vanilla
¼ tsp. salt
1 egg, beaten
2½ cups blueberries
1 unbaked pie shell

Topping:
3 tbsp. all-purpose flour
1½ tbsp. butter
3 tbsp. chopped walnuts

Preheat oven to 400 degrees. Combine sour cream, 2 tbsp. flour, sugar, vanilla, salt, and egg. Beat for 5 minutes, or until smooth and thoroughly combined. Fold in blueberries. Pour filling into pie shell. Bake in 400 degree oven for 25 minutes. Combine 3 tbsp. flour, 1½ tbsp. butter and walnuts. Sprinkle over pie. Return to oven. Bake for 10 minutes. Makes 9-inch pie.

Gwen Johnson

Cantaloupe

WHEN AVAILABLE

August–October

SOME VARIETIES

Muskmelon is synonymous with cantaloupe. Orange, Crenshaw, French Charantais, and green and orange honeydew

PREPARING CANTALOUPE

Wash, cut, scoop out seeds, and slice.

Yield: 1 lb. fresh equals 2¼ cups diced melon.

Nutrition: ½ medium melon has 80 calories and contains large amounts of potassium and vitamins A and C.

Melon and Turkey Salad

2 cups turkey, cooked and cubed
2 cups cantaloupe, peeled, seeded, and cubed
1 cup sliced celery
¼ cup sliced green onions
½ cup toasted cashew nuts (toast 10 minutes in a 350 degree oven)
1 bunch red leaf lettuce

Creamy Yogurt Dressing:
¼ cup plain yogurt
3 tbsp. mayonnaise
3 tbsp. fresh lemon or lime juice
¼ tsp. ground coriander
½ tsp. salt
White pepper to taste

Combine turkey, melon, celery, onions, and cashew nuts in a bowl. Combine yogurt dressing ingredients and toss with salad ingredients. Chill for 1 hour. Serve on a bed of red leaf lettuce. Makes 4–6 servings.

HILLTOP PRODUCE FARM

CANTALOUPE

Whitney Grille's Minted Cantaloupe Soup

6 ripe medium cantaloupe
½ shot Grand Marnier

Sauce Anglaise:
1 egg yolk
1 tbsp. sugar
½ pint heavy cream
Vanilla to taste
2 tbsp. chopped mint plus mint leaves for garnish
Cantaloupe balls for garnish

Seed cantaloupe, purée with Grand Marnier.

Sauce Anglaise: In a saucepan, mix egg yolk and sugar, then add cream. Cook over low heat, stirring constantly. Add vanilla to taste. Cool the sauce. Combine sauce Anglaise with cantaloupe and chopped mint. Serve well chilled. Garnish with cantaloupe balls and mint leaves. Makes 8 servings.

Fruit Kabobs

Any seasonal fruit can be used.

Glaze:
1 tbsp. cornstarch
⅛ tsp. ground cinnamon
3 tbsp. honey
½ cup apple cider or orange juice
2 cups muskmelon, cubed
2 apples, peeled and cut in 1-inch cubes
Wooden skewers (6 inch)

In a saucepan, mix cornstarch, cinnamon, honey, and cold cider. Bring to a boil, stirring constantly, reduce heat, and stir until thick and bubbly. Remove from heat and set aside. Alternate fruit on skewers, brush with glaze, and refrigerate. Brush with glaze again before serving. Makes 6 servings.

CANTALOUPE

Muskmelon Salsa

4 cups melon, cut into 1-inch cubes
1 cup cucumber, cut into ½-inch cubes
3 scallions, chopped fine
2 jalapeño peppers, minced
¼ cup chopped fresh cilantro or mint
3 tbsp. fresh lime juice
Brown sugar and salt to taste

In a large bowl, toss ingredients and serve. Makes 6–8 servings.

Fresh Cantaloupe Relish

Serve hot or cold with spicy ethnic dishes or meat

⅓ cup vegetable oil
2 medium onions, chopped
1 tsp. ground coriander
½ tsp. cumin
½ tsp. ground ginger
½ tsp. ground mace
⅛ tsp. black pepper
4 cups cantaloupe, cubed

In a saucepan, heat oil. Sauté onion until soft. Add spices and stir for 1 minute. Stir in cantaloupe. Cover and cook over low for 15 minutes or until tender. Makes 8–10 servings.

Cantaloupe Jam

2 cups cantaloupe, cubed
1 cup water
1 envelope unflavored gelatin
1 tsp. lemon juice
⅓ cup honey

In a small bowl, dissolve gelatin in 1 cup cold water. Set aside. Place melon cubes in a blender. Cover and process until smooth. Pour melon purée into a medium saucepan. Add lemon juice and honey. Bring to a boil, stirring constantly. Stir in dissolved gelatin and boil for 2 minutes. Ladle into hot sterilized jars. Adjust clean hot lids. Cool. Store in refrigerator. Keeps about 2 weeks. Makes 2–3 pints.

Muskmelon Sundae

This one's from Grandma. It doesn't get any better on a hot summer evening!

1 ripe muskmelon
2 big scoops of ice cream

Slice muskmelon in half and scoop out seeds. Fill each half with a scoop of ice cream. Makes 2 servings.

Duane Lengsfeld

CANTALOUPE

Raspberries

WHEN AVAILABLE
July–frost

SOME VARIETIES
Red, gold, blackberries, summer bearing, and fall bearing.

PREPARING RASPBERRIES
Do not wash until ready to use. Store in refrigerator. Wash and spread out on a paper towel to absorb excess moisture.

Yield: 1 lb. fresh equals 2 cups raspberries.

Nutrition: 1 cup raw has 70 calories and contains calcium, potassium and vitamins A and C.

Spinach Raspberry Salad

This green and red salad is nice for the holidays

1 lb. fresh spinach, stems removed, washed, and drained dry
1 cup fresh raspberries, rinsed and drained dry on paper towels
2–3 green onions, sliced
¾ cup chopped macadamia nuts, toasted (10 minutes in a 350 degree oven)

Dressing:
¼ cup safflower oil
2 tbsp. raspberry vinegar
2 tbsp. seedless raspberry jam or 2 tbsp. sugar
¼ tsp. salt
Dash of black pepper
3 drops Tabasco sauce

Combine spinach, raspberries, and onion in a salad bowl. In a small bowl, whisk dressing ingredients. Pour over spinach. Sprinkle with macadamia nuts and serve. Makes 6–8 servings.

Patty Brand

Easy Raspberry Sauce

1 pint raspberries
Sugar or honey

Process raspberries in a blender until smooth. Push through a strainer, using the back of a spoon, to remove seeds, into a bowl. Sweeten to taste with sugar or honey. Pour over strawberries, melon, yogurt, ice cream, toast, or mix with applesauce. Makes 4 servings.

RASPBERRIES

293

Custard Cream and Raspberry Dessert

Cookies, custard, and raspberries can be prepared ahead of time and assembled before serving.

Sugar Cookies:
2½ cups all-purpose flour
1 tsp. baking powder
¼ tsp. salt
½ cup butter, softened
⅔ cup sugar
1 egg
1 tsp. vanilla
1 tbsp. lowfat milk

Custard:
2 egg yolks
8 tbsp. sugar
⅓ cup half-and-half
1 tsp. vanilla

Topping:
1 quart fresh raspberries
1 cup heavy cream

Preheat oven to 350 degrees.

To make cookies: Sift together flour, baking powder, and salt. Set aside. In another bowl, cream butter and ⅔ cup sugar. Beat in 1 egg, 1 tsp. vanilla and milk until mixture is light and smooth. Add flour mixture. Stir until well mixed. Shape dough into ball. Wrap in plastic wrap. Refrigerate for 1 hour.

To bake cookies: When ready to bake, divide dough in half. Roll each half on a lightly-floured surface to ¼-inch thickness. Cut with 4-inch cookie cutter into about 6 cookies from each portion of dough. If you don't have a cookie cutter, make a circle from cardboard or small saucer to use as pattern. Place cookies on greased cookie sheet. Bake for 15 to 18 minutes. Don't let brown. Cool.

RASPBERRIES

To make custard: Meanwhile, beat 2 egg yolks in small saucepan. Stir in 3 tbsp. sugar and half-and-half. Cook over low heat until mixture thickens, stirring constantly. Do not boil. Stir in 1 tsp. vanilla. Cool and refrigerate.

To serve: Sprinkle 5 tbsp. sugar over raspberries. Let stand a few minutes. Beat whipping cream. Fold into custard. Place cookie on individual plate. Top with sugared berries. Spoon custard over berries. Garnish with whole berries. Makes 12 servings.

Sally Johnson

Raspberry Shortcake Squares

Nice for individual servings

1 pint raspberries
2–3 tbsp. sugar
2 cups all-purpose flour
¼ cup sugar
2 tsp. baking powder
½ cup margarine
1 egg, beaten
⅔ cup lowfat milk

Preheat oven to 450 degrees. Put raspberries in a bowl and mix with sugar. Set aside. In a separate bowl, stir together flour, ¼ cup sugar, and baking powder. Cut in margarine until mixture resembles pea-sized crumbs. In a separate small bowl, mix together milk and egg and add to flour mixture. Stir until just moistened. Spread batter into a greased 8x8-inch square baking pan. Bake for 15 to 18 minutes or until a toothpick comes out clean. Cut out individual squares as needed. Split each square and top with sweetened raspberries.

Fresh Raspberry Pie

1 9-inch baked pastry shell
5 cups raspberries
⅔ cup water
⅔ cup sugar
2 tbsp. cornstarch

Place 4 cups of the raspberries in pastry shell. Put in refrigerator. In a blender, combine remaining 1 cup of the raspberries and water. Cover and process until smooth. In a medium saucepan, combine sugar and cornstarch. Stir in blended berry mixture. Bring to a boil. Cook and stir over medium heat until mixture becomes thickened and bubbly. Cook 1 minute more. Remove from heat and cool for 10 minutes. Carefully spoon raspberry glaze over fruit in pie shell. Chill for 1 hour and serve. Makes 8 servings.

Lydia Waterson

Raspberry Syrup

4 cups raspberries
2 tbsp. water
1 cup sugar
1 cup water

In a medium saucepan, heat raspberries and 2 tbsp. water just to soften berries. Do not cook too long. Force berries through a strainer or jelly bag into medium saucepan. Add sugar and water to berry pulp and reheat. Cook and stir over medium heat until desired thickness is reached. Makes about 2 cups.

JoAn Kaiser

RASPBERRIES

Rhubarb

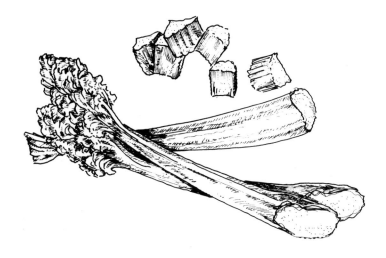

PREPARING RHUBARB

Wash, trim off leaf end, and slice into ¼-inch pieces

Yields: 1 lb. fresh rhubarb equals 4 cups sliced or 2 cups cooked and puréed.

Nutrition: 1 cup raw has 60 calories; contains calcium, potassium and some vitimins C and A.

Easy Rhubarb Sauce

4 cups rhubarb, sliced
½ cup water
½ cup sugar, honey or maple syrup
½ tsp. ground cinnamon (optional)

In a medium saucepan, combine all ingredients and bring to a boil. Reduce heat, cover, and simmer over medium until rhubarb is tender, about 15 minutes. Serve over ice cream.

Rhubarb Dressing for Salad Greens

Especially good with spinach or mixed baby greens

2 cups fresh rhubarb, diced
½ cup sugar
¼ cup white or raspberry vinegar
¾ cup vegetable oil
3 tbsp. green onion, minced
1½ tsp. Worcestershire sauce
½ tsp. salt

In a saucepan, combine rhubarb, sugar, and vinegar; cook over medium heat until the rhubarb is tender, about 6 minutes. Drain through a sieve, squeezing with a spoon to harvest all of the juice. Discard pulp. Pour juice into a jar with a tight-fitting lid; add oil, onion, Worcestershire sauce, and salt. Shake well. Refrigerate. Just before serving add to salad greens and toss to coat. Makes 6–8 servings.

Wendy Marcott

Rhubarb Chutney

2 lbs. rhubarb, chopped finely
1 lb. dates, pitted and chopped
2½ cups brown sugar, packed
1½ tsp. ground cinnamon
1½ tsp. ground cloves
1 cup cider vinegar

In a heavy-bottomed saucepan, combine all ingredients except vinegar. Bring to a boil; reduce heat. Cook slowly for 1 hour. Stir to avoid scorching. Add vinegar and simmer 10 minutes.

Adapted from Helen Nearing's Our Sunheated Greenhouse

Rhubarb Muffins

1¼ cups brown sugar
2½ cups all-purpose flour, sifted
½ tsp. salt
1 tsp. baking powder
1 tsp. baking soda
½ cup vegetable oil
1 egg
1 cup buttermilk
2 tsp. vanilla
1½ cups rhubarb, chopped
½ cup nuts, chopped

Topping:
½ cup sugar
1 tsp. ground cinnamon
1 tsp. melted butter

Preheat oven to 400 degrees. In mixing bowl, combine sugar with sifted flour, salt, baking powder, and soda. In another bowl, combine oil, egg, buttermilk, and vanilla. Add to dry ingredients and mix until just moistened. Gently stir in rhubarb and nuts. Fill greased muffin pans ¾ full. Poke hole in center of each muffin. Combine topping ingredients. Spoon a dab of filling into hole in each muffin. Bake for 20 to 25 minutes. Makes 12 muffins.

RHUBARB

Rhubarb Crisp

3 cups rhubarb, diced

Topping:
½ cup all-purpose flour
¾ cup rolled oats
1 tsp. baking soda
½ cup brown sugar
5 tbsp. butter

Egg Mixture:
2 eggs, beaten
1½ cups sugar
2 tbsp. all-purpose flour
¼ tsp. salt
¼ tsp. ground nutmeg

Preheat oven to 350 degrees. Spread diced rhubarb in the bottom of a greased 9x13-inch cake dish. In a medium bowl, combine ½ cup flour, oats, soda, brown sugar, butter. Mix to make crumbs. Set aside. In a separate mixing bowl, combine beaten eggs, sugar, 2 tbsp. flour, salt, and nutmeg. Beat until well mixed. Pour over rhubarb. Sprinkle with topping. Bake for 30 minutes or until lightly browned. Makes 10 servings.

Mary Peterson

RHUBARB

Rhubarb Torte Squares

Crust:
1 cup all-purpose flour
½ cup butter
5 tbsp. powdered sugar

Filling:
3 eggs, beaten
1½ cups sugar
¼ cup all-purpose flour
¾ tsp. baking powder
½ tsp. salt
1 tsp. vanilla
3 cups rhubarb, sliced thinly

Topping:
¾ cup walnuts, chopped
Powdered sugar for sprinkling

Preheat oven to 350 degrees. Grease a 9x13-inch baking dish. Mix flour and powdered sugar in a mixing bowl. Cut in butter until mixture resembles coarse crumbs. Pat into baking dish. Bake for 15 minutes. Mix flour, sugar, baking powder, and salt in a mixing bowl. Add eggs, mixing well. Add rhubarb and stir to coat. Pour over baked crust. Top with chopped walnuts. Bake for 30 to 40 additional minutes. When cool, sprinkle with a small amount of powdered sugar. Makes 24 squares.

Alice Pieper

RHUBARB

Rhubarb Dessert

Crust:
1¼ cups all-purpose flour
½ cup unsalted butter
2 tbsp. sugar
¼ tsp. salt

Filling:
4 egg yolks, beaten
1½ cup sugar
2 tbsp. all-purpose flour
⅓ cup thin cream (half and half)
4 cups rhubarb, cut fine

Meringue:
4 egg whites
8 tbsp. sugar
¼ tsp. cream of tartar

Preheat oven to 325 degrees. Grease a 9x13-inch glass baking dish. For the crust, mix flour, butter, sugar, and salt in a mixing bowl. Press in baking dish and bake for 15 minutes. For the filling, combine sugar and flour in a medium mixing bowl; add beaten egg yolks and stir to mix. Mix in cream; then add rhubarb, stirring lightly. Pour over baked crust. Bake for an additional 40 minutes. While dessert is baking, beat egg white until soft peaks form. Mix cream of tartar with sugar and gradually add to egg whites while continuing to beat until stiff peaks form. Remove dessert from oven, allow to cool one minute, then spread with meringue. Bake until meringue is golden brown, about 12 to 15 minutes. Cool and cut in squares. Makes 24 squares.

Violet Wuollet

RHUBARB

Rhubarb Cake

This is an easy and delicious coffee cake

1½ cups brown sugar
½ cup vegetable oil
1 egg
1 tsp. vanilla
1 cup buttermilk or sour milk
2 cups all-purpose flour
1 tsp. baking soda
2 cups rhubarb, diced

Topping:
⅓ cup sugar
1 tsp. ground cinnamon

Preheat oven to 350 degrees. Grease and flour a 9x13-inch baking dish. Mix sugar and cinnamon for topping in a measuring cup. Set aside. Combine brown sugar and vegetable oil in a mixing bowl. Add egg and vanilla; beat well. Add dry ingredients alternately with buttermilk or sour milk. Stir in rhubarb and pour into baking dish. Sprinkle sugar and cinnamon mixture evenly over the top. Bake for 40 minutes or until done, when cake springs back when pushed lightly with your finger. Makes 24 pieces.

Lois Neukirch

RHUBARB

Rhubarb Upside-Down Cake

2½ cups all-purpose flour
3 tsp. baking powder
5 cups rhubarb, diced
1 cup sugar
¼ cup light brown sugar
3 tsp. ground cinnamon
1 cup margarine
2 cups sugar
2 eggs, beaten
1 cup lowfat milk, warm

Preheat oven to 350 degrees. In a medium bowl, whisk together flour and baking powder. Set aside. Arrange cut-up rhubarb in a greased 9x13-inch pan. Mix 1 cup granulated sugar and ¼ cup brown sugar with 3 tsp. cinnamon and sprinkle on rhubarb. Cream margarine and sugar, add beaten egg, and beat until fluffy. Add flour mixture alternately with milk. Mix well and pour over rhubarb. Bake for 50 to 60 minutes, until toothpick inserted comes out clean. Cut a piece, flip it over, and top with ice cream, if desired.

Mary Lengsfeld

Rhubarb Pie

2 cups rhubarb, diced
1½ cups sugar
1½ tbsp. all-purpose flour or tapioca
2 egg yolks, beaten
2 egg whites, beaten until stiff
Pastry for double-crust 9-inch pie

Preheat oven to 375 degrees. Dice rhubarb and put in a large bowl. In a small bowl, mix sugar and flour or tapioca; pour over rhubarb and mix well. Add egg yolks and mix. Fold in beaten egg whites. Pour into prepared 9-inch pastry shell. Cover with a lattice crust. Bake for 40 to 50 minutes, until crust is golden and rhubarb is tender.

Mary McDonough

Rhubarb Cream Pie

1 baked 9-inch pie crust
2 tbsp. butter
2 cups rhubarb, diced
1 cup sugar
¼ cup sugar
2 tbsp. cornstarch
2 egg yolks
¼ cup cream
⅛ tsp. salt

Meringue:
2 egg whites
¼ tsp. cream of tartar
6–8 tbsp. sugar

Preheat oven to 350 degrees. Melt butter, add rhubarb and 1 cup sugar. Cook together, stirring until rhubarb is tender. Combine remaining sugar, cornstarch, egg yolks (beaten), cream, and salt. Add to cooked rhubarb and return to heat and cook until thick. Cool and pour into pie shell.

Top with meringue: in a medium bowl, beat egg whites until soft peaks form. Add cream of tartar and sugar while continuing to beat until stiff peaks stand up. Bake until golden brown, about 10 to 15 minutes.

Sheila Gemmill

RHUBARB

Almond-Ginger Biscuit
with Summer Fruit and Rhubarb Compote

This recipe was kindly submitted by Joan Ida, Pastry Chef at Goodfellows Restaurant

For the biscuits:
1½ cups toasted ground almonds
⅔ cup sugar
4 cups all-purpose flour
1 tsp. salt
2 tbsp. baking powder
1 stick cold butter
1 cup cream
½ cup candied ginger, chopped

Preheat oven to 350 degrees. In a mixing bowl, combine nuts, sugar, flour, salt, and baking powder with a paddle. Cut the butter into small pieces and add into the dry ingredients. Mix until you see only a couple of small chunks of butter left in the flour mixture. Mix in cream followed quickly by the ginger. Roll out the dough on a floured surface to a thickness of ¾ inch. Cut with your choice of cutter. Bake for 10–15 minutes. *Optional:* you may brush the tops of the biscuits with cream and sprinkle with sugar before baking.

For the fruit compote:
1 lb. rhubarb
1 pint blackberries
1 pint raspberries
5 pears, peeled and diced
1 cup red wine
1 cup water
1 cup sugar
2 cinnamon sticks
1 vanilla bean, split
1 orange, halved

Clean and wash all the fruit. In a large kettle, bring wine, water, sugar, spice, and orange to a boil. Add rhubarb, reduce heat to a slow simmer and add diced pears. When the pears are tender, add berries. Remove from heat. Cover and chill overnight.

RHUBARB

For the orange sabayon:
8 egg yolks
½ cup sugar
¾ cup orange juice
3 tbsp. Grand Marnier
Pinch of salt
Ice
1¼ cup whipped cream

In a double boiler combine yolks, sugar, orange juice, liquor, and salt. Set over boiling water and whisk like mad until thick. Chill over ice. When cool fold in the whipped cream. Keep chilled.

    To serve: Split biscuits and place halves on dessert plates. Top with fruit from the compote. Spoon orange sabayon over the fruit. Garnish with a mint sprig if desired. Makes 15 servings.

Rhubarb Jam

5 cups rhubarb, diced
3 cups sugar
1 (13-oz.) can crushed pineapple, undrained
1 (3-oz.) box strawberry, cherry or raspberry gelatin

In a medium bowl, combine rhubarb and sugar. Set aside for 30 minutes or until juice forms. Pour rhubarb into a medium saucepan. Bring to a boil. Boil and stir for 10 minutes. Add crushed pineapple. Boil and stir another 5 minutes. Slowly add gelatin and stir until dissolved. Ladle hot liquid into sterilized hot jars. Adjust clean hot lids. Cool. Store in refrigerator. Makes about 4 pints.

For Spiced Rhubarb Jam: Add ½ tsp. ground cinnamon, ⅛ tsp. ground allspice, and ⅛ tsp. ground cloves along with gelatin.

THE VEGETABLE PLACE

Strawberries

PREPARING STRAWBERRIES

Store in refrigerator until ready to use. Wash and remove stems. Pat dry with paper towels.

Yield: 1 lb. fresh equals 2 cups strawberries.

Nutrition: 1 cup, raw has 55 calories and contains some calcium, potassium and vitamin C.

Filled Strawberries
Beautiful on a dessert tray!

6 oz. cream cheese at room temperature
½ tsp. good vanilla
1½ tbsp. sugar
1 quart large strawberries
Toasted almonds for garnish

Whip cream cheese using a hand mixer on medium speed for 2 to 3 minutes, until fluffy. Add vanilla and sugar; mix well. Trim bottoms of strawberries (so they will stand up). Use melon baller to scoop out stems and tops. Fill pastry bag fitted with ½-inch star tip, with cream cheese mixture. Pipe into strawberries until cheese brims over top. Top with a couple of toasted almonds.

Doe Hauser-Stowell

Fresh Strawberry Salad Dressing
This dressing is especially good with a sturdy green salad like romaine lettuce.
Additional hulled strawberries make this salad special

1 medium-sized shallot
1 tsp. dry mustard
1 tsp. kosher salt
8 to 10 fresh strawberries, hulled
⅓ cup white wine vinegar
¾ cup sugar
1 cup vegetable oil

Combine first five ingredients in a blender and purée. Add sugar and blend into the purée. With the blender running slowly, add the vegetable oil.

Donna Cavanaugh
A GOURMET THYME DISTINCTIVE CATERING

STRAWBERRIES

Strawberry Chicken Salad

Marinade:
3 tbsp. extra virgin olive oil
3 tbsp. raspberry vinegar
¼ cup white wine
1 tbsp. coarse ground mustard
1 tsp. fresh ground black pepper
6 green onions

Salad:
4 boneless/skinless chicken breasts
4 cups mixed greens
1 quart strawberries, cleaned and sliced

Vinaigrette:
2 tbsp. extra virgin olive oil
2 tbsp. chopped fresh basil
¼ tsp. white pepper
1 tbsp. raspberry vinegar

In a bowl, mix marinade and pour over chicken breasts. Cover and allow to marinate in refrigerator overnight. Preheat grill. Mix vinaigrette in container. Cover and shake well. Grill chicken breasts and slice thinly. Place 1 cup greens on each plate. Place 1 sliced chicken breast on top of greens. Garnish each plate with ¼ of strawberries. Can be served with chicken hot or cold. Makes 4–6 servings.

GOLDEN FIG EPICUREAN DELIGHTS

Chilled Strawberry Soup

1 quart (4 cups) fresh strawberries, sliced
6 tbsp. honey
2½ tbsp. cornstarch
½ cup orange juice
½ cup yogurt

In a bowl, mix strawberries with 3 tbsp. of honey and let stand 1 hour. Drain berries, reserving juice. Pour reserved juice in a blender, along with half of the berries and purée. Place purée in a 2-quart saucepan and bring to a boil. In a small bowl, mix cornstarch into orange juice and add to boiling purée. Cook 1 to 2 minutes, stirring constantly, until clear and thickened. Add remaining strawberries and honey. For a creamy soup, mix a little yogurt with the soup. Otherwise serve with dollops of yogurt on top. Makes 8 servings.

Fresh Glazed Strawberry Pie

6 cups fresh strawberries
⅔ cup water
⅔ cup sugar
2 tbsp. cornstarch
1 9-inch baked pastry shell
Whipped cream (optional)

Wash, stem, and drain berries. Cut any large berries in half. Set aside. In a blender, combine 1 cup of the strawberries and water. Cover and process until smooth. In a medium saucepan, combine sugar and cornstarch. Stir in berry mixture. Cook and stir over medium heat until it becomes thickened and bubbly. Cook and stir for 1 more minute. Remove from heat and cool for 10 minutes. Arrange strawberries in pie shell and spoon glaze over strawberries. Chill for 1 hour and serve. Top with whipped cream, if desired. Makes 8 servings.

Louise Thoeny

STRAWBERRIES

Strawberry Dessert Crepes

1 quart fresh strawberries
¼ cup sugar
1¼ cups lowfat milk
1 cup all-purpose flour
2 eggs, beaten
2 tbsp. oil or melted butter
2 tbsp. sugar
Whipped cream or powdered sugar

Slice strawberries and put in a bowl. Mix with ¼ cup sugar and set aside. In a medium bowl, combine milk, flour, eggs, oil or butter, and sugar. Beat until well mixed. Brush oil or melted butter onto a 6-inch skillet. A paper towel works well for this. Heat skillet over low heat. Pour in 2 tbsp. of batter and tilt pan to cover evenly. Cook for 1 to 2 minutes, until top is set. Using a metal spatula and your fingers, flip crepe over, and cook for a few seconds. Cook remaining crepes the same way, brushing the skillet with oil between every couple of crepes. Cool crepes on a wire rack and stack. Cover each crepe with a layer of berries, roll up, and top with more strawberries, whipped cream, or powdered sugar. Makes 8 servings.

Mrs. Olson's Strawberry Lefse Roll-Ups

4 lefse
Strawberry cream cheese or yogurt
Sliced strawberries
Sugar

Lay lefse flat. Spread with softened cream cheese or yogurt. Layer with sliced strawberries. Sprinkle with sugar. Roll up. Makes 4 roll-ups.

Mrs. Olson

Strawberry Cream Puff

A very simple recipe, but read directions through, so you can work quickly

Cream Puff Pastry:
½ cup butter
1 cup boiling water
1 cup all-purpose flour, sifted
1 tbsp. sugar
¼ tsp. salt
4 eggs

Filling:
1 quart fresh strawberries, washed, ends plucked, halved
¼ cup sugar
1 pint whipping cream
4 tbsp. powdered sugar
½ cup sliced almonds for topping

Preheat oven to 450 degrees. Grease two large cookie sheets. In a heavy saucepan, melt butter in 1 cup boiling water. Pour in sifted flour, sugar and salt. Cook and stir quickly with a spoon until mixture forms a solid ball. Remove from heat. Cool one minute. Add eggs, one at a time, beating well by hand after each one. Spread dough into three 7-inch circles on the cookie sheets, leaving one inch between circles. You will have two circles of dough on one sheet and one circle on the other. Bake for 15 minutes, then for 10 minutes more at 325 degrees. Cool. While puffs are cooling, combine strawberries and ¼ cup sugar in a bowl. Whip the cream until soft peaks form; then gradually add powdered sugar while continuing to beat until stiff. Assemble in layers—puff, whipped cream, berries, puff, whipped cream, berries, puff, whipped cream. Top with sliced almonds and serve immediately. Makes 6 servings.

Reprinted from Pick of the Patch *by Janet R. Kogler*
PUBLISHED BY NEEDLES OF THE NORTH

STRAWBERRIES

Strawberry Muffins

1½ cups fresh strawberries, chopped coarsely
2 eggs, beaten
¾ cup sugar
½ cup vegetable oil
1½ cups all-purpose flour
¾ tsp. soda
1 tsp. ground cinnamon
¼ tsp. salt

Strawberry cream cheese:
8 oz. cream cheese, softened
2 tbsp. powdered sugar
⅓ cup fresh strawberries, finely chopped

Preheat oven to 350 degrees. Grease 18 muffin cups. Beat eggs and oil together. Add sugar and beat well. Mix in the strawberries. Add remaining dry ingredients and stir just until mixed. Fill muffin cups ⅔ full. Bake at 350 degrees for 20 to 25 minutes. Serve with strawberry cream cheese. To make the strawberry cream cheese, mix the softened Neufchatel with powdered sugar until creamy. Stir in the strawberries. Refrigerate unused portion. Makes 18 muffins.

This is a modification of a recipe from Shelly Jilek,
Inn on the Green Bed and Breakfast, Caledonia

Strawberry Soft Freeze

Frozen strawberries
Juicer

Use a plunger to push frozen strawberries through a juicer and out comes the best soft freeze you've ever had! Any frozen fruit works: blueberries, raspberries, and muskmelon chunks are especially good.

STRAWBERRIES

Strawberry Rhubarb Pie

Pastry for a 10-inch double-crust pie
3 cups strawberries, sliced
4 cups rhubarb, diced
1½ cup sugar
¼ tsp. ground cinnamon
6 tbsp. quick-cooking tapioca

Preheat oven to 375 degrees. Line a 10-inch pie plate with bottom crust. In a large bowl, mix together the strawberries, rhubarb, sugar, cinnamon, and tapioca. Pour filling in pastry-lined pie plate. Place on top crust, crimp edges, and make several slits or prick holes. Bake for 45 to 50 minutes. Makes 8 servings.

Fresh Strawberry Preserves

2 cups fresh strawberries
2 cups water
1 envelope unflavored gelatin
1 tsp. lemon juice
¼ cup honey

Wash strawberries and slice. In a small bowl, mix 1 cup cold water with gelatin. Set aside. In a blender, process half the berries with 1 cup water, lemon juice, and honey until smooth. Pour purée in a medium saucepan and add remaining 1 cup water and strawberries. Bring to a boil, stirring constantly. Remove from heat as soon as boiling is reached. Pour into sterilized hot pint jars. Adjust clean hot lids. Cool and store in refrigerator. Makes 4 cups.

Summer Berry and Greens Salad

6 cups fresh mixed greens, washed and drained dry
2½ pints total fresh strawberries, blueberries, and raspberries
1 cup halved pecans
⅓ cup sugar
1 tsp. salt
1 tsp. coarse ground mustard
1 tsp. dry mustard
⅓ cup raspberry or blueberry vinegar
1 cup extra virgin olive oil
1 tbsp. poppyseeds

Divide greens among 6 plates. Carefully rinse all berries. Slice strawberries.
Place berries and pecans equally on top of mixed greens. Combine remaining ingredients in a covered jar. Shake well. Serve with salad.

GOLDEN FIG EPICUREAN DELIGHTS

Mixed Berry Shortcake

3 pints mixed berries (strawberries, blueberries, raspberries)
¼ cup granulated sugar
¼ cup vanilla sugar
2 cups heavy cream
1 tsp. pure vanilla extract
8 mint sprigs for garnish
8 baking powder biscuits cut in half

Clean and quarter strawberries and carefully rinse and pat dry other berries.
Put in a large bowl. Toss berries with 1 tsp. of each sugar and let sit while you whip the cream. In a medium bowl, whip cream until it holds soft peaks; then whip 1 more minute while incorporating sugars and vanilla extract. Fold in berries and spoon onto bottom half of biscuit. Place top half of biscuit on bottom and spoon another scoop of berries on top. Garnish with fresh mint and serve immediately. Makes 8 servings.

Laurie McCann

Baked Custard with Fresh Berries

This recipe is adapted from Joy of Cooking. *I like it because it's very quick to prepare and very good served with any seasonal fruit*

2 cups lowfat milk
¼ cup honey
Dash of salt
2 eggs, beaten
½ tsp. vanilla
Ground nutmeg
Fresh fruit (strawberries, raspberries, or blueberries)

Preheat oven to 350 degrees. Put first five ingredients into a greased baking dish and heat well. Sprinkle with nutmeg. Bake for 1 hour or until a knife inserted into the edge of custard comes out clean. Center will continue to cook after removed from oven. Serve with fresh fruit—strawberries, raspberries, and blueberries are especially good. Makes 4–6 servings.

Jennifer Drew

STRAWBERRIES

Watermelon

WHEN AVAILABLE
August–October

SOME VARIETIES
Red, yellow, orange, and seedless

PREPARING WATERMELON

Wash, cut, and slice

Yield: 1 lb. fresh equals 2 cups diced watermelon flesh.

Nutrition: 1 wedge has 2 calories and contains potassium and lots of vitamins A and C.

Watermelon Boat

1 large watermelon
2 cantaloupe
1 lb. seedless grapes
1 quart strawberries
1 fresh pineapple, cut in chunks

Cut the ripe watermelon in half lengthwise; take out the fleshy part with melon ball spoon to form balls. Place in large bowl. Do the same with cantaloupe. After balling, scrape out the half shell of the watermelon; this is your boat. Mix all the fruit together gently. Place fruit into watermelon shell half. Keep refrigerated. Makes about 20 servings.

Variation: Marinate the fruit for a few hours with 1 cup of rum

Southwestern-Style Watermelon Salad

½ tsp. ground cumin
½ tsp. salt, or to taste
¼ tsp. chili powder
⅛ tsp. cayenne, or to taste
2 lbs. watermelon, seeds and rind discarded and the flesh cut into ¾-inch
    pieces (about 4 cups)
3 tbsp. fresh lime juice, or to taste
2 tbsp. shredded fresh coriander or basil leaves

In a small bowl, stir together cumin, salt, chili powder, and cayenne. In a serving bowl, toss watermelon with the cumin mixture, lime juice, and coriander or basil until the salad is combined well and serve the salad immediately. Makes 4–6 servings.

Mary Broeker

WATERMELON

Watermelon Popsicles

1 red, yellow, or orange-fleshed watermelon
Small paper cups
Popsicle sticks

Cut watermelon in half and slice into chunks. Seed the chunks and put in blender. Cover and purée. Fill each paper cup ¾ full with purée. Freeze for several hours. Insert popsicle stick when partially frozen.

Watermelon Pickles

12 cups watermelon rind, 1-inch cubes, trimmed
¾ cup canning salt
6 cups cold water

Brine:
3 cups white vinegar
6 cups sugar
3 cups water
6 tsp. whole cloves

Trim off the hard outer skin and any pink flesh still on the rind. In a large stainless steel kettle, mix salt and 2 cups water and add cubes. Cover and soak for 5 to 6 hours. Drain and rinse well. Cover with fresh water and cook until barely tender, about 7 minutes. Drain. In a large stainless steel kettle, combine vinegar, sugar, water, and bring to a boil. Tie cloves in a bag, add to brine, and simmer for 5 minutes. Pour over rind cubes and let stand overnight. Bring to a boil and cook about 10 minutes. Rind will be clear but not mushy. Pack hot cubes into hot sterilized pint jars. Add boiling syrup, leaving ½ inch headroom. Adjust clean hot lids. Process in a boiling-water bath for 10 minutes. Remove and cool. Makes 6 pints.

WATERMELON

Hmong Specialties

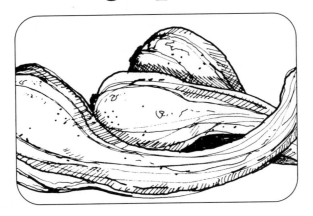

Asian Vegetables

SOME VARIETIES

Asian Cucumber
Start out small and green and grow to become quite large, turning to yellow and, finally, orange. The large orange cucumbers have a sour taste. When grown in warm, tropical climates, the small green cucumbers have a tropical fruity taste. In North America they taste similar to American cucumbers. The Asian cucumbers are very meaty. They are commonly peeled, the seeds scooped out, and sliced in salads or cooked very briefly in stir-frys.

Bittermelon
Tastes bitter. The level of bitterness depends on the size of the melon. The smaller the melon the stronger the taste. It is commonly used in small amounts in soups and stir-frys. Usually the seeds are scooped out and the flesh is sliced thinly.

HMONG SPECIALTIES

Bittermelon Greens
Have a bitter taste. They are almost exclusively used in stir-frys.

Daikon Radish (not pictured)
Considered more mild, juicy, and tender than standard American radishes. They are commonly used in salads, soups, and in pickled Napa cabbage.

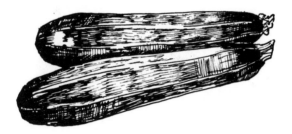

Kuzi Winter Squash
Starts out looking like a zucchini and grows to be as large as a watermelon. A common way to use these is to peel, scoop out seeds, and boil the flesh in water to make a squash drink. They are also used in stir-frys and soups.

HMONG SPECIALTIES

Kukuzi Squash
Grows up to 2 to 3 feet in length and has a long, curved neck. When young it can be used unpeeled like a zucchini. More mature squash are peeled, the seeds scooped out, and then peeled and sliced into stir-frys and soups. They have a taste similar to zucchini.

Lemon Grass
Herb widely used in tea and soups. Small amounts are used in stir-frys to add just a touch of flavor.

Mustard Greens
Come in many different sizes. The larger leaves tend to have a more bitter flavor, depending on weather and variety. They are commonly used in stir-frys, soups, and pickling.

HMONG SPECIALTIES

Oriental Eggplant
There are three types: purple, white, and small round-shaped with white stripes. Except for small differences in texture and taste, there is little difference in the flavor among the three varieties. Commonly used in soups and stir-frys.

Pea Greens
Commonly used in soups and stir-frys. They are also boiled in water to drink the water as tea as well as to eat the greens.

Thai Peppers
Come in green (the mildest), yellow (medium heat), and red (hottest). They are added to dishes when a hot flavor is desired. They are also commonly used to make a pasta.

HMONG SPECIALTIES

Asian Cucumber Drink

This beverage is usually served during a meal. It can also be served alone in a bowl or as a refreshing snack on a hot sunny day. Hmong people use a spoon to drink this.

1 large Asian cucumber, washed
2 cups ice water
Sugar to taste

Cut cucumber in half lengthwise. Scoop out seeds and discard. Using a spoon, scrape thin shavings of cucumber flesh into a bowl until only the shell remains. Repeat with other cucumber half. Add ice water to the cucumber shavings. Stir in sugar to taste. The cucumber shell can also be used as a serving dish. Makes about 2 servings.

Der Thao

Spicy Fruit Salad

1 green pear, peeled, quartered, cut in ⅛-inch slices
1 firm green apple, prepared like pear
1 cucumber, cut into ⅛-inch slices
2 small oranges, peeled, sectioned
1 firm mango, peeled and cut into bite-size pieces
½ pineapple, peeled and cut into ½-inch pieces

Dressing:
½ tsp. chili pepper
3 tbsp. brown sugar
1 tbsp. soy sauce
1 tbsp. tamarind dissolved in 4 tbsp. warm water
In a large bowl, mix fruit and cucumber slices. Combine dressing ingredients in a blender, cover and process until well mixed. Pour the dressing over fruit and cucumber mixture. Mix well. Makes 6–8 servings.

Der Thao

HMONG SPECIALTIES

Daikon Radish and Carrot Salad

1 4-inch piece of daikon radish, peeled
2 tsp. salt
2 medium carrots, peeled
2 cups ice water
3 tbsp. dressing

Dressing:
1 tbsp. soy sauce
1 tbsp. sesame oil

Use a vegetable peeler to peel down the radish lengthwise, making long thin shreds. Put shreds in a bowl and sprinkle with 1 tsp. salt. Cover and refrigerate 1 hour. Cut carrots in half lengthwise. Use a vegetable peeler to peel down the carrot half, lengthwise, making long thin shreds. In a large bowl, combine ice water, remaining 1 tsp. salt, and the carrot and radish shreds. Mix well. Cover and refrigerate for 1 hour.

Make the dressing. In a small bowl, combine soy sauce, sugar, and sesame oil. Stir until sugar is dissolved. Cover and refrigerate until ready to use. Rinse radish and carrot to remove salt. Drain. Put in a bowl and toss with dressing. Chill. Makes 4 servings.

Der Thao

HMONG SPECIALTIES

Winter Squash (or Kukuzi Squash) and Shrimp Soup

4 cups fresh chicken broth
12 fresh shrimp
2 cups winter squash (or kukuzi squash), chopped
1 slice fresh ginger
1 clove garlic
3 inches fresh lemon grass stalk, crushed
½ cup red pepper, chopped
4 whole mint leaves
4 Thai basil leaves, whole
1 green onion, chopped
Salt to taste

In a large pot, heat chicken broth until it comes to a full boil. Add garlic, ginger, and lemon grass. Simmer for 2 minutes then discard garlic clove and lemon grass. Put the shrimp in a large saucepan. Add the broth and bring to a boil. Cook covered over low-medium heat until the shrimp is almost cooked. Add the kukuzi or winter squash and red pepper. Cook for 2 minutes or until squash is tender. Season with salt and then garnish with mint, Thai basil, and green onion. Serve with rice. Makes 4 servings.

Der Thao

Hot Chili Pepper Sauce
Use as a seasoning or dip during a meal

2 chili peppers, chopped finely
½ clove of garlic, minced
¼ cup chopped fresh cilantro, or less
4 tbsp. fish sauce
1 tbsp. freshly squeezed lime juice

In a small bowl, combine chili peppers, garlic, cilantro, fish sauce, and lime juice. Stir to mix well. Store covered in the refrigerator. Makes about ½ cup.

Der Thao

Fried Rice with Vegetables

4 oz. shrimp
3 cups cooked long grain rice
1 tsp. salt
4–5 tbsp. vegetable oil
3 eggs, beaten with salt and black pepper
½ cup peas
½ cup carrots, diced
4 oz. pork or ham, diced into ¼-inch cubes
2 tbsp. light soy sauce
½ tsp. sugar
½ cup green onions, finely chopped
Salt and black pepper

In a wok or skillet heat 2 tbsp. oil, add shrimp, and stir-fry over high heat for 45 seconds. Remove from wok or skillet and set aside. Heat 2 tbsp. oil, add rice, and stir until heated. Quickly make a well in the center of the rice. Add 1 tbsp. oil and add beaten egg. Scramble the egg and then blend with the rice. When rice and egg are blended add peas and carrots, continue stirring. Stir in cooked shrimp, pork or ham, soy sauce, and sugar. Continue stir-frying over high heat until heated through. Add green onion, salt and pepper to taste. Makes 6 servings.

Der Thao

HMONG SPECIALTIES

Bittermelon Greens, Snowpea Greens, and Squash Greens Stir-fried with Chicken Breast

This is a basic stir-fry dish. Once you like the dish and know the taste and texture of the greens you can add other favorite vegetables. Cook the food quickly so it does not overcook. It is also important that the vegetables stay crisp and the chicken stays moist. It is best to serve the dish immediately after cooking.

2 cups bittermelon greens (substitutions: 4 cups snowpea greens or 3 cups
    squash greens)
2 cloves garlic, minced
2–3 tbsp. vegetable oil
1 chicken breast, sliced into strips (1½-inch long by ½-inch wide)
1 tsp. salt
2 green onions, chopped

Wash greens under water. Using your fingers, break off greens into 3-inch portions. Set aside. Heat wok until hot and then add oil followed by garlic. Next add chicken strips and stir-fry quickly over high heat for 3 minutes or until cooked. Sprinkle with salt. Last, add bittermelon greens, and green onions. Cover and steam for 1 minute then uncover and stir to mix. Stir-fry uncovered for additional minute or until greens are tender-crisp. Transfer to a plate and serve with rice. (Note that snowpea greens will cook faster, therefore only cook covered for 30 seconds. Squash greens will take a little longer to cook, so cook covered for 2 minutes.) Makes 4 servings.

Der Thao

Beef Curry with Thai Eggplant and Long Beans

1 tbsp. vegetable oil
2 tbsp. red curry paste
½ lb. beef loin, sliced thinly
1 tbsp. fish sauce
1 tsp. salt
1 tsp. sugar
2 cups coconut milk or light cream
2 cups water
1 stalk lemon grass
1 cup Thai eggplant, diced
1 cup long beans, 1-inch pieces
15 Thai basil leaves

In a large saucepan, heat oil over low heat. Stir-fry curry paste for 2 minutes. Add sliced beef loin and stir-fry for 1 minute. Add fish sauce, salt, and sugar and cook for 2 minutes, stirring a few times. Add coconut milk or light cream, water, and lemon grass and mix well. Cover and simmer for 20 minutes. Add eggplant and cook for 3 minutes, stirring. Add long beans and cook over medium heat until eggplant and beans are tender. Stir in Thai basil leaves. Serve with hot rice. Makes 4 servings.

Mai Vang

HMONG SPECIALTIES

Stuffed Cabbage

14–16 large green cabbage leaves
1 lb. ground pork
2 green onions, minced
½ cup bean thread vermicelli noodles, cooked and cut into 1–2 inch lengths
¼ cup fresh carrot, shredded
¼ cup new potatoes, shredded
1 clove garlic, minced
1 egg, beaten
½ tsp. salt
1 tsp. oyster sauce
1 tsp. soy sauce

Boil cabbage leaves in boiling water 3 to 4 minutes. Drain. Using a sharp knife, remove the ribs of the cabbage leaves. In a wok or skillet, stir-fry pork over high heat until almost cooked and set aside to cool. In a medium bowl, combine green onion, noodles, carrots, potatoes, garlic, egg, pork, salt, oyster, and soy sauce. Mix thoroughly. Divide the mixture into 16 portions. Put a portion of the meat mixture at the end of a cabbage leaf. Fold the two sides of the cabbage inward, then, starting at the end with the meat on it, roll-up. Repeat with the remaining leaves. Place the rolls seam side down on a steamer rack and steam for 15 minutes. Steamed rolls can be served hot or refrigerated and served cold. Makes 14–16 cabbage rolls.

Der Thao

Stir-fried Chicken and Chinese Broccoli

2 tbsp. vegetable oil
5 cloves garlic, minced
1 3-inch piece of fresh ginger root, peeled and minced
2 cups diced chicken pieces
½ cup water
1 small red onion, diced
1 green bell pepper, cut in strips
3 cups broccoli florets
2 green onions, chopped
2 tbsp. Southeast Asian mushroom soy sauce or soy sauce
½ tsp. salt
15–20 whole fresh mint leaves

In a wok or skillet, heat oil. Stir-fry garlic and ginger over high heat until they become aromatic, about 30 seconds. Add chicken pieces and stir-fry until brown. Add water, onion, pepper, broccoli, green onion, soy sauce, and salt. Mix well. Cover and steam over high heat for 1 to 2 minutes or until vegetables are just tender. Sprinkle with mint leaves and stir. Transfer to a bowl. Serve with rice. Makes 6 servings.

Der Thao

Hmong Traditional Medicine Herb Bouquet with Chicken

This is a common recipe that's been in Hmong families for many generations. It can be used as daily dish. The chicken broth that the herbs are brewed in is served warm, accompanied by rice. The broth is used for inner healing and cleansing the body, boosting energy, and relaxing the mind and body. The herbs are edible (optional). Pronunciations for the Hmong herbs are in parenthesis.

3½ cups water
2–3 lbs. fresh stewing chicken, cut up into 2- to 3-inch pieces
1 stalk lemon grass (Toujdub)
2–3 leaves Kouj Liab (kaw lia)
2–3 leaves koj ntsuab (kaw toua)
23 leaves koj rog (kaw touw)
2–3 leaves nte (dee)
2–3 leaves puj qaib (par kai)
2–3 leaves raw (dar)
2–3 leaves nea liab (gou lia)
3 inches of kaw ywm (elephant ear)
2 tsp. salt
½ tsp. black pepper

In a large pot, bring the water to a boil. Add chicken pieces. Cover and cook over high heat for 5 to 10 minutes or until chicken is thoroughly cooked. Place the whole herb leaves on the lemon grass leaf. Roll up and tie packet up tightly with a string. Add herb bouquet to boiling chicken. Cover and boil for an additional 3–5 minutes. Add salt and pepper to taste. Serve with rice.

Miscellaneous

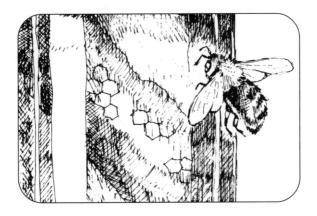

Wild Rice

Harvested in mid August–mid September

PREPARING WILD RICE

Rinse under cold water for 1 minute. For every cup of raw wild rice you will need 3 cups water. Bring the water to boil, add rice, cover, reduce heat and simmer for about 30 to 45 minutes or until water has been absorbed and the rice is tender.

Yields: 1 cup raw plus water equals 2⅔ cups cooked wild rice.

Nutrition: 1 cup cooked has 184 calories and is high in protein, potassium, phosphorous and rich in Vitamin B.

Salad on the Wild Side

1 cup wild rice, uncooked
2 tbsp. salt-free chicken flavor instant soup mix (or use 2 chicken
    bouillon cubes)
4 oz. nearly fat-free cooked ham or turkey ham, cut in julienne strips
¾-cup hot pepper cheese, cut in julienne strips
¾ cup broccoli florets, broken into small pieces
1 carrot, peeled and cut into thin rounds
¾-cup red pepper strips
4 green onions cut into thin rounds
¾ cup walnut halves
Freshly ground black pepper

Dressing:
½ cup canola oil
2 tbsp. lemon juice
2 tbsp. white wine vinegar
½ tsp. dry mustard
½ tsp. curry powder (or more to taste)

To cook wild rice: Rinse wild rice with hot water. Drain. In saucepan, combine rice with 3 cups hot water and instant soup mix or bouillon. Simmer, covered, for 35 to 45 minutes, or until water is absorbed and rice is tender. Cool.

    To mix salad: In large mixing bowl, toss rice with ham, pepper cheese, broccoli, carrot, red pepper, onions, and walnuts. Add a few grinds of black pepper.

    To make dressing: In small bowl, beat dressing ingredients until emulsified. Taste to see if more curry powder is needed. Pour over salad. Toss to mix well. Chill before serving. Makes 6 servings.

Minnesota's own Eleanor Ostman (*St. Paul Pioneer Press*) graciously gave us leave to print this, her prize-winning recipe from her book, *Always on Sunday.*

WILD RICE

Wild Rice Pilaf

1 tbsp. vegetable oil
⅓ cup red onion, chopped
1 cup red bell pepper, chopped
2 cups cooked wild rice
¼ tsp. salt
¼ tsp. black pepper
4 green onions, including some tops, thinly sliced
⅓ cup pine nuts, toasted
¾ cup fresh parsley, chopped
2 tbsp. fresh basil, snipped

In large skillet, heat oil over medium heat. Stir onion and red pepper; sauté until onion is tender. Stir in wild rice, salt and pepper; sauté until heated through. Stir in green onion, pine nuts, parsley, and basil until heated through. Serve immediately. Makes 4–6 servings.

Wild Rice, Pork Chop, and Apple Skillet

This skillet supper-dish features wild rice, pork chops and onion with apples . . . perfect for fall. Add broccoli for a colorful, nutritious meal.

4 pork chops, about 1 inch thick
Oil for frying as needed
1 cup uncooked wild rice
1 large onion, sliced
2½ cups chicken broth
2 large red cooking apples, peeled and sliced

Brown the pork chops on both sides in an electric skillet set at 375 degrees, using as little oil as necessary. Remove chops and sprinkle wild rice in pan. Arrange chops over wild rice. Push the onion slices to separate rings and place these over the rice. Pour chicken broth over all and bring to a boil. Cover and reduce heat to a slow simmer, about 200 degrees, for an hour. Add apple slices and simmer, covered, about 15 minutes more, or until apples, wild rice, and chops are tender. (Do not cook until apples lose their color and texture.) Makes 4 servings.

Recipe is reprinted here with permission of Voyageur Trading Division and is from Beth Anderson's *Wild Rice for All Seasons Cookbook*

WILD RICE

Burger Wild Rice Bake

This casserole has no sauces or soups to add extra calories and sodium

1 lb. lean ground beef
3 ribs celery, sliced
1 large onion, chopped
½ lb. fresh mushrooms, sliced
1 green pepper, chopped
Oil, if needed to sauté vegetables
1½ cups uncooked wild rice
4 cups chicken broth

Preheat oven to 350 degrees. Crumble the ground beef into a large skillet and sauté until the beef loses its color. Drain off any fat. Transfer the meat to a 3-quart shallow, oblong casserole. In the same skillet, adding as little oil as possible, sauté the celery, onion, mushrooms, and green pepper just until the vegetables begin to soften slightly, about 3 minutes. Combine the sautéed vegetables with beef, wild rice, and broth in the casserole. Stir well. Bake, covered, for 1½ hours, stirring once or twice during baking. Uncover during last 15 minutes of baking time to evaporate any excess liquid and brown the top of the casserole. Makes 8–10 servings.

Recipe is reprinted here with permission of Voyageur Trading Division and is from Beth Anderson's *Wild Rice for All Seasons Cookbook*

Creamy Wild Rice and Turkey Casserole

This is a good way to use leftover turkey or chicken.
This casserole can be prepared ahead and refrigerated or frozen until baking time.

6 cups cooked wild rice
1 (about 10-oz.) can cream of mushroom soup
1 (8-oz.) carton dairy sour cream
1 stick (¼ lb.) butter
3 ribs celery, sliced
1 medium onion, chopped
¼ lb. fresh mushrooms, sliced
1 tsp. salt
¼ tsp. ground black pepper
3 cups cooked turkey, cut into large dice or pieces

To prepare the wild rice, use 2 cups uncooked rice. Wash rice in a sieve using cold running water. Drain well. Place in a heavy saucepan with 7 cups of water. Bring to a boil, reduce heat, and simmer 40 to 50 minutes, or until rice is tender. Drain excess liquid and fluff rice with a fork. Do not overcook.

Meanwhile, combine soup with dairy sour cream, stirring to blend well. Melt butter in a skillet and sauté celery, onion, and mushrooms, just until vegetables are slightly limp. Stir in salt and pepper, sour cream-soup mixture, wild rice, and turkey. Spoon into a lightly greased, shallow 3-quart casserole. Bake, covered at 350 degrees about 45 minutes, then uncover and bake another 15 minutes to lightly brown top of casserole. Makes 6 servings.

Recipe is reprinted here with permission of Voyageur Trading Division and is from Beth Anderson's *Wild Rice for All Seasons Cookbook*

Dips, Dressings, and Maple Syrup

Mock Hollandaise Sauce

The classic use for this sauce is steamed asparagus,
but it is also good on just about any green or yellow vegetable

1 cup beef broth or bouillon
½ stick unsalted butter
1 cup whole milk
1 tbsp. cornstarch
2 egg yolks
1 tbsp. lemon juice
1 tsp. sugar
Salt and white pepper to taste
1 tiny pinch of cayenne pepper

In a saucepan, bring broth to a boil, add butter and remove from heat. Beat milk, cornstarch, and egg yolks together. When butter is melted add milk mixture, bring to a boil over medium heat, stirring constantly, boil for one minute and remove from heat. Stir in lemon juice, sugar, salt, and pepper to taste, add cayenne pepper. Makes 2½ cups.

Ulrich Bloecher

Dilly Dipper

Here's a tried and true recipe for a summer veggie dip you'll love

2 cups dairy sour cream or 1 cup sour cream and 1 cup mayonnaise
1½ tbsp. lemon juice
2 tsp. dill weed, chopped
½ tsp. salt
⅛ tsp. ground black pepper

In a bowl, combine sour cream, lemon juice, dill weed, salt, and pepper. Cover and chill. Serve with crisp vegetables such as broccoli, carrots, cherry tomatoes, cauliflower, peapods, cucumbers, mushrooms, radishes, green peppers. Makes 2 cups.

MINNESOTA GROWN

Roasted Red Pepper Dip
Serve this colorful dip with your favorite fresh vegetables

2 red bell peppers, roasted, peeled and seed removed
1 whole head roasted garlic, pulp squeezed out and skins discarded
8 oz. soft goat cheese
2 tbsp. extra virgin olive oil
5 tbsp. fresh basil, minced
1 tbsp. fresh rosemary, chopped
Pinch cayenne pepper
Salt and freshly ground black pepper

In food processor using steel blade, blend peppers, garlic, and cheese. Put in mixing bowl and stir in remaining ingredients. Refrigerate until ready to serve. Makes about 1½ cups.

Doe Hauser

Curry Vegetable Dip
This recipe can easily be made ahead, since it keeps very well refrigerated for several days

¾ cup mayonnaise
1 cup sour cream
1 pkg. dry Italian dressing mix
½ tsp. thyme
1 tsp. curry powder
½ tsp. garlic powder
4 tsp. white vinegar
4 tsp. salad oil

In a bowl, blend all ingredients well. Cover and refrigerate overnight to allow flavors to blend. Makes about 1 cup.

Provincial Dressing

5 tbsp. extra virgin olive oil
1½ tbsp. herbed vinegar
1 tsp. coarse ground mustard
3 tsp. fresh chervil
Salt and ground black pepper

In a mixing bowl, mix vinegar with mustard. Drizzle in oil and whisk until thickened. Add chopped chervil. Season to taste with salt and pepper. Makes about ¾ cup.

GOLDEN FIG EPICUREAN DELIGHTS

Red Raspberry Vinaigrette

¼ cup strong brewed tea
3 tbsp. extra virgin olive oil
2 tbsp. raspberry vinegar
1 tbsp. raspberry preserves
1½ tbsp. coarse ground mustard
¼ cup fresh basil, chopped

Place all ingredients in bowl and whisk well. Makes about ¾ cup

Laurie McCann

Basic Vinaigrette

1 tsp. coarse ground mustard
2 tbsp. good quality flavored vinegar
Dash white pepper
1 tsp. salt
1 tbsp. plus 1 tsp. safflower oil
2 tsp. mild olive oil

In a bowl, whisk first five ingredients together. Gradually add oils. Whisk until well blended. Makes about ½ cup.

GOLDEN FIG EPICUREAN DELIGHTS

Honey-Herb Salad Dressing for Greens

¼ cup vegetable oil
½ cup honey
⅓ cup white vinegar
1 tsp. dry mustard
½ tsp. salt
2 tsp. onion, minced
½ tsp. lemon balm, dried
½ tsp. tarragon, dried

Place all ingredients in a shaker bottle. Shake at intervals until thoroughly blended. Refrigerate to cure for 24 hours. Shake before each use. Makes 1 cup.

Lil Lindig

Fresh Strawberry Salad Dressing

1 medium-sized shallot
1 tsp. dry mustard
1 tsp. kosher salt
8–10 fresh strawberries, hulled
⅓ cup white wine vinegar
¾ cup sugar
1 cup vegetable oil

Combine first five ingredients in a blender and purée. Add sugar and blend into the purée. With the blender running slowly, add the vegetable oil. This dressing is especially good with a sturdy green salad like romaine lettuce. Additional hulled strawberries make this salad special. Makes about 2½ cups.

Donna Cavanaugh
A GOURMET THYME DISTINCTIVE CATERING

Maple Dressing for Tossed Salads

½ cup corn oil
¼ cup white vinegar
¼ cup maple syrup
1 or 2 tbsp. tomato paste
½ tsp. salt
Dash ground black pepper
½ tsp. dried basil, crushed
¼ tsp. dried oregano, crushed

In a medium bowl, whisk together all ingredients. Cover and refrigerate at least 2 hours. Stir will before serving. Makes 1 cup.

Joan Schellinger

Fondurella

This dip for strawberries or raspberries is positively elegant!

1 lb. good white chocolate
1 cup heavy cream
¼ cup 12-year-old balsamic vinegar
3 pints large strawberries or raspberries (or both)

In a double boiler, melt chocolate over hot water (do not boil). Add cream, mix well, then add balsamic vinegar and stir to remelt. Serve warm as a dip for fruit. Makes 3 cups.

Philip Dorwart, Executive Chef
TABLE OF CONTENTS, MINNEAPOLIS

Orange Dip for Fruit

Try using strawberry jam or other fruit jams in place of the marmalade

3 oz. cream cheese
½ cup sour cream
¼ cup orange marmalade
¼ tsp. ground ginger

In a bowl, blend all ingredients. Cover and chill about 1 hour. Makes about 1¼ cups.

Florence Staley

Elaine's Special Dressing for Fruit

½ cup mayonnaise
1 tbsp. honey
2 tsp. white vinegar
1–2 tsp. poppy seeds

In a bowl, beat honey into mayonnaise. Add vinegar and mix well. Add poppy seeds (and chopped nuts if you want to be really excessive). Pour over fruit.

Crystal Bloecher

Fluffy Honey Dressing for Fruit

2 eggs, beaten
½ cup honey
2 tsp. grated lemon rind
2 tbsp. frozen orange juice concentrate
⅛ tsp. salt
¼ cup lemon juice
⅔ cup sour cream
½ tsp. fresh mint leaves, chopped

In a medium saucepan, cook eggs, honey, lemon juice, orange juice, and salt over low heat until thickened. Cool. Fold in sour cream, lemon rind, and mint leaves. Serve on fresh fruit salad. Makes 2 cups.

Bernie Brand

Maple Country Ribs

3 lbs. country style pork ribs
1 cup maple syrup
½ cup applesauce
¼ cup ketchup
2 tbsp. lemon juice
¼ tsp. each of salt, black pepper, paprika, garlic powder, and
    ground cinnamon

Preheat oven to 325 degrees. Put ribs in pot and cover with water. Bring to a boil, then turn down heat to simmer for 10 minutes. Drain ribs and place in greased 13x9-inch pan. In a bowl, mix remaining ingredients and pour half of it over the ribs. Cook, uncovered, for 1½ hours, basting occasionally with remaining half of marinade. Makes 4–6 servings.

MAPLE LEAF ORCHARD

Maple Dressing for Fruit Salads

1 egg yolk
¼ cup maple syrup
2 tsp. lemon juice
¼ cup cream, whipped

Beat yolk and syrup with a wire whip in a small saucepan. Cook over low heat, stirring constantly until slightly thickened. Cool. Fold in lemon juice and whipped cream. Serve over fruit salad. Also good on cake, custard, and gelatin. Makes about ¾ cup.

Joan Schellinger

Maple Toffee Bars

Crust:
2 cups flour
1 cup packed brown sugar
½ cup (1 stick) butter
1 cup pecan halves

Toffee Topping:
⅔ cup butter
⅓ cup packed brown sugar
¼ cup maple syrup
1 cup milk chocolate or semi-sweet chocolate chips

Preheat oven to 350 degrees. In a medium bowl, combine flour, brown sugar, and butter and mix until fine crumbs form. Press into ungreased 13x9-inch pan. Sprinkle pecans over crust. In a small saucepan over medium heat, combine butter, brown sugar, and maple syrup. Cook while stirring constantly until mixture comes to a boil. Continue boiling and stirring for 30 seconds, then immediately drizzle evenly over pecans and crust. Bake 20 minutes (topping will be bubbly and golden). Remove from oven and immediately sprinkle chocolate chips over top; press gently into surface. Cool in pan on wire rack. Cut into bars. Makes 24 bars.

MAPLE LEAF ORCHARD

Maple Walnut Cake

Maple Caramel Glaze:
4 cups heavy cream
2½ cups dark amber Grade A maple syrup

Maple Walnut Layer Cake:
4 oz. (1 stick) sweet butter (unsalted)
2 cups dark amber Grade A maple syrup
3 large eggs
2¾ cup all-purpose flour
1 tsp. baking powder
¼ tsp. salt
1 tsp. ground ginger
1 cup coffee or buttermilk
1 tsp. vanilla extract
8 oz. (1 cup) fresh chopped walnuts

To make glaze: May be made days ahead and kept refrigerated. Combine cream and maple syrup in a tall, heavy-bottomed pot. The glaze boils up quite high as it first cooks, so bring to a boil, watching closely. Simmer slowly until liquid is reduced by half. Set aside. *Note:* If you refrigerate the glaze, reheat it before glazing cake layers.

To make the layer cake: Preheat oven to 350 degrees. Butter and flour three 9x2-inch round cake pans. Have all ingredients at room temperature. Fit a mixer with a paddle attachment. Mix butter in mixer bowl at medium speed until creamy, about 5 minutes. Add maple syrup and combine well. Add eggs, one at a time, until combined, then set-aside. In a large bowl, sift together flour, baking powder, salt, and ground ginger; mix together very well. Add about one third of this mixture to the butter-syrup-egg mixture in the mixer bowl. Combine coffee or buttermilk with vanilla; add one half of this mixture to the batter. Mix just until combined. Add half of remaining dry ingredients; mix until combined. Add remaining liquid, combine; add remaining dry ingredients and combine. Fold in chopped walnuts. Divide batter evenly into baking pans and bake 25 minutes or until done. Cool 5 minutes before removing from pans. Cool layers completely. As you stack layers, spread warm glaze over each, just until a bit drips over the edges.

Susan Dietrich, Pastry Chef
PRAIRIE SWEETS

Meats

A variety of meats are sold all year at the market's downtown location. Several meat selections are organic.

MEATS SOLD AT THE MARKET

Beef
Buffalo
Chicken
Duck
Game Hens
Goose
Lamb
Pheasant
Pork
Turkey
Trout

Butchering Day Hotdishes

We process all our own chickens and turkeys right here at the farm. One way to keep good help is to feed them well. Every week I try to come up with a tasty hearty meal, something memorable. This gives everyone something enjoyable to look forward to. This meal also must be easy to prepare and serve. One of our favorite meals is the "hot dish." Since I'm a native Minnesotan and heavily influenced by Scandinavian relatives and neighbors, I call all casseroles "hot dishes." Proper side dishes to serve with a hot dish include: pickles, cole slaw, and red jello with whipped cream topping. To stray from serving these familiar foods with the hot dish is to invite suspicion and bewilderment by your guests. I've included a few of my most popular hot dishes here. I hope they bring as much satisfaction to you, your families, and guests as they have to all of us Callisters.

Lori Callister

Herb Sausage and Pasta Hot Dish

1 lb. herb chicken sausage
½ of a small onion, chopped
2 cups uncooked pasta
1 can cream of chicken soup
3 soup cans of water
2 tbsp. soy sauce
½ tsp. sage
½ tsp. marjoram
½ tsp. thyme
½ tsp. black pepper
½ tsp. salt

Preheat oven to 350 degrees. Coat 6-quart casserole with cooking spray. Brown chicken and onion in frying pan or microwave oven. Pour into casserole pan. Place raw macaroni in pan with chicken and onion mixture. In a separate bowl mix the soup, water, soy sauce and spices in a large bowl. Pour this mixture over macaroni and chicken. Stir to mix. This can be baked immediately or placed in the refrigerator until needed. Bake covered for 1½ to 2 hours. Serves 6 people.

Lori Callister

Ground Beef and Pasta Hot Dish

1 lb. lean ground beef
½ small onion, chopped
2 cups raw pasta
1 can tomato soup
3 soup cans of water (canned soup and water may be replaced with 1 quart of fresh chopped tomatoes and 1 cup of water.)
2 tbsp. Worcestershire sauce
½ cup ketchup
½ tsp. black pepper
½ tsp. salt

Preheat oven to 350 degrees. Coat 6-quart casserole with cooking spray. Brown ground beef and onion in a frying pan or in a microwave oven. Pour into casserole pan. Place raw macaroni over beef mixture. In a large bowl mix soup, water, Worcestershire sauce, ketchup, salt, and pepper. Pour over macaroni and ground beef in the casserole. Mix well. Bake immediately or place in the refrigerator until needed. Bake covered 1½ to 2 hours. Serves 6 people.

Lori Callister

Beer Can Chicken

1 farm fresh chicken (¾ pound–1 lb. per person)
1 tsp. granulated garlic
1 tsp. paprika
1 tsp. cinnamon
1 tsp. black pepper
1 tsp. oregano
1 tsp. sage
1 tsp. sea salt
1 tsp. onion powder
½ can beer

Mix spices together and rub mixture on outside of chicken. If you have a roasting stand for chicken use it. It holds the bird upright and allows the juices to drip down into the pan. Place the pan in the oven or on the grill first. Pour beer into the bottom of the cooking pan. Place the chicken into the pan. Bake for about 20 minutes per pound at 375 degrees. Juices will run clear. Place a thermometer in the thigh of the chicken. It should read 180 degrees. You can also pour the beer directly into the cavity if desired.

Lori Callister

Easy Fried Chicken

1 farm fresh chicken
seasoning of choice

Cut up chicken and place in large skillet, skin side down. Do not add any oil or liquid–the chicken will make it's own liquid. Sprinkle seasonings on all sides. Place cover on pan. Place pan on largest burners of stove. Set temperature at mediuim. Cook this way without lifting cover for ½ hour (no peeking). After ½ hour remove cover. Turn chicken to brown on other side. Cook another ½ hour. Chicken should be done! Check the temperature in a breast or thigh. It should read 180 degrees. Larger chickens will require a longer cooking time. Wasn't that easy? Tasty too!

Lori Callister

Ground Turkey Tacos

1 lb. ground turkey
1 tsp. cumin
¼ tsp. cayenne pepper
¼ cup key lime juice
½ tsp. sea salt

Brown turkey in pan or microwave. Add remaining ingredients and mix well. Spoon into taco shells. Add fresh lettuce, chopped tomatoes, chopped sweet onions, shredded cheese, sour cream and salsa.

Lori Callister

Callister Family Favorite Meat Loaf

2 lbs. lean ground beef
2 eggs
½ medium onion, chopped
12 soda crackers, finely crushed
½ cup ketchup
1 tsp. black pepper
1 tsp. salt
2 tbsp. Worcestershire sauce
½ cup ketchup

Mix all ingredients thoroughly. Place in a greased loaf pan. Press into loaf shape. Pour ½ cup ketchup over the top. Bake at 350 degrees for 1½ hours. Remove from pan and let rest for 15 minutes before slicing. Serves 6–8 people.

Lori Callister

Turkey Steaks

Turkey steaks

Teriyaki marinade:
½ cup soy sauce
¼ cup vinegar
⅛ cup brown sugar
1 tsp powdered or fresh ginger
1 tsp granulated or fresh garlic

Mix well and pour over turkey steaks that have been placed in a glass baking dish. Turn steaks. Cover dish and let marinate 2 to 4 hours. Grill over hot coals about 6 minutes. Serve with grilled vegetables or steamed rice.

Lori Callister

Leftover Turkey Hot Dish

Don't know what to do with all that leftover turkey at Thanksgiving?
Be a true blue Minnesotan and make a hot dish!

Leftover turkey meat
Leftover dressing
Leftover gravy

Use a 9x13 greased baking pan. Place a layer of dressing on the bottom of the pan. Add a layer of turkey. Top with a thin layer of gravy. Don't add too much gravy or it gets soupy. Cover the pan with aluminum foil. Bake at 350 degrees for 1½ hours. Uncover for the last ½ hour. Serves 6–8 people

Lori Callister

BBQ Pork Ribs

4–5 lbs of pork ribs

BBQ sauce:
2 cups ketchup
1 cup brown sugar
¼ cup vinegar
¼ tsp. Worcestershire sauce
¼ tsp. onion
¼ tsp. garlic

BBQ sauce should not be made until you are ready to use it. Place all ingredients in a glass bowl and mix well. Place in the microwave till mixture comes to a boil. Let boil for 1 minute. If you like your sauce tart add more vinegar. If you like it sweet add more sugar.

Ribs can be cooked in a crock pot on low for 5 to 6 hours. If you prefer the oven, place the ribs in water in a covered roaster pan. Heat oven to 300 degrees and cook for 5 to 6 hours. Remove ribs and place on bottom of broiler pan. Pour sauce over ribs and broil for 5 to 6 minutes.

You can cook the ribs the day before, cover with BBQ sauce and refrigerate over night. Broil or grill 7 to 10 minutes to heat through. When the sauce starts to bubble the ribs will be done.

Linda Noble
FARM ON WHEELS

Beef Brisket

5 lb. beef brisket
1 cup red wine
salt
pepper
2 tsp. basil

Preheat oven to 300 degrees. Place brisket, fat side up, in a roasting pan. Pour red wine into bottom of pan. Salt and pepper. Sprinkle basil over top of brisket. Place in oven and bake for 8 to 9 hours or until done. When you put a fork into brisket it should go in easily and spread apart. Let stand 15 minutes and remove from pan. Slice and serve. For sandwiches tear into small pieces and mix with BBQ sauce. Serves 10.

Linda Noble
FARM ON WHEELS

Easy Summer Dinner

1 lb. ground beef
1 small onion, chopped
1 jar salsa
1 small can black beans
1 bag tortilla chips
lettuce, shredded
tomatoes, diced
cheese, shredded
sour cream

Brown ground beef with onions in a large sauce pan or skillet. Add salsa and black beans and cook until heated. Put over tortilla chips and add lettuce and other toppings as desired.

Linda Noble
FARM ON WHEELS

Pronto Pups

1⅓ cups flour
2 tsp. baking powder
⅔ cup milk
¼ tsp. salt
2 tbsp. sugar
1 egg
8 skin on wieners

Mix all ingredients well. Roll wieners in dough. Deep fry at 365 degrees for 3 to 5 minutes. If using the stovetop use a deep heavy kettle. Do not fill to full with lard as it will boil when you add pronto pups. Use a tong to turn pronto pup to cook all around. Drain on paper towels and enjoy.

Linda Noble
FARM ON WHEELS

Wild Rice Casserole

1 lb. wild rice
1 lb. seasoned pork sausage
1 stick butter
1 small onion, diced
¼ cup flour
1½ cups chicken broth (add 1 bouillon cube and let dissolve)

Cook wild rice according to directions, drain and put into 2-quart casserole dish. Brown pork sausage and drain. Add to wild rice. In a heavy skillet melt butter over medium heat, add diced onions and cook until soft. Add flour to make roux and quickly add chicken broth with dissolved bouillon cube. This will look like gravy. Pour over wild rice and beef mixture. Preheat oven at 325 degrees and bake for ½ hour and serve as a side dish or main course. This is one of our favorite family dishes for the holidays.

Linda Noble
FARM ON WHEELS

Weiner Wrap

1 loaf frozen bread dough, thawed
12 wieners

Preheat oven to 350 degrees. Roll out bread dough to ½ inch thick. Cut into ½-inch strips. Wrap around wieners to look like a weiner bun. Let rise for ½ hour. (Longer if room is cool). Bake for 20 minutes or until golden brown. *Variation:* Add cheese to wiener before wrapping.

Linda Noble
FARM ON WHEELS

Beef Skillet Meal

1 lb. ground beef
1 small onion, chopped
1 tsp. salt
? tsp black pepper
2 tbsp parsley, chopped
2 cups chicken or beef broth
½ lb. angel hair pasta, broken into 3 sections
1 cup green peas, fresh

In a large skillet, brown ground beef and onions. Season with salt and black pepper to taste. Add parsley. Add broth and bring to a boil. Add angel hair pasta pieces and toss gently until pasta is cooked. Stir in peas, cook for 1 minute, and serve. Serves 4.

Linda Noble
FARM ON WHEELS

Sirloin Tip Roast

3½ lb. sirloin roast
½ cup red wine
salt to taste
black pepper to taste
1 tsp. basil, chopped

Preheat oven to 300 degrees. Place roast in roasting pan with red wine. Salt and pepper to taste. Sprinkle basil over top and bake in oven 5 to 6 hours. Let rest 15 minutes before slicing. Pour reserve juice over top of slices before serving. Serve with potatoes or carrots from the market.

Linda Noble
FARM ON WHEELS

Chicken Soup

1 stewing chicken
2 celery stalks, chopped
2 carrots, chopped
1 medium onion, chopped
2 tsp. salt
½ tsp. black pepper
1 tsp. basil, chopped
2 garlic cloves, crushed
4 bouillon cubes
Noodles (optional)
Rice (optional)

Place chicken in a soup pot and cover with water 2 inches above chicken. Cover pan and bring to a slow boil for 5 to 6 hours. Remove from heat and cool down chicken. Remove from pot and reserve the liquid for later. Skim off any excess fat. Bone out chicken and remove skin. Cut chicken into small pieces and put reserved liquid in soup pot. Add celery, carrots, onion, salt, black pepper, basil, garlic, and bouillon cubes. Bring mixture to a slow boil for 20 minutes. If you want noodles or rice add after mixture comes to a boil. This recipe comes from my grandmother.

Linda Noble
FARM ON WHEELS

Best Beer Brats Ever

1 lb. fresh brats
1 can beer
1 onion, chopped (optional)
sauerkraut (optional)
ketchup (optional)
mustard (optional)

Place brats in a small sauce pan and cover with a can of beer. Bring to a slow boil for 5 to 6 minutes. Remove from pan and discard remaining liquid. Place brats on medium heat grill for 1½ minutes per side and serve on a bun as desired.

Linda Noble
FARM ON WHEELS

Swedish Meatballs

1 lb. ground beef
1 lb. ground pork
½ cup onion, chopped
¾ cup bread crumbs
1 tsp salt
⅛ tsp black pepper
1 tsp Worcestershire sauce
½ cup milk
1 tbsp parsley, minced

Gravy:
¼ cup all purpose flour
½ tsp. salt
2 cup milk
1 tsp. paprika
⅛ tsp, black pepper
¾ cup sour cream

Mix together beef, pork, onion, bread crumbs, salt, black pepper, Worcestershire sauce and milk. Shape into walnut sized balls. In a heavy skillet, pour in olive oil. Brown meatballs turning to cook all sides. Remove meatballs from skillet and make gravy in skillet.

Gravy: Mix the ingredients with a wisk and add to the skillet. Stir until it starts to thicken. Place meatballs in a crock pot on low and pour gravy mixture over the top. Increase the heat to medium and cook for ½ hour. Stirring occasionally.

Linda Noble
FARM ON WHEELS

Egg Bake

2½ cups cubed bread (no crust)
1 lb. ham, cubed
1 cup shredded hard cheese
½ tsp. mustard
10 eggs
2 cups milk
¾ tsp salt
Dash of black pepper

In a 9x13 greased pan spread a layer of bread cubes. The cubes should cover about halfway up the side of the pan. Spread a layer of ham over bread cubes. Spread cheese over meat. Blend mustard, eggs, milk, salt, and black pepper together and pour over other ingredients. Cover and refrigerate for several hours or overnight. Bake at 325 degrees for 55 to 60 minutes or until set. A knife should come out clean and the egg bake will be slightly browned.

Variation: In place of ham or with it you can add crisp bacon, chopped broccoli, cooked seasoned pork, or sausage.

Linda Noble
FARM ON WHEELS

Beef Stew

2 lbs. stew meat
1 medium onion, chopped
1 clove garlic, crushed
1 cup carrots, chopped
1 large potato, diced
½ cup celery, chopped
1 tsp. olive oil
1 cup red wine
1 cup fresh mushrooms
1 cup peas
1 large tomato, diced

Brown stew meat in oil in a heavy skillet over medium heat with onion and garlic. Turn down heat and add the rest of the ingredients. Cover and simmer for 1 hour. Check moisture level occasionally and add water if necessary.

Linda Noble
FARM ON WHEELS

Down Home Lamb and Dumplings

4 onions, chopped
4 tbsp. butter
3 lbs. lamb stew meat
2 tbsp. paprika
½ tsp. salt
½ tsp. sea salt
1 tomato, diced
1 green pepper, diced
½ cup beef broth
2 cups sour cream

Dumplings:
1½ cups all purpose flour
2 tsp. baking powder
½ tsp. salt

1 tbsp. parsley flakes
3 tbsp. shortening
1 tsp. minced onions
¾ cup milk

Saute onions in melted butter. Add lamb stew meat, paprika, and salts. Stir until lamb is brown. Add tomatoes, green pepper, and beef broth. Cover and cook slowly until meat is tender, about 1 hour. Season with salt to taste. Stir in sour cream. Heat slowly but do not boil. Serve with steamed dumplings.

Dumplings: Mix flour, baking powder, and salt together. Add in parsley and mix well. Cut in shortening until mixture resembles fine cornmeal. Stir in just enough milk to make a thick batter. Use a wet spoon to pick up batter and drop into bubbling stew. Cover and reduce heat to low. Cook 15 minutes.

PROMISED LAND FARM

Lamb Tortilla Lasagna

1 lb. ground lamb
1 pkg. taco seasoning
1 tomato, diced
1 cup sour cream
1 cup cheddar cheese, shredded
1 tbsp. all purpose flour
1 pkg. flour tortillas
1 onion, sliced thinly
1 cup cheddar cheese (optional)

Brown ground lamb, drain, and mix with taco seasoning and tomatoes. Mix sour cream with shredded cheese and flour. Spray a 9x13 pan with non-stick spray. Layer as directed: Line dish with 2 or 3 tortillas, add meat mixture, onions, sour cream mixture. Repeat 2 to 3 times starting with tortillas. Sprinkle top with cheese if desired. Bake at 350 degrees for 45 minutes.

PROMISED LAND FARM

Lamb Meatballs

1 lb. ground lamb
1 egg
½ cup bread crumbs
¼ cup onion, chopped
½ tsp. garlic powder
1 tsp. salt
1 tsp. black pepper
1 tsp. oregano
1 tsp. basil
½ tsp. thyme

Mix well and let stand in refrigerator, covered tightly, at least one hour. Form into meatballs. Brown in skillet or bake 30 minutes in 350 degree oven. Drain. These can be combined with noodle stroganoff or spaghetti sauce. Once baked these meatballs freeze well for quick preparation.

PROMISED LAND FARM

Lamb Marinade

½ cup soy sauce
¼ cup water
2 tbsp. vinegar
1 tbsp. oil
½ tbsp. ginger
½ tsp. garlic powder

Stir together and pour marinade over your favorite cut of lamb. Keep in your refrigerator for a maximum of 12 hours.

PROMISED LAND FARM

Quick and Easy Lamb Kabobs

1 lb, lamb, cubed
1 green pepper, cubed into 1½" pieces
3 small onions, cut into wedges
1 lb. whole mushrooms
Wooden Skewer

Assemble lamb kabobs by alternating lamb cubes, green peppers, onions, mushrooms. Grill on electric skillet or outside grill for 8 to 10 minutes. Turn over half way through. Serves 4.
PROMISED LAND FARM

Tips for Using Honey

- Substitute ⅔ cup honey for 1 cup sugar. The amount of liquid is then reduced by ½ cup. One-half (½) tsp. baking soda is recommended to cut acidity. Reduce the oven temperature by 25 degrees.
- Store honey at room temperature in a dry warm place.
- Honey can be liquified by placing the container in warm tap water until liquid.
- Honey may be warmed lightly in the microwave oven, but be careful not to scorch.
- A squeeze bottle of honey is very handy to have in the kitchen for sweetening coffee, tea, also for drizzling over cereal, toast, fruit, and ice cream.
- Add 2 tbsp. of honey to cake mix for moistness. For best results, add the honey in a fine stream as you mix the cake.

Tips for Using Cheese

➤ Best served at room temperature. Remove from refrigerator an hour or two before serving. Cream cheese is best when served soft but chilled.

➤ Gouda melts beautifully. Use it in omelettes, pizza, lasagna, and cheeseburgers. It also adds a delightful taste to hotdishes, salads, soups, cheese soufflés, and whatever you'd like.

➤ Refrigerate to preserve flavor and texture, 34–38 degrees.

➤ Cover cut surfaces with plastic wrap to keep from drying out. Covered refrigerator dishes should be used for highly aromatic cheese.

➤ Hard cheeses—Cheddar, Swiss—may be kept for 4–6 weeks. Semisoft cheeses—Butternip, Monterey Jack, Muenster, Brick—may be kept for 2–4 weeks under proper storage conditions. Soft cheese—Camambert, Brie, cream cheese—keeps about 1–2 weeks.

➤ Should surface mold develop, trim it off as soon as possible. It will not harm the remainder of the cheese, nor affect the flavor. Cut deep enough to remove all mold.

➤ Cheese can be frozen–thaw it in the refrigerator.

➤ Small pieces of dried-out ends can be shredded and kept refrigerated in a covered jar. Use on salads, soups, and cooked dishes.

➤ Always cook over low heat—prevents toughening, stringing, and separation. When melted, it's fully cooked.

➤ Grate cheese with a rotary-type grater. One-half pound of cheese yields about 2 cups.

➤ Shred cheese with a kitchen shredder. For garnish, cheese shreds should be long and fluffy.

➤ Slice cheese with a wire cheese slicer. If a knife is the tool available, select one that's very sharp and thin-bladed.

Index